PRAISE FOR *THE MINISTRY OF UNGENTLEMANLY WARFARE*

'One of the most extraordinary stories of World War II is also one of the least commonly known ... an eloquent and welcome tribute to their selfless, sometimes reckless courage – a howitzer of a tale that more people should know about'

Brian Viner, *Daily Mail*

'One of the most remarkable stories in the history of Special Forces' operations'

Daily Express

'Modern drama at its best'

Mail on Sunday

Damien Lewis

THE MINISTRY OF UNGENTLEMANLY WARFARE

THE MAVERICKS WHO PLOTTED HITLER'S DOWNFALL, GIVING BIRTH TO MODERN-DAY BLACK OPS

QUERCUS

First published in Great Britain in 2014 by Quercus Editions Ltd
as *Churchill's Secret Warriors*

This paperback edition published in 2024 by

QUERCUS

Quercus Editions Ltd
Carmelite House
50 Victoria Embankment
London EC4Y 0DZ

An Hachette UK company

A CIP catalogue record for this book is available from the British Library

PB ISBN 978 1 52943 952 6
Ebook ISBN 978 1 84866 854 6

Every effort has been made to contact copyright holders.
However, the publishers will be glad to rectify in future
editions any inadvertent omissions brought to their attention.

Plate section credits (plates numbered in order of appearance)
Imperial War Museum, London: 1, 2, 3, 7, 10, 13, 14, 15, 16, 17, 18, 19 and 20
The National Archives, Refs HS9/48/1; HS9/680/5(1); HS2/89/2(1): 4, 5 and 6
Bundesarchiv/Bild 183-B10713/Krempl/Sammelplatz: 9
Reproduced by kind permission of Jack Mann: 8, 11 and 12

Text designed and typeset by IDSUK (DataConnection) Ltd
Plates designed by Rich Carr

10 9 8 7 6 5 4 3

Typeset by Jouve (UK), Milton Keynes

Printed and bound in Great Britain by Clays Ltd, Elcograf S.p.A.

Papers used by Quercus are from well-managed forests and other responsible sources.

'There comes out of the sea from time to time a hand of steel which plucks the German sentries from their posts with growing efficiency'

Winston Churchill

Acknowledgements

Very special thanks are due to those veterans who I was able to interview, or who granted me access to their interviews, and in many cases gave of their time, their memories and opened their archives to me freely, not the least of whom is Jack Mann. Thanks also to Iain Farmer and Anders Sandberg, producers of the forthcoming film *Raiders*, which tells of the life of Anders Lassen and his fighting men, who first inspired me to look further into the extraordinary story as told in these pages. Thanks also to Paul and Anne Sherratt for reading the early drafts and for perceptive and constructive criticism and feedback.

I am especially grateful to my publishers, Quercus, and to Richard Milner, Josh Ireland, Charlotte Fry, Patrick Carpenter, David North, Jane Harris, Dave Murphy, Ron Beard, Caroline Proud, Hannah Robinson and everyone who helped bring this book to fruition. I am again grateful to my researcher, Simon Fowler, for exhaustive research work in The National Archives, The Imperial War Museum and at various other venues. Thank you, once again, for unearthing those untold stories and those secrets that were waiting to be found.

I am also indebted to those authors who have previously dealt with the topics that I have covered in this book and on whose work I have relied here. In alphabetical order they are: W. E. Benyon-Tinker (*Dust Upon The Sea*); Thomas Harder (*Anders Lassen's War*), Peter Kemp (*No Colour Or Crest*), Charles Koburger (*Wine-Dark, Blood Red Sea*), James D. Ladd (*SBS – The Invisible Raiders*), Mike Langley (*Anders Lassen VC, MC*), Suzanne Lassen (*Anders Lassen VC*), Brian Lett (*Ian Fleming and SOE's Operation Postmaster*; *The Small Scale Raiding Force*), John Lodwick (*The Filibusters*) and Gavin Mortimer (*The SBS In World War Two*).

Thanks – once again – to my wife, Eva, and to David, Damien Jnr and Sianna-Sarah, for putting up with Dad being locked away in his study, writing.

Cork, Ireland, 2014

Author's Note

There are sadly few if any survivors from the Special Forces operations of the Second World War depicted in these pages. Throughout the period of the research and writing of this book I have endeavoured to be in contact with as many of those who do exist, plus surviving family members of those who have passed away. If there are further witnesses to the stories told here who are inclined to come forward, please do get in touch with me, as I may be able to include further recollections on the operations portrayed in this book in future editions.

The time spent by Allied servicemen as Special Operations Executive (SOE) agents and/or Special Forces operators, or as captives of the enemy were often deeply traumatic, and many chose to take their stories to their graves. I am very grateful to those few who felt able to provide their testimonies (some of whom have now sadly passed away). Memories tend to differ and apparently none more so than those concerning often confused and frenetic operations behind enemy lines. The few written accounts that do exist of such missions also tend to vary in their detail and timescale, and locations and chronologies are often contradictory. That being said I have done my best to provide a comprehensible sense of place, timescale and narrative to the story as told in these pages.

Where various accounts of a mission appear to be particularly confused the methodology I have used to reconstruct where, when and how events took place is the 'most likely' scenario. If two or more testimonies or sources point to a particular time or place or sequence of events, I have opted to use that account as most likely. Where necessary I have recreated small sections of dialogue to aid the story's flow.

The above notwithstanding, any mistakes herein are entirely of my own making, and I would be happy to correct any in future editions. Likewise, while I have endeavoured to locate the copyright holders of the photos, sketches and other images used in this book, this has not always been straightforward or easy. Again, I would be happy to correct any errors in future editions.

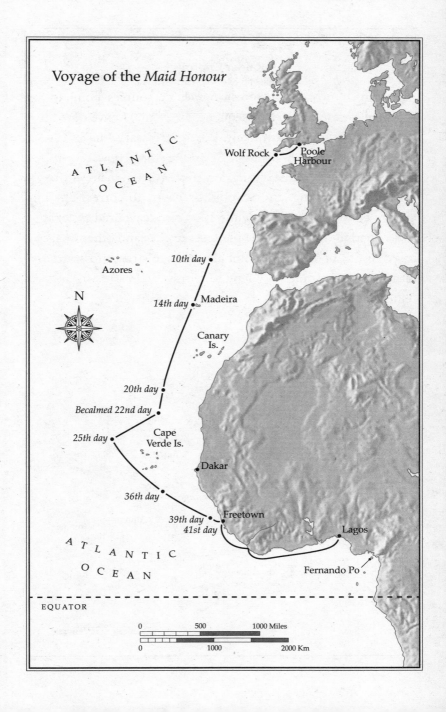

Voyage of the *Maid Honour*

ATLANTIC OCEAN

Wolf Rock
Poole Harbour

10th day

Azores

14th day Madeira

Canary Is.

20th day

Becalmed 22nd day

25th day

Cape Verde Is.

Dakar

36th day

39th day
41st day Freetown

Lagos

Fernando Po

ATLANTIC OCEAN

EQUATOR

0   500   1000 Miles

0   1000   2000 Km

N

Raider Central:
Eastern Mediterranean
and the Aegean

Lake Comacchio:
The Last Stand

Venice

Argenta
Gap
*Lake
Comacchio*

Comacchio
Ravenna

YUGOSLAVIA

A D R I A T I C   S E A

I T A L Y

Rome

0   50   100 Miles

0   100   200 Km

SICILY

Catania

*(Appleyard lost near
here July 1943)*

N

For Jack Mann,
whose hand of steel remains firm to this day.

And for those other butcher-and-bolt raiders
who have sadly passed away.

We will remember them.

Chapter One

The goats wandered across the dry, dusty terrain nibbling here and there at whatever vegetation they could find. Ahead of them loomed the wire-mesh fence of the German airbase. A low bush still possessing some succulent greenery grew right on the fence line. It drew the hungriest animals. To get to the highest branches they had to stand on their hind legs, fore-hooves resting on the wire itself.

Two figures followed in the animals' wake. They were dressed like local goatherds, wrapped in traditional loose, dirty-grey robes and shawls. As they tried to restrain the animals, pulling them back from the wire without much success, a pair of Junkers Ju-87s landed on the airstrip, the roar of their propellers drowning out the goatherds' cries to their animals.

The two men eyed the hated Stuka dive-bombers, whose *Jericho-Trompete* screaming sirens could strike terror into even the most hardened of operators. There were six further Ju-87s sitting on the runway, plus a handful of the larger Ju-88 *Schnellbombers* – Hitler's much-vaunted warplanes.

No doubt about it, Kastelli Airbase was getting busy. Along with the handful of sleek Messerschmitt fighter planes and

Storch reconnaissance aircraft that also dotted the runway, there were a plethora of juicy targets to choose from.

As the roar of the Stukas died away, from somewhere inside the airbase a voice yelled out a challenge in German. A guard had spotted the goats clambering on the perimeter fence. He started pounding on the wire with his rifle butt.

'Hey! You there! Get your animals off! *Schnell! Schnell!* Get them off!'

Beneath their disguises Anders Lassen, a Dane by birth, but now fighting with Britain's Special Forces, and Nereanos Georgios, his Greek resistance-fighter guide, stiffened. Unlike Georgios, Lassen was a fluent German speaker and could understand every word – but both men tried to act as if they were entirely ignorant of the meaning.

Lassen fingered the Luger pistol he had tucked under his robes, flicking the safety catch to 'off'. While Georgios could easily pass as the local that he was, Lassen's straw-blond hair and piercing blue eyes were a dead giveaway, that's if the German guard got close enough to get a proper look at them.

'Get your damn goats off the wire!' the German yelled again. 'Get out of here! Or I shoot!'

It had seemed like a good idea to use the goatherd cover to do a close recce of the airfield, but Lassen hadn't taken into account the inate stubbornness of the animals, especially when they were hungry. As he and Georgios used their sticks to beat the animals back, the German guard seemed suddenly to grow more suspicious.

'*Kommen Sie hierher!*' – come here. '*Kommen Sie hierher!*'

Lassen's grip on his weapon tightened, but it was then that Georgios took the initiative. He splayed his hands in a helpless gesture.

'We don't understand!' he shouted back at the guard, in Greek. 'We don't understand!'

The guard raised his rifle angrily and mimed shooting the goats. Then he switched his gun-sights across to the two men. The message couldn't be clearer: *get the hell out of here*. Lassen figured they'd seen enough. Together the two men dragged the last of the animals off the fence and beat them back with their sticks.

The guard gave them a long, lingering scowl, before continuing with whatever were his duties.

'Perfect,' Lassen muttered, as soon as they were out of earshot. 'The fence isn't electrified.'

As they drove the herd further away, he took the odd, surreptitious glance at the wider fortifications surrounding the airbase. The nearest guard tower – a wooden structure built up to a height of around 50 feet – had a searchlight peeping out between the outer posts, one that could be operated by those manning the tower.

'See that,' Lassen whispered. 'Searchlights all face outwards.'

Georgios flashed him a look. 'Perfect to see us coming. How does that help?'

Lassen's mouth offered a thin smile, but there was no corresponding warmth in his eyes. There was only the ever-present, visceral hatred of the German enemy, plus the wide-eyed, wired stare of a man burning through the Benzedrine. Benzedrine – more commonly known as 'bennies' – is a

3

powerful amphetamine. Ever since they'd landed on this Greek island, Lassen had been handing out the pills like Smarties. It was the Benzedrine that was keeping him and his men going.

'It means we can go about our work unseen,' Lassen muttered. 'Once we're on the airfield—'

'That's if we *get* as far as the airfield,' Georgios cut in.

'Don't worry,' Lassen countered, his Danish accent still evident. 'Ve vill get there.'

From the skies to the east a faint, juddering beat drifted on the air. It grew into a powerful rhythmic roar as an aircraft approached. Over the far end of the airbase, for a brief moment, three silhouettes hung in the air almost as if they were floating. But within seconds they were thundering towards where Lassen and Georgios were standing.

'More *Schnellbombers*!' Lassen hissed, excitedly. 'First the Stukas and now these! They must be clearing Heraklion.'

The flight of Junkers-88s thundered low overhead, the sheer power of their twin BMW engines coupled with the sensation of the downdraft scattering the goats. The *Schnellbomber* had been designed to fly too fast for Allied fighters to intercept or shoot it down, and had proved to be one of the most versatile aircraft in the war. Known in the Luftwaffe as 'Mädchen für Alles' – the Maid of all Work – the Ju-88 was used as a bomber, a night fighter, a heavy fighter, a reconnaissance aircraft and even as a torpedo bomber.

Recently, the *Schnellbombers* had been used in that latter role from Crete, flying anti-submarine and anti-ship patrols, searching for any Allied vessels that might be lurking in the

Mediterranean. As Lassen and his men had been dropped at the start of this operation by a British warship operating under the very noses of the Germans, taking out those *Schnellbombers* would be a delicious irony.

Lassen let out a wild laugh. 'It's all here! Looks like Holmes and his lot'll be attacking empty runways and hangars!'

Some several dozen kilometres across the German-occupied island of Crete lay Heraklion Airbase – the target for a sister group of raiders, led by Ken Lamonby and Dick Holmes. Holmes was Lassen's arch-rival in D Squadron, their Special Forces unit, and the Dane thrilled to the idea that Holmes might arrive at Heraklion to find no targets to strike.

Two hours later he and Georgios made it to the bare and sun-blasted ridgeline lying high above the airbase. They'd left the goats with one of Georgios' brothers at a pre-arranged rendez-vous, where they'd also dumped their local dress.

On seeing them Ray Jones, who was lying in a hidden sentry position, called out the coded challenge: 'GARAJ!'

'SLAVE!' Lassen replied.

As with everything, they kept it simple: the codewords were made up from the first few letters of the men's name and rank. There were five raiders on the Kastelli mission – Georgios included – so it was simple enough to remember five code-words based upon such easy details. Recently, they'd been ordered by Raiding Force Headquarters to resort to a more complex and arguably unbreakable code system, but as with most things Lassen liked to keep it idiot-proof. He gave those orders he disagreed with the scant attention they deserved.

Lassen and Georgios rejoined the main body of men, lying-up in the shade of a patch of rocky scrub just outside the entrance to their cave. All apart from Jones were feverishly busy constructing the tools for the coming night-time attack. Mostly these were Lewes bombs – a DIY blast-incendiary explosive made by mixing diesel oil with 'Nobel 808', a plastic explosive, plus thermite, a metal-based gunpowder.

It was Lieutenant Jock Lewes, one of SAS founder David Stirling's stalwarts, who had invented the Lewes bomb. Stirling's men had needed a device light enough to carry into the field, yet powerful enough to damage and set fire to aircraft. Placed within a small canvas bag, the Lewes bomb could be hidden inside a cockpit or on a wing, in close proximity to the fuel tanks, so as to ignite the aviation fuel – which was exactly how Lassen and his men intended to use them tonight.

Lassen squatted down among his band of fighters. He grabbed a half-eaten K Ration pack and pulled out some hard biscuits. While the rest of the British Army was issued with the so-called British 'Compo' Rations, Lassen had managed to blag some of the US Army paratroopers' 'K Rations' for his men. Far lighter and more portable than Compo, they were borderline edible, and provided just enough energy and calories to keep a soldier going in the field.

Of course, Lassen was largely fuelling himself with the Benzedrine, but he needed something solid in his guts with tonight's mission almost upon them. He started to sketch a map of the airbase, describing in a series of sharp, staccato sentences what he and Georgios had found. His eyes were wide and staring, and his men could sense the blood lust that was coursing through his veins. For all of them, the thought of blowing that airbase to smithereens was a delicious one – only with Lassen, it was the idea of killing Germans that really got his blood pumping.

'We keep it simple,' Lassen declared. 'We go in tonight and cut the perimeter wire. There will be good cloud cover. Little moonlight. Nicholson and Greaves, you move in from the east and hit the fuel and ammo dumps. Jones – you and me go in from the west and we hit as many aircraft as we can. We go through the wire at 0100 hours. We should be in there for no more than twenty minutes. Set the timers for 0200 hours, so we get a good distance away before it blows.'

'But what about me?' It was Georgios.

'Go back to your village,' Lassen told him. 'Go back home.'

'But I can fight!'

'Not tonight. Not with us. When the base blows we run like the wind. You do not want to be with us. Anyway the Germans may try to take revenge. Go back and make your people ready.'

In spite of his cold-blooded demeanor, Lassen had a real affinity with the locals, and especially the women – the dark-eyed, raven-haired beauties of this captivating Greek island. He shared a common bond with the Cretans, who nurtured a level of hatred of the German enemy as deep as his own.

'But I want to fight,' Georgios insisted. 'I am *resistance fighter*. I want to fight. The Germans, they already have killed many of my people.'

Lassen's voice softened. 'Go back where you are needed. Protect your family. Trust me, we could not have come this far without you.'

'But when you run you will need guide,' Georgios argued. 'You get nowhere without me. You attack: I attack. You go in; I go in. You come out, I show you the way.'

'Andy, Georgios is right,' Sergeant Jack Nicholson cut in. 'We'll be buggered on the way out without him.'

'All right,' Lassen relented. 'Georgios, you go with Nicholson and Greaves. But stay outside the perimeter wire to guide us out again.'

'Yes!' The Cretan's fist punched the air. 'Andy, we will fight like the brothers!'

'What's the plan if things go wrong?' Nicholson asked. 'What if we're spotted on our approach under the searchlights? Or once we're on the base setting the charges?'

Lassen's killer stare returned. 'No one is going to get seen during the approach.' He was silent for a beat. 'Make sure of that. And if we are spotted once on the airbase, blow it all to hell and get moving. You all know the emergency RV?'

Lassen reached into his pocket and pulled out a crumpled map. He took a pencil and tried to scribble 'Rendezvous' on their agreed emergency rallying point, should they get split up. But English wasn't his first language, nor spelling his strongest suit. He tried again, scrubbed it out in frustration, and scrawled one word in capitals: 'MEAT'

'Got it?' he queried.

There were a series of grunts in the affirmative.

'If any one of us does not make the RV, we do not go back for him. Understood?'

Again, the grunts of agreement.

Lassen nodded. 'Good. Now the fight.'

The night trek to the airbase went without a hitch. The four raiders were dressed in 'light order', carrying only their day sacks stuffed with Lewes bombs, and armed with pistols, grenades and knives. They'd left their heavier Tommy Guns and German Schmeisser machineguns behind – the key with such a mission being able to move fast and unseen. They'd never win a stand-up firefight with the enemy, who tonight numbered some two hundred mixed German and Italian troops.

Instead, the aim was to be in and out like ghosts.

At around five hundred yards out from the airbase Lassen's group split from Nicholson's, the latter skirting southwards through a vineyard towards the humped, blocky silhouette of the fuel dump. Lassen led Jones towards the airstrip, dropping to a cat-crawl as they emerged from the cover of the vines, a couple of hundred feet short of the wire. A searchlight swept the night, the sentries on the nearest tower staring into the thin beam that probed the sea of darkness around them.

For an instant the blinding spear of light seemed to pierce Lassen and Jones, pinning them to the ground. The two raiders burrowed on their bellies into the dry dirt and the sparse, scrubby undergrowth, as they tried to escape the searchlight's pitiless glare. Being trapped under that intense illumination was spine-chilling, especially as there wasn't a scrap of real cover anywhere around.

After several tense seconds the light moved on and Lassen urged Jones forward. The Dane reckoned it was movement that drew the eyes of the guards, so if they made like statues whenever the light swept past no one would detect their presence.

The next time the searchlight swung around he and Jones froze in their tracks, and after a tense moment the beam of light continued its steady sweep across the hillside. As they pushed ahead Lassen was trying to keep his natural exuberance in check. He was never happier than when on the hunt, especially stalking much sought-after prey.

He'd been this way since he was a small boy, when he'd tracked deer with a bow-and-arrow on his parents' grand country estate, hunting silently and swiftly. But now his native Denmark was occupied by the German enemy, the Danish people – his family among them – crushed under the heel of the Nazi jackboot, just like the Cretans.

It fed his hatred of the Nazis, and fuelled his lust for revenge.

Finally, he and Jones reached the wire. A hundred yards or so to their south Lassen could make out the skeletal form of the main gate, with one of the six guard towers rearing above it. A match flared in the thick darkness, betraying where a sentry was positioned atop it. The flame was passed between the guards as each lit a cigarette, forming four pinpricks of fiery orange as they puffed away.

In the glow of the flaring match Lassen had caught the gunmetal-blue form of a Maschinengewehr 42, the German's fearsome 'Spandau' general-purpose machine gun. A belt-fed 7.92 mm weapon, it could put down a stunning volume of suppressive fire. They'd better hope the sentries were less than alert, for Lassen's men were going in with a few pistols, knives and two dozen Lewes bombs between them.

For a few seconds Lassen and Jones scanned the terrain to their front. The squat forms of the Stukas were some two hundreds yards away, separated from them only by the wire. *So near and yet so far.*

As their eyes probed the darkness, Lassen spotted a pair of sentries executing a foot patrol past the line of aircraft. The enemy had pitched tents on the mown grass that lined the runway, so they could camp out under canvas and keep permanent guard on their warplanes. Clearly, they had men standing permanent watch over the aircraft, in addition to those positioned in the guard towers.

The sentries out on foot had their weapons slung over their shoulders, but Lassen could sense that they were alert and on-task. He knew the Germans to be professional and motivated fighters, as opposed to their Italian comrades, who tended not to have their heart in the fight. It would be well not to underestimate them.

Lassen put two fingers to his eyes, then pointed towards the foot sentries and held up two fingers – indicating to Jones where to look and the number of the nearest enemy. By the silent nod he got in return he figured Jones had seen them. On Lassen's signal Jones reached up to the fence with a pair of wire-cutters and began to snip the strands, slicing through a section up to about three feet in height.

He forced it apart and was just reaching higher, when from out of the darkness to their right a match flared again. This was much closer. The flame revealed a sentry who had paused to light up. It looked as if they had guards out walking the wire, on perimeter patrols – a third layer of security.

Lassen and Jones went to ground, forcing their faces deeper into the dry dirt. The sentry paced closer along the fence-line, and for some reason he chose to pause right opposite where the raiders had cut their hole in the wire. Perhaps he had heard them doing so, the sharp snips of the wire-cutters carrying far in the still darkness.

Lassen cursed under his breath.

They'd 'blacked-up' earlier, using first camouflage cream and then a burned cork to smear their faces, but that wouldn't hide the whites of their eyes. The sentry took a long drag of his cigarette, and exhaled. The June night was balmy, and the soldier seemed in no hurry to move. Quite the opposite: his attention seemed glued to the section of fencing that Lassen and Jones had just been cutting.

If the two raiders didn't get going soon, Nicholson's lot would already have set their charges, and Lassen and Jones would be caught on the runway as the ammo and fuel dumps blew. Without a sound, Lassen slid out of his backpack and reached for the fence. Moving like a cat, his lithe, wiry form wriggled through the narrow hole, the handle of his heavy 'stiletto' fighting knife gripped in his right hand.

He rose into a crouch and flitted through the darkness towards the sentry. Once, during training with fellow Special Duty recruits in Scotland, Lassen had stalked and killed a deer with his knife. Those who had watched him were amazed at his hunting prowess. It was a large stag, and he and fellow trainees had feasted on its flesh for days. Lassen possessed an uncanny ability to creep up undetected on just about any kind of prey, and to kill it with his bare hands.

He came up silently behind the sentry. In one swift move he slipped his left arm around the neck and mouth in a savage chokehold, blocking off any possibility of a cry, jerking the chin upwards and to the left at the same moment. Simultaneously, his right arm came around in a savage thrust, sinking the blade of his fighting knife up to the hilt through the man's neck, before punching forward to slice through the artery.

For several seconds Lassen gripped the stricken figure in a vice-like hold, as his life drained out of him, before lowering his body to the blood-soaked dirt. An instant later he was back beside the fence, the dead man's submachine gun slung across his bloodied shoulder. He crouched low and lent all his weight on the wire, widening the narrow hole for Jones.

'Come on! Let's go!'

By now Lassen had killed enough Germans at close quarters that another death wasn't exactly going to damn his soul. But the first time he'd killed a man with a knife he had found it difficult. A year earlier, during a raid on the Channel Island of Sark, he'd knifed to death a lone German sentry.

He'd written in his diary about it: 'The hardest and most difficult thing I have ever done.'

A lot had happened since then.

Jones wriggled through. Together, the two men moved ahead at a low crouch, sticking to the darkest shadows. They skirted past the dead sentry, his body lying in a pool of thickening blood, before coming up at the rear of a hangar, with an attached barracks block. Inside, it was a hum of chatter and laughter, as the aircrew, technicians, aviators and guards enjoyed a little downtime. It was a Saturday night, and no doubt their minds had drifted to thoughts of loved ones back home.

Lassen led Jones around the side of the block, keeping away from the light. To the front was another machinegun, this one positioned in a sandbagged bunker, the gun facing outwards to protect the aircraft at its back. Lassen eyed the planes hungrily.

Not far now.

Jones reached for a second line of fencing, one that segregated the airstrip itself from the rest of the base. The wire was thicker here, offering more resistance, but they had to cut a passage through. The only other way in was via the main gate, and no way did Lassen want to have to bluff his way past that.

Straining with the effort, Jones snipped the first few strands of wire. Beside him, Lassen used his hands to pull up the cut ends and bend them backwards, forming a hole just big enough to crawl through. With his purloined German machinegun covering Jones, Lassen waved the man on. Only when Jones had reached the far side did Lassen slide his gun under and wriggle through himself.

With Lassen in a crouch and covering him, Jones knelt to twist together the wire in a makeshift fix, just as he'd done at the outer fence. At first glance no one would notice that it had been cut.

They were at least two hundred yards inside the base by now, and practically in among the aircraft. As Jones worked feverishly at closing the wire, Lassen felt certain they would be spotted. With so many sentries posted on the airstrip it was going to be nigh-on impossible to flit unseen among the airframes.

After what seemed like an age Jones turned away from the wire and gave a thumbs-up. Lassen breathed out a sigh of relief. For a few seconds he kept watch, tuning his senses to the rhythm of the German sentries on duty. Once he had a feel for the pace of their march, he was ready.

Using hand signals he sent Jones to his left, to deal with the aircraft on the near side. He would move ahead-right, to plant his charges on the second rank of Stukas. But then, under the glare of a distant floodlight Lassen spotted a more remote, but juicier target. Parked on the grass beyond the Stukas he could just make out the form of a twin-engine Junkers-88 *Schellbomber*.

Lassen's pace quickened. Painted on the side of the sleek fighter-bomber was a white square bisected by a black cross, marking it out as an aircraft of the hated *Luftwaffe*. The insignia shone out in the darkness, drawing Lassen to it like a moth to a candle flame.

He glanced left and right, as he steeled himself for a dash through the open. The sentries were nearing the end of their patrol leg, whereupon they'd do an about-turn and come around to face him. In the few seconds remaining Lassen darted forwards. He scuttled across the bare brightness of the grass strip running alongside the runway, trying as far as possible to keep under cover and out of view.

The next moment he pounded onto an open stretch of tarmac, his felt-soled boots passing silently over the unyielding surface, before he darted onto the grass on the far side. One last dash and he slipped into the cover of the larger aircraft – moments before the first of the sentries turned. They were no more than two hundred yards away and nearing the ends of the runway – which meant Lassen and Jones had just minutes in which to complete their task.

Lassen glanced left, confirming what he suspected – that this was the first in a row of six Ju-88s. He clambered up the steel ladder set against the aircraft's flank, and from there slid onto the wing.

Lassen inched ahead on his belly, the rucksack held before him, his hands crabbing about inside for two Lewes bombs, plus a timer. This being a big old bird he wanted to make doubly sure that he'd blow it sky high. He'd noted how closely the Ju-88s were parked. If he could just get the fuel tank of this one to go up, it should ignite the next and the next, like a row of falling dominoes.

Hands working feverishly he slid the two bombs into position, shoving the same fuse into both of them. That done, he turned to eye the nearest sentry, whose hobnail boots he could hear clicking their way back towards his position. Lassen was now lying on the Junkers' wing facing back the way he'd come, with Jones in front of him.

Lassen watched his fellow raider freeze as he heard the approaching footsteps, then press himself down onto the wing of his chosen Stuka. Each man was carrying several more charges that they'd yet to lay, and they forced themselves to remain motionless as the sentry approached. Unfortunately, like most of the men in his unit, Jones was a compulsive smoker, and as the lead sentry moved forwards he let out a stifled cough.

The sentry stiffened. He turned to glance in Jones's direction. 'Friedrich? Friedrich?'

The sentry stared at Jones's Stuka for a long moment. Jones was doing his best to force his body into the hard steel of the wing, but it was slick with the first drops of dew, and he was sick with worry that he was going to slip and fall.

'*Friedrich?*' the sentry called again, more insistent this time.

He slipped the rifle off his shoulder, flicking the safety to off and levelling it at the hip. Keeping it there, he reached into his pocket for his torch.

As he did so, a silent figure sprinted along the wing of the *Schellbomber*, sailed thought the air, and landed with a crushing impact on the German's shoulders. Even as he hit the deck Lassen jerked the sentry's head up and to the left with one hand, the other driving his fighting knife into the man's throat, forcing it savagely downwards.

As he'd fallen the sentry's rifle had clattered to the ground, making a harsh metallic crack as the barrel hit the concrete.

His fellow sentry stiffened in alarm. He called out, voice thick with alarm. 'Oli? Oli?'

The dying man gurgled horribly as he fought against Lassen's hold. Moments later, Lassen rose to his feet, the dead man's rifle gripped in his hand.

'Hey! Friedrich! It's me!' He was speaking fluent German. 'Like a fool I tripped over my own weapon.'

'Dummkopf!' The sentry laughed, but there was a nervous edge to his laughter. Maybe he'd noticed that Lassen didn't exactly sound like the Oli he knew. 'I thought maybe there was trouble?'

'Only my two left feet,' Lassen replied.

He shouldered the rifle and moved forward as if continuing with his patrol. They were a dozen paces apart when Lassen saw the sentry falter, and his hand go towards his weapon. In one smooth movement Lassen drew his Luger and fired, unleashing one sharp shot from the hip, using the weapon Shanghai Style as he'd been taught in their 'school for bloody mayhem and murder'. The bullet struck the guard full in the chest, perfectly aimed to drill his heart.

As the echoes of the shot faded Lassen heard a muffled cry of alarm from the machinegun nest a couple of hundred yards away. He sprinted through the darkness towards Jones, as the gunner called for a searchlight to sweep the airstrip in the direction from which the lone shot had come.

A searchlight fingered the darkness. Confused shots rang out across the airbase, as nervous guards loosed off at shadows. None of the fire yet seemed to be directed at Lassen and Jones, but it was clear that their mission was blown. The Germans would send a search party to look for Oli and Friedrich; two missing sentries wasn't something to be ignored.

Lassen ran over to Jones, who was crouched in a dark slice of shadow beneath one of the Stukas. 'Change of plan,' he hissed. 'Get as many aircraft rigged with charges as you can. We need a distraction to cover us, so we can get the hell out of here. Leave that to me . . . And if we get split up see you at the RV.'

Without another word Lassen turned and moved at a crouching run towards the barracks building. Jones scuttled off towards the remaining aircraft. As the Dane neared the barracks end of the runway, a barrier lifted in the fence-line and a

Kubelwagen – a German open-topped jeep-like vehicle – nosed through. It was loaded with four soldiers, presumably those who had come to investigate the lone shot and the two missing sentries.

Lassen slipped into the shadow of the last Stuka in line. He waited for the vehicle, his right arm gripping a grenade with the pin already removed. He was known for being a 'grenade man' – he loved the weapon, and he never missed a chance to use it. As the Kubelwagen neared the first of the dive-bombers he let out a cry in German.

'Idiots! Sentry change isn't for another thirty minutes!'

The Kubelwagen slowed, and Lassen stepped forward and threw the grenade. It arced through the air, landing in the rear of the open-topped jeep. An instant later a savage blast tore through the vehicle, jagged shards of shrapnel ripping apart its thin metal skin and human occupants alike. The Kubelwagen kept rolling for a few seconds, as the flames engulfing it fizzed and boiled, before coming to rest hanging half in the shallow drainage ditch running beside the runway.

Before the vehicle had stopped Lassen was running for the nearest machinegun nest, crying out: 'Partisans! *Schnell! Schnell! Schnell!*'

The machine-gunner swung his weapon around towards Lassen, but the yelled German words made him hesitate for just an instant. In that moment Lassen fired with the Luger from the hip, three bullets spitting out of the weapon in rapid succession and smashing into the German gunner. It was a classic 'double-tap' – two to the body and one to the head, as he'd been taught – the gunner slumping forward over his weapon.

An instant later Lassen vaulted into the machinegun nest, heaving the dead man to one side. In one smooth move he swung the Maschinengewehr 42 around, and opened fire with the belt-fed 7.92 mm weapon.

As he did so, all hell broke out across Kastelli airfield.

Chapter Two

*25 August 1941, The Atlantic Ocean, 400 miles off the
Coast of North Africa*

In the blackness of the open water a battered ship rolled on the oily swell – her tall twin masts, four knife-cut sails, vertical prow and finely-raked stern marking her out as an old but graceful-looking fishing trawler. At first sight she appeared utterly deserted, but upon closer inspection a number of shadowy figures could be seen moving across the night-dark deck.

Feverish preparations were underway.

Bare-chested and dressed in a motley collection of civilian clothing, each member of the ship's crew bristled with half-hidden weaponry – pistols, grenades, coshes and knives lashed to belts and stuffed into trouser pockets – so much so that they looked more like a gang of bloodthirsty pirates than the honest fishermen one might expect to find on such a vessel.

In reality, the mystery boat was no standard Brixham trawler. She was a small, clandestine British warship – a 'Q-Boat', the 'Q' standing for secrecy and bluff more often than not perpetrated in breach of all the known and accepted rules of war.

She had been selected and modified for the present mission with extreme care and attention to detail. Brixham trawlers are strong and robust for their size, having a three-skin hull, with four-inch planking on the outside covered in cement up to the waterline. She was judged as being seaworthy enough to make a 3,000-mile journey across the capricious Atlantic Ocean without breaking up – that's if her crew could avoid the enemy and successfully navigate her to their target.

The eight-berth ship possessed sails as well as an engine, making her perfect for undertaking long voyages on limited supplies of fuel, or silent night operations under the very noses of the enemy. With her wooden hull she could ply the world's oceans largely immune to the magnetic mines that menaced steel-skinned vessels. But most importantly, to any marauding enemy warplanes she would appear as a harmless fishing boat, one hardly worth a bombing or a strafing run.

Yet her innocent-looking deck could be collapsed within minutes at the tug of a lever, the plywood wheelhouse folding away to reveal a 40mm QF (quick-firing) Vickers cannon, capable of unleashing 115 rounds-per-minute of high explosive, armour-piercing shells. Twin Lewis machineguns had been mounted on a specially lowered section of the deck, so they could be fired unseen through the scuppers – the openings that allow water to drain off a ship's deck.

As if that weren't enough, four experimental Blacker Bombard spigot mortars – a short-range anti-tank weapon developed chiefly for Home Guard use – could be fired from her deck. Armed with a 20-pound airburst shell, the spigot mortars were intended for short-range attack against enemy submarines. Lastly, high above the deck a fake crow's nest had been erected, constituting a fire-platform from which the crew could rain down bursts from their Thompson machineguns – the so-called 'Tommy Gun' favoured by 1930s gangsters and 1940s elite operators alike.

In theory, the ship could hold her own against an enemy U-boat, should one decide to surface and use its deck gun to try to sink her. But fighting wasn't her first line of defence: that lay entirely in trickery and deception.

In short, she was the perfect ship for the kind of small-scale, guerrilla operation such as that on which she was presently embarked – taking a handful of highly trained elite operators far behind enemy lines, to sabotage, plunder, murder and steal. Some 2,000 miles away lay a target of breathtaking audacity, one that her six-man crew were tasked to neutralize, while at all costs avoiding any responsibility being laid at Britain's – and Winston Churchill's – door.

To that end each man had signed an agreement prior to departure, recognizing that they were to be disowned by the British government in the event of their death or capture. In effect, they were on their own. Being taken alive didn't bear thinking about, for they would very likely be treated as spies – tortured and executed. Indeed, one of the first standing orders in the ship's log read: 'Avoid a fight if humanly possible, but resist capture to the last.'

Incongruous words, considering they were scribbled in a standard hardback *Log Book For Yachts*, printed by Thomas Reed publishers and carried by many a weekend sailor.

Tonight the atmosphere aboard ship seemed unusually tense – more so than at any stage of the perilous journey so far. The tiny vessel was nearing her first landfall. Ahead of her in the darkness lay the neutral Portuguese territory of Madeira, an island lying some four hundred miles off the coast of north-west Africa. There the ship intended to put into the Port of Funchal – undoubtedly the greatest test yet of the crew's cunning and nerve, not to mention the Q Ship's bluff and disguise.

At the wheel of the ironically named *Maid Honour* stood a whippet-slim, aesthetic-looking figure, his moustache unable to hide the scar disfiguring his lip where a horse had once bitten him. In another life Gus March-Phillipps might have been the ace thriller-writer and professional horseman that he aspired to be. But not now. Now the world was at war, and Captain March-Phillipps – a battle-scarred veteran of Dunkirk – was leading a band of brigands and desperadoes on a mission the likes of which the world had never seen: the very first deniable operation of the Second World War.

Ahead of March-Phillipps and beneath the main mast stood the distinctive figure of Anders Lassen, a fearsome 'Danish Viking' who alone would account for more Germans than just about any other soldier of his kind in the war. But right now Lassen – the twenty-year-old scion of an aristocratic Danish family – had yet to see any action. The coming mission would constitute his first taste of battle.

To further the bluff and subterfuge they would employ tonight, Lassen proceeded to run up the Swedish flag. It was left fluttering from the masthead – a yellow cross against a bright blue background silhouetted against the barely lightening sky. Some years prior to March-Phillipps requisitioning the *Maid Honour*, her owner had converted her into an ocean-going pleasure cruiser, and the six men now crewing her were posing as a group of Swedes embarked upon a sailing holiday. Sweden being a neutral country the cover story was seen as having merit, and the flag might at least add a little extra authenticity.

Lassen however refused to put all his trust in their claims to Swedish neutrality. Before setting sail from Poole Harbour, in the south of England, Lassen had shinned up the sixty-odd feet to the apex of the topmast, and there nailed on a piece of dried dolphin's tail. He swore that he'd been given it as a sailor's lucky charm, and he for one believed they were in dire need of any good-fortune it might bring.

'We are doomed,' Lassen had pronounced. 'I will never see any of you again. We are sailing without an escort. We haven't a hope.'

Lassen's gloomy fatalism didn't reflect any lack of keenness on his part to go to war. Quite the reverse. In spite of his youth he was actually one of the most experienced seamen aboard the *Maid Honour*. After school, he'd more-or-less run away to join the merchant navy, and it was via that route that he'd found his way to Britain. But from his experiences on the high seas he was convinced that any ship sailing without an escort was dead in the water.

Yet so far, Lassen's worries had proved distinctly ill-founded. Without any form of escort, operating on strict radio silence and with no qualified navigator – prior to departure March-Phillipps had undergone a largely self-taught crash course in sea navigation – the *Maid Honour* had succeeded in making her way 1,267 miles to this remote island outpost, where they needed to take on fresh water and food. The hectic preparations now taking place above and below decks were to make the ship appear as much as possible like an innocent Swedish pleasure cruiser, once dawn and landfall were at hand.

Across from the shadowy figure of Lassen, Lieutenant Geoffrey Appleyard and Lieutenant Graham Hayes busied themselves stowing away the *Maid Honour*'s weaponry and ammunition. It would need to be very well-hidden. Upon entering Madeira's Funchal Harbour the *Maid Honour* was bound to be subjected to a rigorous inspection by the Portuguese naval authorities. In a war that was fast spreading to the four corners of the world, the Portuguese – like their Spanish neighbours – were desperate to preserve their neutrality.

Known to all simply as 'Apple', Appleyard was a strikingly handsome twenty-three-year-old Yorkshireman. Like March-Phillipps he was a nature-lover and keen amateur ornithologist. He was also supremely fit and combat hardened, being another veteran of the retreat from France. In fact, Appleyard had first met March-Phillipps purely by chance, as both men had sheltered in a foxhole on the bloody beaches of Dunkirk. March-Phillipps and Appleyard had hated the taste of impotence and failure that Dunkirk had left in their mouths. They had vowed to strike back hard against the German enemy, and it was their chance meeting that had given birth to the present, daring undertaking.

March-Phillipps was an inspired and driven commander, one forever inclined to think the unthinkable – qualities that made him well suited to the task at hand. His deputy, Appleyard, was the calmer, more methodical planner and thinker, though no less brave and spirited for it.

Graham Hayes, the man now helping Appleyard stow away the *Maid Honour*'s guns, was third-in-command of the diminutive vessel. Lieutenant Hayes had grown up alongside Appleyard in the Yorkshire village of Linton-on-Wharfe, and they'd formed a close childhood friendship. A wood-sculptor before the war, Hayes was a quiet, charming, fearless dynamo of a man, and he'd been recruited for the present mission at Appleyard's personal behest.

To aid in their collective subterfuge – that this was nothing but a Swedish trip – March-Phillipps had recruited Private Frank 'Buzz' Perkins, a boyish-looking seventeen-year-old, as the fifth member of the crew. He'd been stuck with the childhood nickname Buzz, all because his baby sister, unable to pronounce 'brother', had taken to calling him 'buzzer'. Blond, fresh-faced and gangly, Buzz was the son of a good friend of the *Maid Honour*'s captain – one who'd somehow been persuaded to grant permission for his child to set sail on such a perilous venture.

As they neared Portuguese waters, Buzz was ordered to act like a ship's boy for all he was worth.

His other job aboard ship was to keep her single engine in good working order – something that had become a thankless and excruciating task. The underpowered four-cylinder petrol motor was deeply unreliable, but somehow Buzz had managed to nurse it across a thousand-plus miles of storm-swept sea.

In the months leading up to their departure each of these men had been taught to wage war in what was then a very un-British way – fast and dirty, with no holds barred. At the revolutionary Experimental Station 6, the codename for the seemingly genteel Ashton Manor, just south of Stevenage, in Hertfordshire, they'd been taught to fight 'without a tremor of apprehension, to hurt, maul, injure or kill with ease'. Their instructors were the legendary William Fairbairn and Eric 'Bill' Sykes, veterans of policing British interests in what was then the wild Treaty Port of Shanghai, which lies at the mouth of China's mighty Yangtze River.

On that city's lawless waterfront and in its twisting streets and alleyways Fairbairn and Sykes had learned how to injure and kill at close quarters. At the outbreak of war they had been recalled to Britain, to teach all they knew to the crew of the *Maid Honour*, and others volunteering for such missions. From Wilkinson Sword they'd commissioned a specially made knife, with a seven-inch blade, a heavy handle to give firm grip in the wet, a cross-guard to prevent hand slip, plus two razor sharp edges and a sharp, stiletto stabbing profile.

Some 250,000 of these knives would roll off Wilkinson Sword's London production line during the war years, each etched with the words 'The Fairbairn Sykes Fighting Knife' on its square head. Fairbairn and Sykes taught the *Maid Honour* crew how to stalk a man silently from behind, to snake an arm around his neck choking off any cry, while jerking the head sideways and driving the blade deep into the soft area between the neck and shoulder blade in a savage down-thrust.

They demonstrated how if a main artery was severed, a man would quickly lose consciousness and die – drowned within seconds in his own blood. Most importantly, Fairbairn stressed, there was no more deadly a weapon at close quarters than the knife, 'and it never runs out of ammunition.' In what became known as their 'school for bloody mayhem' they demonstrated methods of silent strangulation, how to disable with a single blow from fist or boot targeting vulnerable points like the kidney or spine, and how to wield a pistol fast and deadly from the hip, 'Shanghai Style'.

They stressed how most pistol duels take place at very short range, a matter of a few feet separating the two sides. They showed how the man who was quickest on the draw would doubtless win, no matter how accurate was his aim. By drawing and firing Shanghai Style – bracing the pistol butt against the hip and aiming from there – the shooter could get the drop on his opponent. They taught the double tap – two bullets fired rapidly from the hip, in the general direction of the target's torso, to disable, then one fired with more careful aim into his head.

In short, they emphasized how in war, 'one cannot afford the luxury of squeamishness.' What they taught at Station 6 wasn't fair and it wasn't pretty, but it certainly delivered. And Anders Lassen for one had taken to this school for bloody mayhem like a fish to water.

But right now as the sun rose above the glittering ocean and March-Phillipps set a course for Madeira's Funchal Harbour, it was subterfuge and deception that was needed most of all.

Landfall was approaching.

With the jagged profile of Madeira hoving into view – the volcanic peaks of the island rise to over 6,000 feet at their highest – even Lassen was persuaded to discard and keep hidden all of his weaponry. Being a fluent Swedish speaker, the blond-haired

Dane – along with Hayes, who spoke a smattering of Swedish, and Buzz the 'cabin boy' – would spearhead their Scandinavian deception.

Cover papers were hastily gathered together. These included false passports and fake seaman's documents, all of which identified the crew as Swedish civilians off on a transatlantic jolly.

With weapons concealed and papers made ready, the *Maid Honour* swept into the seemingly idyllic harbour, which lies at the southern end of the island. The distinctive white steeple of Santa Clara church seemed to keep watch over the harbour's breakwater, which reaches like a crooked arm far into the bay. But it was other watchful eyes that March-Phillipps feared. Madeira had attracted the unwanted attention of the Germans during the First World War, and she was bound to have done so again now.

In December 1916 the German submarine U-38 had sailed undetected into Funchal Harbour and torpedoed and sunk three British and French ships. She'd then bombarded the town with her gun, before shore batteries had forced her to withdraw. In that war Portugal had fought alongside the British, and the German enemy had been unwelcome in all Portuguese territories. But right now, in August 1941, Portugal remained neutral. As with many neutral nations, its capital, Lisbon, was known to be crawling with German spies. Likewise, Funchal, this strategically placed mid-Atlantic harbour was bound to have its own complement of enemy agents.

If the *Maid Honour*'s true nature and purpose were discovered, a British Q Ship bristling with concealed weaponry would be far from welcome here. The vessel would be impounded; her crew seized, imprisoned and left bereft of any hope that the British government would come to their rescue. But without replenishing their fresh water and food supplies, the crew wouldn't last the two thousand miles of their epic journey to come.

It was Funchal Harbour or bust.

On March-Phillipps' order the vessel drifted to a halt, and dropped anchor in the lee of the breakwater. *Now the wait.*

The first vessels to appear on the water were the traditional 'bum-boats', crewed by locals and carrying fresh provisions – fruit, eggs and vegetables – to sell to the visiting seamen. But among their number the crew could make out the sleek form of a Portuguese coastguard launch, complete with her uniformed officials.

The launch bore down on them fast. Playing his part to perfection, Lassen welcomed the Portuguese captain aboard, deliberately adopting a thick accent and faltering English, which seemingly convinced the man that this was indeed a Swedish vessel. For a long and tense moment the captain seemed to linger by the fake wheelhouse – the 40mm QF Vickers cannon just one pull of a lever away from erupting into view. In spite of its fake door, the 'wheelhouse' could only be entered from below, and if the Captain asked to see inside Lassen would have to come up with some cock and bull story as to why it couldn't be opened.

As luck would have it, Lassen – with Hayes and Buzz Perkins in support – managed to steer the coastguard party past the main danger points. By the time the inspection was over the Funchal authorities seemed happy that this vessel was what the crew claimed her to be – an innocent pleasure yacht, one crewed by fellows from a sister neutral country, Sweden. The coastguard captain urged the crew to take on-board whatever supplies they required for the journey ahead, stamped their – entirely false – documents and wished them 'bon voyage'.

The *Maid Honour* had passed her first real test – the deception had held good. Hastily re-provisioned, the crew wasted no time in setting sail once more, heading south towards the coast of West Africa. Fresh trade winds whisked the ship along at a spanking pace, and the crew was more than a little relieved to leave Portuguese waters behind them. By the time she was two days out from Funchal the *Maid Honour* was making seven or eight knots. A day later she topped ten knots, and the crew were able to indulge in a meal of fresh flying fish, which had made the mistake of blundering into the ship's rigging.

Averaging 146 miles a day the *Maid Honour* swept further southwards. As she approached the Cape Verde islands she was forced to turn west, to give the West African nation of Senegal a wide berth. With the Germans victorious in France, a significant proportion of the French people had opted to throw their lot in with the German invaders. Vichy France had been formed and those parts of France in league with the Axis powers encompassed swathes of southern France, plus many of her overseas colonies. Senegal was in Vichy hands, as was the French Colonial Navy stationed at Senegal's Dakar naval base, and the Vichy French administration was known to be virulently anti-British.

In September 1940 a powerful British fleet had set sail to seize Senegal by force of arms if the Vichy French defenders refused to capitulate. In Operation Menace the aircraft carrier HMS *Ark Royal*, accompanied by two battleships, several cruisers, destroyer escorts and troop carriers laid siege to Dakar naval base. But the Vichy French defenders had used their shore batteries, plus their own light cruisers *Georges Leygues* and *Montcalm* to repulse the attack. With the help of a hundred or more shore-based warplanes the British task force was finally beaten off.

Eleven months later Senegal remained in Vichy French hands, its fleet of warships still a potent fighting force – hence March-Phillipps' detour west, to avoid her waters. Just when he least needed it, the *Maid Honour* drifted out of the corridor of southerly trade winds and found herself becalmed. She was still some three hundred miles north of the Cape Verde islands, and well-within interception range by the Vichy French warships sailing out of Dakar. The *Maid Honour* was a sitting duck. Should an enemy vessel steam onto the horizon, becalmed as they were, their puny, unreliable petrol engine would give them little chance of escape.

March-Phillipps urged his crew to keep an eagle-eyed watch on sea and sky, as they rotated their sentry duties, standing six-hours on and six off. Tired though they all were from the constant need for vigilance, the last thing they could risk right now was to let an enemy warship sneak up on them before they could un-mask and bring to bear their guns.

The *Maid Honour* was six days out from Madeira and still marooned in a windless calm, when the lookout on the mast-head fire-platform cried out the dreaded warning.

'Ships off the port bow! Ships off the port bow!'

The two vessels were as yet too distant to be identified, but one was clearly a merchant ship, while the other had the unmistakable – and chilling – silhouette of a battle cruiser. From the direction of their approach it was most likely that these were Vichy French vessels. If so, the warship had to be either the *Georges Leygues* or the *Montcalm*. Light cruisers of some 9,000 tonnes, each boasted a 31-knot top speed, nine massive 152mm guns, plus twenty-four 40mm cannons.

There seemed no way in which the cruiser would pass them by. Indeed, the more March-Phillipps studied the course set by the commander of the distant warship, the more he became convinced that it was sailing on an interception bearing.

The *Maid Honour*'s captain considered his options. They may have fooled a handful of Portuguese coastguard officials back at Funchal Harbour, but a Vichy French cruiser was a completely different matter. Even if she didn't identify the *Maid Honour* as a hostile vessel from distance, she was sure to send across a boarding party to thoroughly check her over.

March-Phillipps made a snap decision. The hour for deception was clearly past.

'Man the guns!' he cried. 'Man the guns!'

Figures dashed across the deck. The dummy wheelhouse was collapsed, and the Vickers 40mm cannon loaded and brought to bear. She had an accurate range of around 4,000 metres, though what damage her two-pound shells might inflict on a Vichy French cruiser with 120mm-thick side-armour was open to debate. The Lewis machineguns were unmasked, and the crew took up battle stations as they waited for the warship to come within range.

March-Phillipps was determined to be the first to open fire, but he could only do so once he'd made a positive identification that this was indeed an enemy warship. Even then it was surely only a matter of time before the *Maid Honour* was blasted out of the water. It looked as if Anders Lassen's grim prediction – *we are doomed; we are sailing without an escort; we haven't a hope* – was about to be proved horribly accurate.

And so the six men waited, hunkered down behind their weapons, and determined to go down all guns blazing.

Chapter Three

Even as the crew of the *Maid Honour* awaited a seemingly deadly confrontation, a power struggle was playing out at the highest level in London, and all concerning the diminutive vessel's daring mission. As the British Expeditionary Force had retreated from the French beaches, so Churchill had issued an extraordinary order to his Chiefs of Staff: 'prepare hunter troops for a butcher-and-bolt reign of terror.'

Under Churchill's order the British military was tasked to do something that didn't quite come naturally to it – to raise a raiding force to strike the enemy in hit-and-run attacks, using all possible measures. Every man aboard the *Maid Honour* was one of Churchill's 'volunteers for Special Duties', and March-Phillipps had been given 'absolute power' to pick and choose his number. He'd gone for individuals formed in his own image: fiery, disdainful, rebellious and individualistic, and with little respect for the formal hierarchies that defined the established military.

Indeed, March-Phillipps' authority – and that of his entire crew – flowed not from the regular armed forces, but from an organization born of Churchill's iron will and formed wholly in the shadows. In the summer of 1940 Britain's wartime leader had given the green light for the founding of the highly-secretive

Special Operations Executive (SOE). Its remit went way far beyond butcher-and-bolt raiding. Its mission was to set ablaze enemy-held Europe – and the wider world – launching subversion and sabotage missions wherever possible.

The SOE wasn't part of the wider military. It was formed under the Ministry of Economic Warfare, and it was more akin to a separate branch of the Secret Intelligence Service (SIS). So clandestine was its existence that it operated under a cover name – the innocuous sounding 'Inter-Service Research Bureau.' Those who began working at its grey, nondescript 64 Baker Street, London, headquarters referred to the SOE as variously 'The Firm', 'The Org' or, perhaps most suitably, 'The Racket.'

Officially the SOE didn't exist, and neither did its agents nor its missions, which meant that *anything was possible*. The *Maid Honour*'s key crew – March-Phillipps, Appleyard, Hayes and Lassen – had been exhaustively checked and vetted, and contracted to utmost secrecy prior to their departure for Africa.

The Official Secrets Act, signed by all four of the *Maid Honour* stalwarts, warned them that: 'Any person who is guilty of a misdemeanour under the Official Secrets Acts 1911 and 1920 shall be liable upon conviction or indictment to imprisonment with or without hard labour . . .'

Lassen's 'Minute Sheet', detailing his SOE vetting, recorded him as 'Danish – passed by M.I.5 and Scotland Yard'. His MI5 vetter, a Captain Strong, wrote of Lassen: 'NOTHING RECORDED AGAINST" – i.e. no negative trace had been found on the prospective SOE recruit.

The SOE operated on a strict need-to-know basis and it wasn't bound by the regular military's labyrinthine rules and red tape. Its agents were paid in cash, to prevent banking and wage slips leaving any kind of a paper trail. It had its own James-Bond-like dirty tricks department, producing exploding attaché cases and pistols disguised as pens, and numerous other similarly innovative means of doing harm to the enemy.

In truth, the SOE was formed to carry out operations seen as being too politically explosive, illegal or unconscionable as to be embraced by the wider British establishment. This was Churchill's answer to his edict to set the lands of the enemy ablaze – though he'd perhaps little-imagined that his extraordinary call to arms would manifest itself in the form of a wooden trawler sailing half-way around the world, crammed full of such an odd assortment of piratical raiders and desperadoes.

As well as being highly-trained commandos, the *Maid Honour* crew were secret agents working under direct orders from the SOE. The *Maid*'s present mission had first been dreamt up in the bowels of the SOE building, by March-Phillips and Appleyard, working together with Brigadier Colin McVean Gubbins, the SOE's Operations and Training Director – better known to all as simply 'M'.

In the previous year Gubbins had been sent into Norway to organize Striking Companies to fight a guerrilla war to hold-up the advancing Germans. They had blown up bridges, sabotaged railway lines, mined tracks and generally spread as much destruction and mayhem as possible. In Norway Gubbins had learned the craft of guerilla warfare well, and he was one of its diehard advocates. And as far as Gubbins saw it, the *Maid Honour*'s mission absolutely fitted the bill.

But when he'd rubber-stamped the founding of the SOE, Winston Churchill had little appreciated the resentment and anger that it would cause in some circles. Having trained his special agents, M had experienced grave problems actually getting them deployed. The *Maid Honour* Force had been no exception. In scoping out various options for the Force's inaugural mission – and the very first deniable operation of the SOE – M had run up against some spirited opposition from the highest echelons of the British military, not to mention Churchill's foremost political adversaries.

Decrying the lawless nature of the *Maid Honour*'s master and crew, not to mention their modus operandi and intentions, the Royal Navy had managed to get them banned from all European theatres of operations – but not from Africa.

Gubbins, and all involved in the conception of the mission, knew that the stakes were high. If the crew of the *Maid Honour* succeeded in their present task, it would be proof that the SOE's concept of high-octane risk, coupled with an absolute disregard for international law, was workable, and capable of achieving spectacular results and reaping stupendous rewards. But if it failed, the consequences were unthinkable . . .

The target of the tiny Q Ship now becalmed off the coast of West Africa lay some two thousand miles eastwards, on the small Spanish colonial territory and island nation of Fernando Po (now called Bioko). Lying in the Gulf of Guinea – the very armpit of Africa – Fernando possesses Santa Isabel harbour, a port of equal strategic import to that of Funchal, the *Maid Honour*'s recent re-supply stop-over.

The British powers feared that Santa Isabel harbour was being used as a covert re-supply point for German U-boats stalking Allied shipping along the African coast. A mission to raid Santa Isabel risked stirring up a hornets' nest of international outrage, for in theory at least Spain remained a neutral party in the war. But recent developments in the region had convinced Brigadier Gubbins, Winston Churchill and his War Cabinet that such a raid – *if fully deniable* – might actually be worth the risk. If all went well, it would also represent an invaluable propaganda coup for a British nation desperately in need of positive news from the war.

The war in the North African desert was presently in full swing, and victory hung in the balance. Air cover was seen as being crucial to the fortunes of both sides – the British on the one hand, and the German-Italian Axis Powers on the other. With the Mediterranean menaced by enemy U-boats and warplanes, the safest route to get aircraft and spare parts into North Africa was via convoys to Britain's West African ports, from where they were flown north to those airstrips still in British hands.

Or at least it had been. But by the summer of 1941 German U-boat attacks along the West African coast were threatening the safety of those convoys – many of which had been forced to re-route thousands of miles across the Atlantic.

Spain's Falangist government under General Franco was seen as being neo-Fascist, and an enthusiastic, if secretive supporter of the Axis Powers. During the Spanish Civil War Italian troops had fought alongside Franco's forces, and German Stuka dive-bombers had provided devastating air support. In short, while Franco's Spain paid lip service to her much-vaunted neutrality, Fernando Po's Santa Isabel port was suspected of being a clandestine German U-boat refuelling and rearming depot.

What gave added weight to those suspicions were the three enemy ships – one flying the German Swastika, one the Italian flag – seemingly permanently anchored in Santa Isabel harbour. The largest, the *Duchessa d'Aosta* was an 8,000-tonne Italian passenger liner-cum-cargo ship, manned by an Italian crew of between forty and fifty. Her hold was stuffed full of valuable war materials – including copper ingots, plus a quantity of materials any further details of which the ship's Captain had refused to divulge.

A copy of the ship's manifest had been obtained by the SOE, but it was the missing page that proved most tantalizing: 'The manifest as forwarded contains six pages,' the SOE reported, 'It is understood, however, that a seventh page is missing . . . The Spanish port authority requested a copy of the missing sheet from the ship's master, who declined to produce it but offered no explanation.'

The repeated refusal by the *Duchessa*'s captain to divulge the nature of the materials detailed on the seventh page of the manifest fuelled speculation that his ship was in truth carrying weaponry, and possibly even spare parts for German submarines.

The second largest vessel moored in Santa Isabel harbour was a modern German tugboat, the 200-tonne *Likomba*, which came complete with German captain and crew. The *Likomba* was the perfect kind of vessel for going to a crippled U-boat's aid, and towing her to the shelter of the nearest hidden tropical lagoon or 'neutral' harbour. Moored alongside the *Likomba* was a luxury pleasure yacht, the *Bibundi*, which was also presumed to be a German vessel.

Whatever the three ships and their crew might be up to – with the suspected connivance of the Spanish port authorities – a decision was made that they had to be stopped.

The SOE had been formed entirely so that its actions could be disowned by His Majesty's Government. It was clear that any mission to raid Santa Isabel Harbour and to take out the three enemy vessels would have to be carried out by SOE agents – for this of any mission called for absolute secrecy coupled with total deniability.

At the SOE headquarters various options for the assault – codenamed 'Operation Postmaster' – had been considered. Bombing the ships from the air was unthinkable, for British warplanes would be wholly identifiable. Such a wanton breach of neutrality would almost certainly provoke Spain into joining forces with the Axis powers, after which Portugal would very likely be forced to follow suit, with potentially disastrous consequences for Britain's fortunes in the war.

Infiltrating the port and sinking the vessels where they lay at anchor was the next most obvious option, but that wouldn't provide the knockout blow. The harbour was comparatively shallow with a firm, rocky bottom, and a vessel the size of the *Duchessa d'Aosta* would simply settle a few feet onto the seabed. It would be possible to repair and re-float her, and possibly also the German tugboat. And so the mission had become a 'cut-out' tasking – one designed to free the vessels and spirit them into British hands, and all without any responsibility being laid at Britain's door.

The plan for the cut-out mission involved March-Philipps sailing his ship into Santa Isabel Harbour under cover of darkness, whereupon he and his men would overpower the ships' crew, seize the vessels, blow their anchor chains and spirit them away to one of the nearest British ports, lying some 1,500 miles across the Gulf of Guinea.

If spotted, the *Maid Honour* would simply appear as an unidentifiable fishing trawler, albeit one sporting some unusual weaponry for such a ship. If she was captured – and this was to be avoided at all costs – the *Maid Honour* might still maintain the bluff of being of Swedish origin. If any of her crew were taken alive – death was considered far preferable; like all SOE agents the crew carried what had been nicknamed 'holy communion', a hidden suicide pill to be taken in case of capture – they were to stick to their cover story at all costs. If all of that failed the mission would be vehemently denied by the British government, who would blame 'rebel elements' for carrying out the attack wholly without official sanction.

Upon first consideration such a mission appeared nigh-on impossible; looking at the port's defences there was every likelihood of failure. There were reports of increasing numbers of Spanish troops and armaments arriving on Fernando Po. Its vital strategic position made the island a tempting target for both Germany and Britain – for whoever controlled Fernando Po pretty much controlled the Gulf of Guinea. The Spanish had garrisoned the island with forty of their officers, commanding some five hundred native troops, with one hundred or more reservists of European nationality to call upon if need be.

There were a dozen 4-inch guns stationed around the island, and in Santa Isabel itself the Customs House, barracks and main public buildings had machine guns positioned overlooking the harbour. The Spanish Governor of the island was known to be strongly pro-Nazi and thus hostile to British interests.

Needless to say, if *Maid Honour* Force made it to Fernando Po their mission would entail violating just about every rule of war. The cut-out job would represent an outrageous act of piracy and kidnapping on the high seas; it would violate the 'neutrality' of Spain; and in wearing no uniforms the raiders 'deserved' only to be treated as spies, if captured.

If March-Phillipps was successful, Britain – Churchill – needed to be able to deny absolutely all knowledge and culpability. Otherwise, Spain might be provoked into granting Germany access to invade the British territory of Gibraltar, and her vital ports. If Germany took Gibraltar, that would mean the war for the Mediterranean would be all but lost; defeat only be a matter of time.

Accordingly, there needed to be a plausible explanation as to how on earth two German and one Italian ships had fallen into British hands. Working closely with Ian Fleming, then SOE's liaison at the Admiralty – and the future author of the James Bond books – M set about coming up with just such a ruse. The cover story finally agreed upon by M, Fleming and others in the know consisted of several sophisticated and interlocking elements.

The British destroyer HMS *Violet*, stationed in the West African port of Lagos, in Nigeria, would steam into the Gulf of Guinea to intercept the three vessels once they had been 'cut-out' of port. It would be claimed that the Italian and German crews had mutinied, severing their own anchor chains and sailing away of their own accord. Officially, *Violet* would seize the ships and their crew in international waters, and escort them into British custody at Lagos harbour.

Need-to-know and convincing theatre was absolute paramount with this element of the cover story. The captain of HMS *Violet* would be given sealed orders for his eyes only, and told to open them only once at sea. He wouldn't know the nature of his mission until he had embarked upon it. The entirety of his officers and crew would be left believing they were tasked to intercept a genuine 'enemy flotilla', and heavily-armed boarding parties would be sent to disarm and subdue all aboard.

Once the three ships had been 'seized', the captain of HMS *Violet* was to send a coded radio message: 'Postmaster Successful'. That would trigger the next stage of the cover story, to be orchestrated from London. The BBC would broadcast a story in English, Spanish and Portuguese, based upon a press-release issued by the Admiralty. It would detail how three enemy vessels had been intercepted by a Royal Navy warship. The crews had mutinied due to poor pay and conditions in Fernando Po, and the vessels had been seized as prizes of war.

*

The success of this clandestine raid, and of the cover stories, was of paramount importance. In recognition of this, during recent weeks M had visited the *Maid Honour* Force at their Poole base on numerous occasions. As a result, he was convinced that if anyone, March-Phillipps and his crew had the training, the skills and the sheer guts to pull off such a mission.

However, the Admiralty remained suspicious of a force that it viewed as something of a 'loose cannon'. Shortly before the *Maid Honour*'s departure Ian Fleming had been sent down to Poole to do his own investigation. Whatever Fleming's conclusions about *Maid Honour* Force, the Admiralty had chosen not to stand in the way of their setting sail for Fernando Po – perhaps believing the raiders could do little harm if sent off on such a harebrained scheme so far from home.

Yet, as the *Maid Honour* made her way towards her target, other powerful forces conspired to block her path. Admiral Willis, the Navy's overall commander in the South Atlantic – the waters through which the Q Ship was steaming – was not best pleased upon learning of her coming mission. General Giffard, the British Army's overall commander in West Africa, was even less enamoured with the proposed raid on Fernando Po. Both commanders bemoaned the potentially ruinous ramifications should Operation Postmaster fail.

Even as the *Maid Honour* sat becalmed off West Africa, General Giffard and Admiral Willis made it clear to London that in their view the risks were unacceptable, and neither commander had much if any desire to assist with such an undertaking – one that might turn the very fortunes of the war.

Of course, for those crewing the *Maid Honour* the consequences of failure would be far more immediate and deadly. Perhaps inevitably, some twelve months on from its formation the existence of the SOE had become known to Hitler, as had its mission to send agents deep into enemy territory. In a chilling order issued in response to its earliest activities, Hitler decreed that SOE operatives and their resistance colleagues were to disappear into the *Nacht und Nebel* – into the Night and Fog.

Captured SOE operatives were to be shown no mercy. After unspeakable torture, they were to be hanged – on specific instructions issued by the Führer – using piano wire, to make their deaths as slow and degrading as possible. The aim of this was two-fold: one, *pour décourager les autres*; and two, to extract every last drop of intelligence from those agents, to aid in the tracking down of their SOE colleagues.

As the *Maid Honour* lay becalmed with a warship fast approaching, her crew feared they were about to disappear into the night and the fog.

Chapter Four

March-Phillipps – the man braced at the *Maid Honour*'s wheel urging his men to a spirited, if hopeless defiance – was also known as SOE agent W.01. 'W' stood for West Africa, the region to which he was deployed, and '01' denoted that he was the first SOE agent assigned to that territory. The '0' prefix also signified that March-Phillipps was a 'zero'-rated agent, meaning that he was trained and licensed to use all means to liquidate the enemy.

But right now March-Phillipps' means of liquidating the enemy were somewhat limited. In spite of his standing order in the ship's log – *avoid a fight if humanly possible, but resist capture to the last* –the *Maid Honour* appeared doomed. Becalmed, there was nowhere that she could run to using her one small and unreliable motor. She had no option but to stand and fight, even against the fearsome weaponry of the fast-approaching La Galissonniere-class cruiser.

Or at least March-Phillipps presumed that was the identity of the mystery warship, for as he swept his field glasses across her deck he noted the massive guns set in twin-turrets forward of the superstructure, the rear-most battery positioned higher than that in front, so they could put down devastating salvoes in unison. Agents W.02 and W.03 – otherwise known as Appleyard and Hayes – were equally convinced that this had to be one of the Vichy French warships that had survived Operation Menace, Britain's abortive attack on Dakar.

Minute by minute the powerful battle cruiser bore down upon the diminutive Q Ship. Five sets of eyes scanned the vessel for clues as to her identity, while the tension mounted and the men remained poised at their battle stations.

It was then that those armed with field glasses noticed an anomaly. As she drew closer, her prow cleaving the water in a furl of white, it became clear that the mystery vessel was bigger and more potent than a French cruiser – more akin to the size of a full battleship. Surely, the 9,000 tonne *Montcalm* and *Georges Leygues* were smaller than the approaching vessel, which appeared to be more the size of a 30,000 tonne behemoth. The massive superstructure placed amidships also didn't fit the sleeker, lower profile of the modern French La Galissonniere-class cruisers, and neither did the almost vertical cut of her prow.

It was the distinctive form of the White Ensign fluttering from the ship's rigging – a red St George's cross against a white background, with a Union Jack set in one corner – that finally decided it: she had to be of British origin.

A yell of relief echoed across the *Maid Honour*'s deck, as news of the warship's likely identity was relayed among her crew.

The clipped style of March-Phillipps' entry in the ship's log typically downplays the moment: '4.30 p.m. Hove to. Boarded and questioned. English.'

Under cover of the battleship's guns, a heavily armed party was sent across to the *Maid Honour* and her captain questioned rigorously. March-Phillipps was able to satisfy the boarding force commander to such a degree that he and his men were invited aboard the British battleship. Hot baths, drinks and a supply of fresh food were provided to the five hardy seamen, before the companies parted and their vessels went their separate ways.

But the *Maid Honour's* onward journey proved far from easy. As she rounded Africa's western bulge and began to push east towards the Gulf of Guinea the temperature soared to a debilitating 135 degrees Fahrenheit. Alternately becalmed, roasted and suffering repeated bouts of engine failure, fresh water became a real problem, as did food. The experienced merchant seaman Lassen had his own answer to the latter problem – homemade fish bombs. He removed a piece of calcium carbide from one of the ship's carbide lanterns – which burn acetylene gas – placed it inside an old but shiny tin, and tossed the whole lot over the ship's side.

'Look! Vatch!' he called to his shipmates. 'Fish steaks coming up!'

The warm sea was teeming with life, especially shoals of barracuda. They were drawn to the shiny glitter as the tin slowly sank, before the water made contact with the carbide, releasing acetylene gas in a violent explosive reaction. Fish stunned by the blast floated to the surface. They were gathered up, finished off with a cosh, gutted and sent below to the ship's galley to be filleted and barbecued.

By such unorthodox means and with the wind finally freshening, the crew were sustained and the *Maid Honour* made it to their destination port – Lagos Harbour, in the British colonial territory of Nigeria (after a stop-over in Sierra Leone). The *Maid Honour* had completed an epic journey of over 3,000 nautical miles.

As Lassen recorded in his diary of their arrival: 'I don't think it is an exaggeration to say that in a small boat it was a distinctive achievement. One of the finest of its kind performed in recent years.'

Their target destination, Fernando Po, lay four hundred miles east across the Gulf of Guinea. Santa Isabel Harbour and the three enemy ships were well within their grasp. Six more of the *Maid Honour* Force stalwarts were flown out to Lagos, to reinforce the existing Operation Postmaster crew – including Leslie Prout, making the fourth officer among them. Prout had been a schoolboy champion at rugby and boxing. After school he'd trained as a mechanic, but at the outbreak of war he'd joined up with the Army. He'd served alongside Appleyard in France, and as with the others he'd been recruited by personal recommendation.

Prout was accompanied by five more junior ranks – Thomas Winter, Ernest Evison, Jock Taylor, Dennis Tottenham and the Free Frenchman Andrew Desgranges. The eleven *Maid Honour* crew were boosted by a further six SOE agents now permanently based in Lagos – making seventeen in all. One of those, Agent W.10 Leonard Guise, had already played a crucial role in furthering the aims of Operation Postmaster. Guise wasn't a '0'-rated agent, so unlike the *Maid Honour* Force he wasn't trained to kill. What Guise and other SOE agents like him excelled in were the subtle arts of subterfuge, trickery and deception.

Under the cover of being a British government courier delivering post to the British Consulate, located in Santa Isabel Harbour, Guise had been dispatched to Fernando Po. There he'd busied himself rowing 'mail' to and fro across the baking hot harbour, pausing at the anchor chains of the three target vessels, apparently to catch his breath. In the process he'd managed to use his handspan to make a working measurement of the thickness of each of the chains – crucial information if the ships were to be freed from their moorings.

The assault force could ill afford to get such matters wrong. All the charges would need to explode at exactly the same moment, to maintain the vital element of surprise. But if any one charge failed to detonate or to cut its target chain, setting replacement explosives would take precious seconds. Once the first blasts had been heard, the ships' crews and the harbour defence force would surely be alerted to the raiders' presence.

The more March-Phillipps studied the targets and the harbour defences, the more it became clear that while the *Maid Honour* would have been perfect for sneaking into the harbour and sabotaging the vessels, she could play little role in towing them away. With hostile crews potentially locked below decks, the only means to steal a ship like the *Duchessa d'Aosta* would be to use a tugboat to drag her out of the harbour and onto the high seas. The same was true of the *Likomba* and the pleasure yacht tied up next to her.

Fortunately, there were vessels stationed in Lagos Harbour that would be ideal for the job. One was the powerful British tugboat the *Vulcan*, captained by a very able and willing commander, Tugmaster Coker. The Operation Postmaster plan was re-written. The *Vulcan* would be used to tow out the large passenger liner-cum-cargo-ship, the *Duchessa d'Aosta*. Meanwhile a smaller tugboat, the *Nuneaton*, under Lieutenant Goodman would haul off the German ship, the *Likomba*. Thereafter the tugs would tow their charges to the planned rendezvous with the British destroyer, HMS *Violet*, at which stage Britain could formally 'seize' the vessels and their 'mutinous' crew.

The *Duchessa d'Aosta* had eight officers plus some forty crew aboard, and the *Likomba* was likewise manned by German officers. Once the element of surprise was lost, the men of the *Duchessa* in particular could mount a sustained defence, potentially fighting a running battle across her twin steel decks, plus there were hundreds of mixed Spanish and local soldiers and police ashore. Bearing in mind how heavily outnumbered the raiders were, further layers of deception were written into the Operation Postmaster plan, to even up the odds a little.

A second SOE agent, W.25 Richard Lippett, was dispatched to Fernando Po, with a very special mission to fulfil. Under the cover of being a businessman working for the Santa Isabel office of the British trading company, John Holts, Lippett's role was to discover some means via which he might spirit the Italian and German officers off their respective ships on the night of the assault. Without their officers to lead them, it was hoped the ships' crew would put up less of a fight when faced by piratical British commandos bristling with weaponry.

Lippett set about being sociable and making himself as well-liked as possible among the Santa Isabel locals. In particular, he sought out any Spaniards who might be anti-Franco and anti-Falangist – the kind of people who might have fought on the side of the Republicans in the Spanish civil war. Those kind of Spaniards might be sympathetically inclined to the sort of sabotage and skullduggery March-Phillipps and crew intended – although Lippett, like all involved in Operation Postmaster, knew only as much as he needed to carry out his side of things.

Lippett struck up a friendship with the assistant manager of the Santa Isabel hardware store, a young Spaniard called Abelino Zorilla. Zorilla spoke fluent English, and over many a game of badminton or a pleasant stroll around the Santa Isabel harbour, Lippett deduced that Zorilla was sympathetic to the British cause. The first thing that Lippett sought was a means to neutralize Governor Sorulace, the Spanish overseer of Fernando Po, whose police and soldiers maintained a round-the-clock watch on the premises of the British Consulate.

Such hostile scrutiny hampered enormously the work of SOE agents Lippett and Guise, plus others in the Consulate working to further the Operation Postmaster cause. The method the SOE hit upon to neutralize the Governor was the tried and tested means of blackmail. The Governor was found to have a local mistress – a very beautiful black African lady. Unbeknown to him he was duly photographed stark naked in an upstairs bathroom showering his beloved from a watering-can, prior to whatever else he might have in mind.

Once the Governor was confronted with the compromising photographs he agreed to cease forthwith any surveillance of the British on Fernando Po. He was even persuaded to allow some over-flights of the harbour using his private aircraft, for the supposed purposes of taking photos of its 'scenic beauty'.

Those photos were sent back to Lagos and used to brief March-Phillipps and his team. From those images the exact location of the three vessels was plotted, as were the key buildings ranged around the harbour at which the Spanish defenders, with their machineguns and 4-inch cannons were stationed. The house of the British chaplain then resident on Fernando Po was identified, from which would be sent a pre-arranged message on the night of the assault, to signal the all-clear for the raiders to enter the harbour.

But Lippett's most important task remained to get the German and Italian officers off their ships come the night of the attack. The ruse he finally set upon was to organize a dinner party at one of Santa Isabel's best restaurants, to which all notables in the local community – ship's officers included – were to be invited. To help deflect suspicion from the British, Lippett's Spanish friend, Zorilla, agreed to act as the party's apparent host. He also agreed to drag Heinrich Luhr, a doctor and notable German island resident, into the fray, by allowing him to be seen to pay for the party – unwittingly handing over money that was in truth SOE funds.

Agent Guise – W.10; the man who'd rowed about the harbour gauging the width of the anchor chains – was to guide the tugboats in during the night of the attack. Presuming Lippett had succeeded in luring the officers ashore, he and Guise would have accounted for two absolutely vital elements of Operation Postmaster. Without those elements being in place M, and all at SOE headquarters, believed the mission would have a less than fifty percent chance of success – without which it would not be given the go-ahead.

In one last crucial act of preparation March-Phillipps and his team of licensed-to-kill agents were sent up-country, deep into the Nigerian bush. There, at a tiny jungle settlement called Olokomeji, they joined a secret SOE school training black Africans in guerilla warfare. The Operation Postmaster plan called for the anchor chains to be blown from the ship-side, as opposed to shore, so that none of the raiding force ever set foot upon Spanish soil. Using shaped charges of plastic explosives the raiders set about blowing apart different diameters of chain, while trying to ensure that the blasts would do minimal damage to the ships themselves.

Hinged 'bracelet' charges were found to be the most effective. Three such charges could be slipped around an anchor chain, detonators and fuses inserted, with the whole lot wired to explode simultaneously. But even if all the charges exploded and cut the chains, simply spiriting away the *Duchessa d'Aosta* in particular represented a massive challenge. She was a 7,872-tonne rudderless deadweight, and she would need to be towed out of the shallow harbour via the one narrow channel leading to the open sea.

At 464 feet in length, the *Duchessa d'Aosta* would present an easy target to the shore-based guns, especially as she was moored just one hundred feet or so from the harbourside, making her highly vulnerable to the 4-inch cannons. In one of several worst-case scenarios the crew could barricade themselves below her steel decks while the shore-based defenders would rake the ship's bridge with fire.

A further worrying scenario was that the anchor chains would fail to blow, and the ships would be stuck fast. In another, the raiders would be detected and fired upon before they reached the target ships – and the defender's four-inch guns could do serious damage to the tugboats. In yet another, the tugs would fail to navigate the ships out of the shallow harbour and they would run aground. If a Spanish vessel was moved in to block the harbour exit the assault force would be trapped, at which point all guns could be turned upon them.

Any which way those planning Operation Postmaster looked at it, the chances of failure seemed to far outweigh those of success. While M and his political taskmasters in London still felt it worth the risk, the two powerful regional commanders remained unconvinced. Admiral Willis and General Gifford repeatedly cabled London and otherwise made it clear that they did 'NOT, repeat NOT agree operation should take place.'

When London issued categorical orders that the raid was to go ahead and they were to furnish all possible help, Admiral Willis acquiesced and green-lit the Royal Navy's part in the mission.

But General Gifford, the more obdurate of the two, found an eleventh-hour means via which to frustrate Operation Postmaster. March-Phillipps reckoned that he needed seventeen extra hands, both to help crew the tugboats and to execute the cutting-out assault. General Gifford was asked to provide those extra men, but all he would offer *Maid Honour* Force was his 'best wishes for the success of the operation'. As to committing any Army personnel to Operation Postmaster, he declined.

With just days to go before the mission was scheduled to proceed, March-Phillipps had half the force that he required. Winston Churchill had been briefed at all stages on the progress of the mission, as had his War Cabinet. Not surprisingly, frustration was boiling over with the local delays. Under guidance from London March-Phillipps and Victor Laversuch, the SOE's top agent on the ground in Nigeria, held a meeting with His Majesty's Governor of Nigeria, Sir Bernard Henry Bourdillon, to air their grievances.

Sir Henry was a man of principle and verve who had supported SOE operations in the area from the very start. He'd served as a Major in the First World War, before going into the Colonial Service, and he'd been the Governor of Nigeria since 1935. In short, he was a fifty-eight-year-old veteran of war, intrigue and diplomacy, and he would become one of the many unsung heroes of Operation Postmaster.

Sir Henry listened to March-Phillipps and Laversuch as they outlined their predicament, after which he proposed a solution as dynamic as it was innovative. They should raise a force from within the ranks of his Colonial Service, which included many ex-military types. Sir Henry asked Laversuch and March-Phillipps to draw up a proposed list, which should include the 'toughest individuals in the Public Service in Nigeria.'

SOE agent Guise described the new recruits thus: 'as choice a collection of thugs as Nigeria can ever have seen'. Those chosen included three policemen, three from the Education Branch, four from Public Works, and one each from Land and Survey and Accountancy. The oldest Colonial Administration amateur invited to join the raiding force was fully 52 years of age. Their cover story was that they had been called away for two weeks leave, and in truth they would only learn the nature of the coming mission once they had departed on the tugboats for Fernando Po.

So it was that thirty-four raiders – together with a force of African stokers feeding the furnaces in the bowels of the tugboats – readied themselves for departure. Each was dressed in dark clothing and issued with a pair of soft-soled Plimsolls – perfect for stealing aboard an enemy ship. Only a handful knew anything about the wider mission: they had been told they were volunteers on an undertaking of a military nature, which would be arduous and potentially dangerous, but would boost the war effort mightily.

March-Phillipps finally had his assault force at the ready. He received a telegram from Brigadier Gubbins – better known as 'M' to the assembled SOE agents. It read:

Good hunting. Am confident you will exercise utmost care to ensure success and obviate repercussions. Best of luck to you and all MH and others. M

All that remained now was to set sail and execute the cut-out mission. There was little time for training and no time to delay.

The assault was to go ahead under cover of a waning moon, when the night would be at its darkest.

Chapter Five

In spite of his Danish crewmember's youth and his borderline madness – betrayed by the unwavering stare of his ice-blue eyes – March-Phillipps was glad to have Lassen in his number. He was something of a loner, possessed of a self-belief that often made him appear arrogant, but March-Phillipps recognised in the Dane a natural-born warrior and a potential fellow leader of men. Over the preceding months the two men had grown close, and the *Maid Honour* Force commander had given Lassen a leading role in the coming attack: he would be the first to board the *Duchessa d'Aosta*.

If the coming operation proved successful, Churchill's concept of ultra-deniable law-breaking coupled with butcher-and-bolt terror raids would have been vindicated, and the SOE and *Maid Honour* Force would come of age. March-Phillipps would need leaders to command a much-expanded outfit, and he had Lassen earmarked for just such a role – as two apparently unremarkable tugboats set sail for Fernando Po to launch a most unorthodox form or warfare.

The *Vulcan* and *Nuneaton* had set out early and for a very specific reason. March-Phillipps needed time at sea in which to give his new recruits a crash course in covert raiding. He had four days before the night of the assault, time in which to train his crew in their individual roles and to meld them into a fighting force.

He also had on board three Spaniards who were die-hard anti-Fascists, and who had fought with the Free French against the Germans. They had joined his crew at the last minute at the suggestion of the SOE, who argued they could furnish useful cover were the assault force to be challenged as they sailed into Santa Isabel Harbour.

At Santa Isabel itself plans for the coming deception were well underway. SOE agent Lippett had got his friend Zorilla to inveigle Frau Luhr, wife of the prominent German resident, into their plans. One dinner party had already been held for Santa Isabel's notables – a kind of dry-run – and it had gone down a storm, with a return drinks party being held aboard the *Duchessa d'Aosta*. Now Frau Luhr was persuaded to book the Valencia Restaurant – a very private venue tucked away in the back streets far from any view of the harbour – for a follow-up dinner.

Frau Luhr extended invitations to the Italian and German ships' officers, and all were persuaded to accept. As far as Lippett was concerned, the deception plan was going swimmingly. Perhaps inevitably, Zorilla sensed that something was up. Clearly, Lippett was organizing and bankrolling something more than an innocent dinner party. Zorilla asked his British friend if he would be running into danger once the evening had run its course. Lippett couldn't deny that he might be.

The brave and spirited Spaniard made it clear that whatever blow they were about to strike against Hitler, Mussolini and Franco, he was all for it. But he suggested that it might be best if he made a quiet getaway the night of the dinner party. With Lippett's blessing and help, Zorilla arranged for an African fisherman to be at the ready with a native canoe. Once the festivities were well underway, he would get the fisherman to paddle him across the Gulf of Guinea – a journey the local boatmen did occasionally undertake – and to drop him on Nigerian (then British) soil.

Lippett now turned to his next task – arranging the all-clear signal for the raiding force. Reverend Markham, the English Chaplain resident in Fernando Po was asked to take some leave ashore. There was a Church Synod taking place in Nigeria, which offered him the perfect excuse to do so. The Reverend's house happened to sit in a prime position overlooking the entrance to Santa Isabel Harbour. It was from his window that the final green light would be given.

All seemed set from Lippett's perspective, but three days before the attack the wife of the Valencia Restaurant owner fell ill. The dinner booking was cancelled. The only alternative venue was the Casino Restaurant, where the previous dinner party had been held, but it sat on a raised terrace providing a splendid view over the entire expanse of the harbour, with the target vessels nestling in the bay nearby.

Lippett reminded himself of his number one priority: it was to get those German and Italian officers off their ships. Accordingly, he had Zorilla move the dinner booking to the Casino Restaurant. He drew up a detailed seating plan, ensuring that all the ships' officers would have their backs to the sea. He also made sure to place a pretty woman opposite each of them, which hopefully would hold their attentions. Lippett made it clear to Zorilla that money was no object. The partygoers were to be plied with alcohol – as much as they could get down them – and for those so inclined the SOE's funds would even stretch to covering a drunken roll or two in the local brothel!

The more ships officers who could be tempted to sneak away for a little carnal refreshment the better, as far as Lippett was concerned. *Needs must, old boy.*

Lippett also sought to use the light to his advantage. Each night shortly before midnight the electricity supply to Santa Isabel was shut down, to save power. It was then that March-Phillipps' raiders intended to sail into the darkened harbour, to steal away the ships and their crew. If Lippett could get the terrace of the Casino Restaurant rigged with Tilley Lanterns – pressurized paraffin lamps – the diners would be entombed in a sea of light, blinding them to whatever was taking place in the dark waters below.

As Lippett and Zorilla went about crafting their elaborate onshore deception, so training got underway aboard the assault vessels at sea. March-Phillipps split his crew into five separate teams to prepare them for what was coming – something that SOE agent Guise described as: 'A cut-out operation. In other words, simple theft.' The men were divided into a cable party, an engine room party, a boarding party, back-up boarding party plus the all-important towing party.

DIY coshes were handed out, consisting of long metal bolts sheathed in rubber – for a nervous government in London had stressed that they wanted minimal casualties, especially among the Spanish population.

'Whenever possible, intimidate,' March-Phillipps urged his men. 'If not, use force. Speed is essential.'

The largest weaponry possessed by the assault force were some Bren guns – a 0.303 calibre light machinegun – mounted on their bipods on the tugboats' bows. Likewise, the Bren gunners were urged: 'Deal with any boats. Shoot across bows. No useless slaughter.'

March-Phillipps and Appleyard would command the attack from the decks of the larger tugboat, the *Vulcan*, while Lassen would lead the assault force onto their target boat, the *Duchessa d'Aosta*. Meanwhile, *Maid Honour* Force stalwart Leslie Prout would be in charge of the African stokers in the ship's boiler room, ensuring they didn't down tools and run when the explosions and gunfire started. The *Vulcan* would need all the power she could muster to drag the massive bulk of the Italian ship free, and it was vital the stokers kept shoveling the coal into her engines. The three Spaniards were also stationed on the *Vulcan*, so they could cry out friendly greetings in Spanish, if challenged.

The smaller tugboat, the *Nuneaton*, was charged with seizing the German ship, the *Likomba*. *Maid Honour* Force veteran Graham Hayes – part of the five-man crew who had sailed the *Maid Honour* out from Britain – would command and lead the assault from her decks. He had with him SOE agent Guise, plus the youthful Buzz Perkins. Two District Commissioners, a Mr Newington and Mr Abell, formed part of the civilian volunteer force supporting them.

At first the weather was stormy and the Colonial Service volunteers were terribly seasick. But by day two the sea had calmed, and the first day's training aboard the *Vulcan* got underway. It was vital that the wire hawsers were made fast to the *Duchessa d'Aosta* swiftly, so she could be hauled out of the harbour with all due alacrity. While Tugmaster Coker concentrated on schooling his raw recruits in tow-wire drill, Hayes gathered his volunteers on the *Nuneaton*'s sun-washed deck, to demonstrate one of the most important skills of all – how to use a Tommy Gun.

The Thompson submachinegun was over twenty years old by the time the war began. However, it remained a favourite of elite raiding forces for several reasons – some of which are reflected in the weapon's various nicknames: 'Trench Sweeper', 'Trench Broom' and 'The Chopper'. It was of simple, reliable design, had a high volume of fire, and its .45-calibre cartridge delivered real stopping power. When fitted with a 30-round stick magazine, or a 50-round drum, it really was possible to sweep an entire enemy trench with fire from a Thompson – not to mention the deck of an enemy ship.

But as the would-be raiders unleashed bursts of Tommy Gun fire at targets tossed in the sea, disaster struck. The *Nuneaton* was under tow from the *Vulcan*, to conserve fuel stocks – both being coal-fired vessels. All of a sudden the *Nuneaton* heeled over violently and seawater flooded into the wheelhouse, pouring into the engine room below. Various ship's supplies tumbled over the side as the men clung on for dear life. The *Nuneaton* had swung too far to one side on her towrope, until she all-but capsized.

As the *Vulcan* ploughed ahead she was dragging the smaller ship further into trouble, water cascading over her deck. It was

Lassen the experienced seaman who saved the day. Seeing the *Nuneaton* heeling over disastrously, he grabbed an axe, ran to the *Vulcan*'s stern and hacked through the tow-rope. Freed at last, the *Nuneaton* finally righted herself. Two men had ended up in the sea, and they were pulled out as quickly as possible, for sharks had been sighted in the area. When the vessels finally got underway again the *Nuneaton* was doing so under her own steam.

Training resumed. A pair of folbots – collapsible canoes – were assembled and painted a dull camouflage grey for night-time operations. March-Phillipps and Appleyard had decided that the *Likomba* could be boarded from those, for she sat so much lower in the water. The advantage of the folbots was that they allowed for an utterly silent and stealthy approach, as long as those crewing them knew how to paddle and steer them properly.

Hayes and Winter – the *Maid Honour* Force regulars – were old hands at such work. They would crew the first folbot, with District Commissioners Newington and Abell in a backup canoe. It took a degree of skill to master the two-man craft. With both vessels hoved to, District Commissioner Newington lowered himself into the narrow, canvas-skinned folbot, with his customary pork pie hat perched on his head and his pipe clamped between his teeth. A large and avuncular man, Newington proceeded to paddle with gusto towards the *Vulcan*, which right now was acting as the target ship.

He promptly capsized.

Undeterred, and with hat and pipe still in place, he began to swim his folbot back towards the *Nuneaton*. It was then that the sharks began to circle. Those on deck were yelling warnings at Newington, but presuming it to be nothing more than good-natured banter he continued on his slow but steady way. Luckily he made it back in one piece, but he turned as white as a sheet once he realized how close the sharks had been.

It was now their third day out from Lagos, and Operation Postmaster was scheduled to take place just before midnight on the morrow. March-Phillipps decided it was time to reveal to his newest recruits the exact nature of their mission. He outlined where they were headed, what the targets were, and the kind of forces and weaponry they were up against – both the shore-based defenders and the ships' crew themselves. He explained how he was putting the *Maid Honour* Force regulars at the tip of the spear – with Lassen, Appleyard and Hayes leading the charge, and tasked with blowing the anchor chains to free the two vessels.

The Colonial Service volunteers would form a second wave of boarders, charged with overcoming and subduing the ships' crew. March-Phillipps stressed that it was impossible to predict the level of resistance they would encounter. To aid in the taking of the *Duchessa d'Aosta* a platform had been rigged up protruding from the *Vulcan*'s wheelhouse. Four men could fit on the planking, and from there they could spring onto the larger ship's deck. The boarding parties were arranged in parties of four, and one after the other they practised using the plat-form as the launch-pad for the attack.

The following day dawned fine and clear. By mid-morning the jagged 10,000-foot Santa Isabel Peak – the highest point on Fernando Po – had been spotted. A cold lunch was served, for the galley was being used to prepare the plastic explosive charges to blow the anchor chains. That afternoon the final kit issue began. Each man forming the boarding parties was handed a torch, a pistol and a Tommy Gun. They were cautioned to use their non-lethal coshes wherever possible, especially as gunfire would alert the harbour defenders to the attack.

The *Maid Honour* Force regulars were armed with a further assortment of weaponry, including their fearsome Fairbairn-Sykes fighting knives. Lassen carried a back-up Beretta pistol tucked away in the rear waistband of his trousers, in case all other weapons failed him. Faces were blacked up, so they would blend in with the darkness. One of March-Phillipps' regulars, the Free Frenchman Desgranges, bedecked himself in a loincloth, complete with multi-coloured headscarf tied over his dark curly hair – in keeping with the raiding force's piratical image.

Night falls quickly in equatorial Africa. It was a moonless one, and the two tugboats showing no lights were able to sneak across the water like phantoms. Under cover of darkness the *Vulcan* and *Nuneaton* altered course, steaming directly for Santa Isabel Harbour. The *Nuneaton* was scheduled to take the lead, for she had further to go to reach her target and she had to launch her folbots once there.

Four miles out from Santa Isabel the *Nuneaton* crept into the lead, SOE agent Guise taking up his place in the bows to guide her into the harbour. Even in the thick darkness he was confident he could steer the Nuneaton through the various buoys and markers, getting her safely to where she needed to be.

Zero Hour for the attack was 2330 hours – as soon as the electricity supply to the port had been cut.

Four miles across the dark sea a group of dinner guests at Santa Isabel's Casino Restaurant were having a fine time indeed. The merry party consisted of some two dozen diners, among whom were eight Italian officers from the *Duchessa d'Aosta*, including the ship's Acting Captain, Umberto Valle. Beside him sat the distinctive figures of the two German officers from the *Likomba*, one of whom was the ship's commander, *Kapitan* Specht. The stubborn and opinionated Specht had refused to attend the previous party. Naturally suspicious, it was only when that one had passed off without incident that he was willing to accept an invitation to a second.

Zorilla remained only for long enough to ensure that all ship's officers were present and properly seated – all with their backs to the sea – and that the alcohol was flowing freely. Around 11.00 p.m. the Spaniard quietly slipped away. Down on a hidden part of the shoreline a canoe was waiting to spirit him to safety, but no one on the terrace of the Casino Restaurant seemed to notice his departure. Too much fine drink and food was being served, as the Tilley Lanterns glowed gaily and the conversation was batted to and fro.

SOE agent Lippett, meanwhile, had dined quietly with a Spanish friend at a quayside eatery, after which he took his customary 'digestive stroll' around the harbour. Final checks done – there was no unusual activity, bar the noisy party on the terrace of the Casino Restaurant – he strolled back to his hotel accommodation. The night was dark as pitch, apart from the odd flash of lightning on the distant horizon, as a tropical storm raged over what looked like the jungles of the mainland.

Hoping that Zorrila's voyage across the Gulf of Guinea would be untroubled by such storms Lippett retired to his hotel room and laid down to rest. Orchestrating all the subterfuge, lies and intrigue of the past few weeks had been a hugely stressful and exhausting high-wire act, and SOE agent W.25 Richard Lippett was soon fast asleep.

But as Lippett slumbered, secure in the knowledge that he had done everything possible to prepare matters shore-side, an unforeseen and potentially ruinous drama was playing out at sea.

It was all down to timing.

Understandably perhaps, March-Phillipps and Appleyard had assumed that Fernando Po was in the same time zone as nearby Nigeria. It wasn't. Perversely, the island ran on Madrid time, which meant that it was one hour behind the nearby African mainland. The problem only became apparent as the two vessels rounded a headland and the harbourside town hove into view. It was midnight by the British operators' watches, but the lights of the houses and streets of Santa Isabel remained stubbornly ablaze.

The assault force was heading into target an hour too early. Clearly if they sailed into the harbour while the entire bay was lit up the results would be disastrous. Operation Postmaster depended on the cloak of darkness hiding the raiding force until the very last possible moment, and on striking with total shock and surprise. All of that would be lost, and the mission would have come to grief due to the most elementary of errors.

The lead ship, the *Nuneaton*, slowed to a dead crawl as a row broke out on the bridge of the *Vulcan*. March-Phillipps was apoplectic. How could the SOE's intelligence – which up until then had been faultless – have failed to warn them of the time difference? A gifted leader of men, one whose fearlessness, brilliance and integrity drew others to him, March-Phillipps had one major flaw: his temper. It could flash in an instant as it had done now, the man exploding into a paroxysm of rage. He also had a slight stammer, one that would worsen noticeably with his mood.

'Will you get a b-b-bloody m-m-move on!' his voice yelled out across the still waters. 'Get a bloody move on or get out! I'm coming in!'

On the bridge of the *Nuneaton* the ship's commander, Lieutenant Goodman, took decisive action. He swung his vessel across the bows of the *Vulcan* and cut his engines, so halting the larger ship in her path.

Under Appleyard's calming influence March-Phillipps was persuaded of the suicidal nature of sailing into Santa Isabel before the lights went out. There seemed to be no option but to remain where they were, just a few hundred yards off shore, engines idling and hoping they wouldn't be spotted.

And so the raiders waited for the town to go dark – faces black as the night, silent and poised to strike.

Chapter Six

As luck would have it, Richard Lippett had also worked his magic with the man whose job it was to cut the town's electricity supply as the midnight hour approached. By suitably unorthodox means – a glittering financial incentive; a clandestine lover seeking a passionate tryst under cover of darkness – Lippett had persuaded the town's electricity engineer to flick the switch a good few minutes early.

At around 2315 Madrid time the first of the lights around Santa Isabel town blinked out, and one by one the windows all around the bay went dark. No sooner had they done so than the two waiting vessels began to inch their way forwards. The *Nuneaton* took the lead with Guise in the bows, gesturing this way and that as he studied the buoys marking the safe passage into the harbour. The *Vulcan* came tight on the *Nuneaton's* stern, as Tugmaster Coker followed the course that Guise steered through the shallows.

The harbour seemed as quiet and dark as the grave. Two pinpricks of light drew the eye. One was the terrace of the Casino Restaurant, from where uproarious laughter and the odd burst of singing in Italian echoed across the silent waters. The other was the window of the Reverend Markham's house, at which a Tilley Lantern burned, its light reflected in a yellow ribbon of brightness that stretched across the bay towards the hidden ships.

As the *Nuneaton* and *Vulcan* crept ahead all eyes turned to that lone window. Sure enough, just as the men had hoped it would be, a blind was raised and lowered before the Tilley Lantern – the prearranged signal that all was as it should be in Santa Isabel Harbour, or at least, as the raiders intended it to be. A mug of fortifying rum was handed around the boarding parties, as both vessels cut their engines. Whether they'd started this mission as highly-trained agent-commandos or Colonial Service volunteers, they were all seadogs and desperadoes to the last now.

Rum downed, the men lay facedown on the deck as the tugboats drifted forward, the gentle lap of the water under their hulls seemingly deafening in the silence. The progress appeared painfully slow and the tension was unbearable. The same thought was on every man's mind: would they sneak past unseen and make it to the target ships undetected?

After what seemed like an age the *Nuneaton* drifted to a stop in the heart of the harbour. The darkness was so intense that Hayes and Winter, the lead boarding party, could barely see their hands in front of their faces. Working largely by feel alone the first folbot was lowered into the sea. The two raiders climbed aboard, whereupon agent Guise pointed out the bearing they needed to take to get them to the *Likomba*. The bay was a mass of impenetrable shadow.

Dipping their paddles into the still water, Hayes and Winter – the vanguard of the raiders – set out. Behind them, the two District Commissioners-turned-brigands lowered themselves into their tiny vessel. Pistols, coshes and Tommy Guns firmly stowed, they too began to paddle. At first they seemed to be heading in entirely the wrong direction, before Guise cried out a muted course-correction. Their role was to act as the vital back-up to the lead raiders. If Hayes and Winter ran into trouble, the District Commissioners were to provide brute force and firepower.

In the forward canoe Hayes and Winter had to keep their wits absolutely about them. They had their weaponry hidden and a cover story ready to hand. If a sentry aboard the *Likomba* were to challenge them, they were to claim to be *Kapitan* Specht and his fellow German officer returning from a thoroughly enjoyable dinner party ashore.

After five minutes paddling they brought their canoe along-side the *Bibundi* – the pleasure yacht tied to the side of the larger German ship – so as to better screen their approach. But as they did so a torchlight pierced the darkness and a voice yelled out a challenge.

'Who goes there? Identify yourselves!'

The blinding light was coming from the deck of the *Likomba*, and it was fully upon Hayes, in the fore seat of the folbot. Whoever it was that had cried out, they were clearly hyper-alert, for he and Winter had made practically no noise whatsoever as they paddled towards the two ships. Hayes opted to use the cover ruse, rather than to reach for his Tommy Gun. He was painfully aware that if he opened fire now he would blow the mission wide-open, before the force manning the *Vulcan* had the time to board the *Duchessa d'Aosta*.

74

Using a few words of broken Spanish and German, Hayes grunted a suitably inebriated-sounding reply.

'*Kapitan* Specht . . . Party . . . Returning to ship.'

In response two figures came forward, as if to help 'their *Kapitan*' aboard. Both were local African members of the ship's crew. But just as soon as they spied a blackened-up Hayes, they realized this wasn't their ship's officer. There was a moment of confusion, before the second folbot emerged from the gloom, District Commissioners Newington and Abell with their Tommy Guns leveled over the side.

No sooner had the two watchmen realized they were staring down the gaping barrels of two .45-calibre machine-guns, than they turned and ran. They sprinted forward, dived off the *Likomba*'s bows and began to strike out for land some fifty yards away. Fortunately, the shock and surprise must have been so complete that neither man had thought to raise the alarm.

That suited the raiders just fine. After all, they were supposed to minimize casualties. *No useless slaughter.* But it did raise the worrying possibility that the sentries would alert the shore-based defenders, once they reached dry land.

Hayes – the boarding force commander – had no time to worry about that now. The four men surged aboard the larger ship, Hayes and Winter making a beeline for the anchor chains. Each had a rucksack bulging with pre-made explosive charges, and each carried enough to cut all the moorings, should either be put out of action. They bent to their task fore and aft, as the two District Commissioners hurried through the length of the vessel, Tommy Guns and coshes at the ready.

To their rear the *Nuneaton* closed in, inching her way alongside. With the first target ship declared clear of enemy forces, the towrope had to be attached, ready for the getaway. Charges set, Hayes and Winter steeled themselves to wait for the appointed moment – so they could blow the anchor chains as the main assault force surged across the decks of the *Duchessa d'Aosta*.

Lashed to the side of the *Likomba*, the 70-tonne pleasure yacht, the *Bibundi*, presented Hayes with a real dilemma. If it was a Spanish vessel and they towed her away along with their main prize, a diplomatic incident was surely in the making. The words of M's telegram – *Am confident you will exercise utmost care to ensure success and obviate repercussions* – echoed through his mind.

Hayes was tempted to cut the *Bibundi* free. But in the main cabin his fellow raider, Winter, discovered damning evidence as to the vessel's identity: photos of the *Bibundi* flying a Swastika, with a lady – presumably the owner's wife – posing beside it.

'Let's take her, Graham,' Winter whispered, showing Hayes the photos.

Hayes agreed: the *Bibundi* deserved to be seized as a prize of war.

They were ten minutes into the assault, and still there hadn't been so much as a cry of alarm from the shore. Sound carries well across still, night-dark waters, yet the bay remained a crucible of calm.

Such peace was about to be well and truly shattered.

Hayes detected the first muffled cries echoing across the water. Presumably the *Vulcan* was nearing her target – the giant

Italian liner-cum-cargo ship. Assuming the boarders were about to swarm aboard her decks, he decided it was time to blow the *Likomba* free and make their getaway. At the same time the young Buzz Perkins and SOE agent Guise were about to jump across to the German tugboat, towrope in hand.

Guise and Perkins were weighed down with Tommy Guns and Mills bombs – pineapple-shaped hand grenades – so it was some leap to make. As Hayes and Winter set the fuses alight on both fore and aft anchor chains, Perkins and Guise leaped across from one vessel to the other; Guise with a grenade gripped in his hand, in case of any trouble. But as they landed on the *Likomba's* bows Hayes cried out a frantic warning – for he and his fellow raiders had just taken cover in anticipation of the coming blasts.

There was a violent flash and the first explosion tore across Santa Isabel Harbour, ripping the peace of the night apart. It took a deal of plastic explosives to cut a large steel hawser in two. As the first charge detonated the blast caught Perkins and Guise in the open, plucking them off the *Likomba's* deck and hurling them into the darkness.

The two men disappeared from view, – Hayes convinced that he had killed both of them.

Just a few hundred feet to the east of the *Likomba* lay the massive form of the *Duchessa d'Aosta*. Indeed, the entire expanse of the U-shaped harbour was little more than 3,000 yards across. That first explosion flashed across the compact confines of the bay, the punching roar of the blast thundering across the Italian vessel's decks, rebounding off the sheer volcanic rock of the harbour walls and echoing back and forth across the water.

Aboard the *Vulcan* Anders Lassen – as always armed to the teeth – heard and felt the blast's power, as he tensed himself to jump. Beside him on the makeshift assault platform were Appleyard and March-Phillipps, laden down with explosive charges, while above them on the roof of the bridge a pair of Bren-gunners hunched over their weapons. All eyes scanned the shadowed form of the Italian ship for any crewmen drawn to her decks by that first explosion.

Even before the *Vulcan* bumped alongside the *Duchessa d'Aosta*, the nimble form of Lassen made the leap, a line grasped in one hand and his free arm making a grab for the ship's rope-ladder. As his feet made contact with the rungs, a second explosion from the direction of the *Likomba* threw a momentary blaze of light across the bay, for an instant blinding the eyes of the raiders.

March-Phillipps, Appleyard and Haggis Taylor – March-Phillipp's batman – followed on Lassen's heels, making a mad dash for the all-important ship's bridge. A sure-footed Lassen looped the line around the nearest ship's bollard, tossed the loose end back through the darkness towards the *Vulcan*'s bridge – which was level with the larger ship's main deck – giving an exultant yell as he did so.

'Pull! Pull Robin! Pull like fuck!'

Robin Duff, the *Vulcan*'s second in command, grabbed the line, dragged it tight and made it fast.

'All fast!' he cried back to Lassen. 'All fast!'

Finally, the British tugboat and the biggest prize – the Italian liner-cum-cargo-ship – were lashed together.

A bamboo ladder was lowered to bridge the eight feet or so separating the two vessels, and the remainder of the boarding party – *Maid Honour* Force veterans, SOE agents, plus Colonial Service volunteers – streamed across. But as the boarders rushed fore and aft of the 464-foot vessel, one of the SOE agents went crashing to the deck, felled by a powerful but unseen assailant.

Fearing that the ship's crew had woken up to the assault and were fighting back, agent W.30, Captain Desmond Longe, struggled to his feet, pistol in one hand and knife gripped in the other. But worried, and distinctly inhuman squeals, revealed that his attacker was actually a large pig running loose on deck, one of three such porkers no doubt intended for the ship's kitchens.

The only sentries that appeared to have been set were two Africans, one of whom dived into the sea at the sight of the fearsome raiders, while the other allowed himself to be taken prisoner without a fight. The main deck of the *Duchessa d'Aosta* had been seized by total surprise, and without a shot being fired.

With March-Phillipps safely installed on the ship's bridge and the main deck clear, Appleyard and Free Frenchman Desgranges were able to dash forward with their charges, in readiness to blow the forward anchor chain. To the rear Desmond Longe – fully recovered from the pig attack – accompanied by a *Maid Honour* Force regular, crouched at the stern, as they prepared to set their charges.

They had six stern cables to deal with, and time was clearly against them. Now that the explosions from the *Likomba* had rung out across the bay, they feared it was only a matter of moments before the power was switched back on in Santa Isabel town – and they would be lit-up like ducks in a shooting gallery.

On the ship's bridge March-Phillipps was desperate to get the below-decks area locked down. He was acutely aware of the number of Italian crewmen ensconced down there, who by now surely must have realised they were under attack. As long as they could keep the Italians trapped below, they should be free to blow the anchor chains and drag the *Duchessa* towards the darkness of the open sea, and victory.

As the SOE had been at pains to point out, the Italian ship would represent 'the richest prize of the war so far'. Just as March-Phillipps was savouring such thoughts, a cry of challenge rang out in Italian from somewhere below him.

Equally as quickly came the fearsome roar of a response: 'Get 'em up! Get 'em up!'

It sounded as if the Italians had finally mustered their forces to mount some kind of resistance.

Directly across from March-Phillipps there were problems aboard the *Vulcan* too. In the bowels of the tugboat, the African stokers – sweating buckets as they shoveled coal, bringing the boilers to maximum pressure – had reacted to the explosions that thumped across the water just as Leslie Prout, the *Maid Honour* Force champion boxer, had feared they might.

The stokers, of course, had not been included in the need-to-know loop, and they had little idea what the assault force was up to. Those two powerful blasts, plus the cries from above decks, struck the fear of God into them. For all the stokers knew it was their ship that was being fired upon and attacked. Prout was both a prizefighter and a consummate manager of men. Using a mixture of threats and promises of a massive pay bonus for each man, he managed to keep the stokers bent over their shovels, the sweat cascading down in rivulets.

The explosions that thundered across the harbour had taken the diners on the Casino Restaurant terrace by complete surprise. No amount of drunken singing or laughter could drown out a blast that was powerful enough to sever a steel anchor hawser.

An instant after the first detonation swept across the terrace all voices – even those of the most-inebriated – fell silent, the diners wondering whether their ears were playing tricks on them. But as heads swivelled towards the bay and all eyes turned on the water, the second blast ripped apart the night, as the rear anchor chain of the *Likomba* was cut.

The momentary burst of light was gone in an instant, as all returned to blackness out on the water. But the German officers in particular realised that whatever was taking place, it was happening on *their* vessel. Some four hundred yards from the terrace there had been two mystery blasts aboard the *Likomba*, and it was only the large amount of alcohol that *Kapitan* Specht had imbibed that prevented him from acting more swiftly.

The Tilley Lanterns served to keep the terrace bathed in light, and as there was no fire or further explosions from the direction of his ship, the drink-befuddled Specht was at a loss to determine exactly what was happening. It was the frantic bugle call ringing out across the harbour that cemented Specht's alarm. An alert was being signalled from Government House – the seat of the Spanish Colonial Administration in Fernando Po.

Figures rushed to man the machineguns positioned on the roof, their barrels sweeping the waters of the bay below. But until the gunners could see to properly assess the threat, they were at a loss as to who or what they should open fire on. No one had yet made the decision to get the town's power switched back on. After all, if this were an attack from the air it would be better to keep the lights off and the town swathed in darkness.

A short distance further around the bay SOE agent Lippett had been woken in his hotel room by the first explosion. A glance at his watch showed 2335 hours. From his window he could see the streets rapidly filling up, as the citizens of Santa Isabel rushed outside to see what was happening. The hotel balcony was thronged with guests and all eyes were staring with alarm at the dark waters of the bay.

Lippett, the only man among them in the know, decided to keep a low profile and stay exactly where he was.

Across from Lippett's hotel window Buzz Perkins and SOE agent Guise were coming back to their senses. Blasted through the air by the first explosion aboard the *Likomba*, they'd been hurled back onto their own ship – one of them landing on the *Nuneaton*'s deck, the other being thrown across a ship's bollard. Hayes was certain he'd killed both men, but miraculously neither had suffered any worse than a few broken ribs. Fortunately for all, the grenades they had been carrying had failed to explode.

Yet Buzz Perkins and Guise had still failed in their task, and the *Likomba* and *Bibundi*, relieved of their anchor chains, were drifting with the wind and current towards shore. Hurt and suffering from shock though they were, Perkins and Guise steeled themselves to attempt a second jump. This time they were able to get the tow-rope aboard and securely fastened to the *Likomba*.

On the *Nuneaton*'s bridge, her commander, Lieutenant Goodman, ordered his stokers to pile on the power. His tug took up the strain and moments later all three ships were underway, moving towards the safe channel leading through the harbour entrance and into the open sea.

The route steered by the *Nuneaton* would take her close by the *Vulcan*. As the smaller tug steamed past her larger sister ship, Graham Hayes – the first to board the enemy vessels – caught sight of the party on the *Duchessa's* bows, readying themselves to blow the forward anchor chain. In the triumph of the moment, and forgetting the supposedly deniable nature of their mission, he let out a spontaneous cry in English.

'We've got 'em, Apple! We've got 'em!'

Appleyard's reply echoed back from the *Duchessa's* bows, equally high-spirited . . . and in English.

'Head for the open sea!'

Below the *Duchessa's* decks the raiders had been hard at work. By now they'd rounded up twenty-eight Italian prisoners, several of the more uncooperative ones having been coshed into submission. A few doors had also needed kicking in, behind one of which they'd discovered a distinctly German-sounding female crewmember. Gilda Turch was so shocked to find the blacked-up raiders thundering into her cabin that she had fainted on the spot.

Ms Turch was carried into the open, so the fresh air might revive her. The Italian crew – many still in their pyjamas – were likewise corralled on the open deck. They were laid face down, where they could be covered with the raiders' Tommy Guns. No quarter could be given and no mercy shown. If one man cried out a warning to the shore – and the harbourside was now thick with watching eyes – the consequences would be disastrous.

Chapter Seven

March-Phillipps gave the signal to cut the anchor chains – blowing one sharp blast on a whistle strung around his neck.

To fore and aft of the *Duchessa* there were the distinctive sharp cracks of steel being cut by plastic explosives, as one after another the charges detonated – the flash of the blasts throwing the winding harbour-side streets into stark light and shadow, rendering the worried crowds of onlookers a ghostly white. The quayside watchers ran in panic from the almighty explosions that roared across the bay.

The charges set on the *Duchessa* were considerably larger than those used on the *Likomba*. They had to be, to cut through the far more substantial mass of her anchor chains. As the blasted metal fell away, lengths of steel crashing into the water, it was as if Santa Isabel Harbour was being pounded by salvoes of bombs dropped from the air. Indeed, the scenario of a concerted air attack appeared all too convincing to the petrified townspeople and the harbourside defenders. To them, this had all the hallmarks of an aerial bombardment.

Aboard the *Duchessa* March-Phillipps, Appleyard, Lassen and their fellow raiders stiffened, as the first staccato shots hammered out from the direction of the shore. All of a sudden, guns positioned around the bay began to open fire, releasing volley after volley. As the *Vulcan* went to full power, her screws thrashing the boiling waters and straining to get the massive ship at her stern to move, the muzzles of the harbourside cannons punched through the darkness, spitting long tongues of fire.

But strain as she might, the *Vulcan* couldn't get the massive deadweight of the *Duchessa* to budge one inch. Somehow, she remained stuck fast. It was Appleyard who realized what had happened. One of the forward charges had failed to explode, which meant that the *Duchessa's* bow remained firmly tethered to the seabed. As salvo after salvo resounded from the harbour-side guns, Apple dashed forward, laid a replacement charge, lit the fuse and threw himself into cover.

Kerboom!

An instant later the massive Italian vessel began to inch forward. From the bridge March-Phillipps let out an exultant cry: 'My God, she's free!'

It was all up to Tugmaster Coker now.

As the *Vulcan* gathered speed, Leslie Prout urged the sweating stokers to shovel on more coal, and the safety lever was physically held in place to prevent it cutting in and reducing the pressure on the dangerously overloaded engines. Demanding maximum power from his vessel, Tugmaster Coker got it. He managed to get both ships underway at a speedy 3 knots, as he began to steer the 7,872-tonne rudderless mass lying at the end of his towrope through the treacherous shallows.

All around the quay total confusion reigned. With the shore-batteries unleashing fire into the heavens, rhythmic flashes pulsed across the bay. The momentary beats of illumination revealed to *Kapitan* Specht and his Italian comrade, Acting Captain Umberto Valle, glimpses of a terrible sight out on the bay. Somehow, their vessels seemed to be slipping out to sea.

It was unbelievable. Almost 10,000 tonnes of German and Italian shipping – *their ships* – was being spirited away beneath their very noses. As the *Likomba* and *Duchessa d'Aosta* melted into the darkness and cannon shells and gunfire rent the skies above Fernando Po, the Captain of the Spanish Colonial guard dashed hither and thither crying out: 'Que pasa? Que pasa?' – *what's happening*.

Panic gripped the townspeople, wild cries of 'Alerta! Alerta! Alerta!' rising up from the harbourside. Any hope of mustering some kind of concerted action to save the fast-disappearing vessels seemed lost, and the marvelous deception at the heart of Operation Postmaster appeared complete.

Out on the waters of the bay the more powerful *Vulcan* over-hauled and passed the *Nuneaton*, as both dragged their prizes further and further towards the open sea. In the stern of the *Duchessa* Lassen, Longe and Haggis Taylor kept their Tommy Guns trained on the quayside, in case any form of last-minute resistance was mounted by either the Spanish defenders, or the German and the Italian ships' officers.

It was fast becoming clear that the seemingly impossible had transpired: Operation Postmaster had been successful beyond anyone's wildest imaginings. The raiders had stolen away the three target ships and while fierce gunfire still illuminated the sky above the town, not a shot seemed to have been directed their way. Apart from a few bruised and battered Italian captives they had not caused a single casualty – just as M had called for. The only shot fired by the raiders had been a negligent discharge – a revolver fired accidentally – and no one had been harmed.

As the ships drew further and further out to sea, it was as if a midnight firework display was underway above Santa Isabel town. Indeed, it was only just past the witching hour as the five ships powered past the buoys that marked the exit to the harbour and turned towards the open sea. The raid had taken just thirty-five minutes to execute.

Ashore in Santa Isabel town someone finally had the gumption to turn the power back on. Just as soon as the lights around the bay blinked into life it was clear what was missing from the harbour. Where the *Duchessa d'Aosta* and the smaller *Likomba* had stood there was now only open water. It was also abundantly clear that no Allied warplanes were thundering through the skies above the town, unleashing bombs.

The shore-side batteries ceased firing into the skies. In the comparative silence that followed, everyone was asking the same question: who had attacked the harbour and stolen the ships away? No one had the faintest clue. Some spoke of as many as five massive battleships stealing in under cover of darkness to execute the daring theft. Others remained convinced that the *Duchessa* and the *Likomba* had been somehow targeted from the air.

To add to the confusion, a handful of distinctive hats were seen lying in the water where the Italian and German ships had been cut free from their moorings. Fished out of the sea, they proved to be Free French naval hats. As the Free French were in effect stateless persons fighting to retake their homeland, what reprisals could the Spanish possibly take against them? A few onlookers spoke darkly of English voices being heard from across the water, but no one could be certain.

There was one exception, however. *Kapitan* Specht, until a few minutes ago the proud commander of the *Likomba*, had no doubt whatsoever who was responsible for the loss of his ship.

Kapitan Specht had refused to attend that first dinner party, for he had always maintained that one German officer should remain aboard his fine little vessel. It was only Frau Luhr's charms that had convinced him to make an exception this time. As a result he was now a Captain bereft of both crew and ship, and he was convinced that both Herr and Frau Luhr must be undercover British agents.

Specht was spitting blood. Well-oiled and with his face puce with rage, he made his way directly to the one obvious target on which to vent his anger – the British Consulate building. He stormed in, marched through the pantry and came face-to-face with Peter Lake, Britain's Vice Consul in Fernando Po. Lake was in truth SOE agent W53, a man personally recruited by M to oversee Operation Postmaster from the Santa Isabel side of things.

Specht let fly with a string of foul-mouthed curses, before yelling out: 'Vere is mine ship?'

'If you think . . .' Lake replied, but he was immediately interrupted.

'Who is drunk? Who is drunk?' an enraged Specht demanded.

'*You are*,' Lake retorted. 'Now get out! This is British sovereign territory. Get out!'

Specht totally lost control. He punched Lake in the face, which gave the twenty-six-year-old SOE agent the excuse he'd been looking for. Lake proceeded to knock seven bells out of the German *Kapitan*, who eventually found himself staring down the barrel of a revolver. At the sight of the gun leveled at his head, Specht promptly collapsed, split his trousers and soiled what was left of them.

The police were called. Specht was dragged away and thrown in gaol, while a round-the-clock guard was placed at the Consulate to prevent any such further incidents. Word quickly reached Lake that Specht was threatening to kill him and his colleagues, but he wasn't overly worried. He'd got the measure of the German *Kapitan* during the punch-up, and if anything he would relish a return match.

Lake was also determined to make the most out of the German captain's intemperance. He immediately penned a letter to the island's Spanish Governor, decrying Specht's breach of international law. He demanded that there should be no repeat performances, and that all British citizens then present on Fernando Po be afforded Spain's full protection. In doing so, Lake had foremost in his mind fellow SOE agent Richard Lippett, the chief architect of the Santa Isabel end of the Operation Postmaster deception.

Sorulace, cowed by the threat of the compromising photos in Lake's possession, offered immediate assurances that Lake's request would be given every priority. More to the point, he refrained from any suggestion that it was actually the British who might be responsible for the shocking breach of international law represented by that night's daredevil raid.

On the blacked-out bridge of the *Duchessa d'Aosta*, March-Phillipps was feeling understandably exultant as he stared out to sea. The entry he made in his ship's log reflected the quiet, understated sense of satisfaction that he was feeling. At last he and his men had struck back hard against the enemy. 'Boarded and captured and towed out *d'Aosta*, *Likomba* and *Bemuivoi*', he noted. 'No casualties. Cutting out went according to plan.' In the fast pace of the moment, it seems he got the name of the captured German pleasure yacht slightly wrong, but the sentiment was entirely heart-felt nonetheless.

March-Phillipps turned to a tall figure standing at his side on the bridge. It was Longe, the SOE agent who had survived the pig assault.

'This is a wonderful thing for the old country, you know,' March-Phillipps remarked. His voice was thick with emotion and touched with a quiet pride.

And indeed it was wonderful: stage one of Operation Postmaster was complete – a five-star, gold-plated cut-out operation. But stage two, in which the British had to formally 'seize' the ships that the invisible raiders had liberated, was yet to be executed, as was the sophisticated information operation that would be orchestrated from London.

March-Phillipps appointed the skilled seaman Lassen as the *Duchessa's* Second Officer, while he kept overall command of the purloined vessel. Under the young Dane's ferocious gaze the

Italian crewmen-captives were put to work to make the ship as seaworthy as possible. All haste had to be made to the planned rendezvous with HMS *Violet*, which was set some forty miles west of Fernando Po. The pigs were captured, corralled and tethered, in preparation for a celebratory feast, once it was mission accomplished.

March-Phillipps wanted to make as much as possible of the journey under the protective cover of darkness. It wasn't inconceivable that the Spanish Governor of Fernando Po might call for Axis air power to scour the sea in search of the missing ships, or there might be vessels in Santa Isabel Harbour capable of giving chase.

Matters took a turn for the worse when the *Nuneaton* started suffering engine trouble. The *Vulcan* ploughed ever onwards, dragging the *Duchessa* after, but the flotilla of three smaller ships fell further and further behind. As the first hints of dawn washed the eastern horizon with a pale light, the sharp form of Santa Isabel Peak became visible, silhouetted against the coming sunrise. The *Nuneaton* – with her engines out of action, and her two ungainly prizes in tow – remained just a few miles off the coast, and well within Spanish territorial waters.

Wracked with worry, March-Phillipps made the difficult decision to make an about turn. He transferred to the *Vulcan*, the tow-line was released, and the *Duchessa* was left to drift under Lassen's command, as the powerful tugboat steamed back to find the missing ships. March-Phillipps discovered the *Nuneaton* in serious trouble, and together with her prizes she was drifting back towards Fernando Po.

Hayes and the *Maid Honour* Force commander discussed whether the *Vulcan* should take the three vessels under tow. But Hayes and his crew remained convinced they could restart the *Nuneaton*'s engines. It was crucial that March-Phillipps did not lose sight of their bigger prize: the *Duchessa*. And so he made the difficult decision to leave the three ships drifting, as the *Vulcan* turned westwards once more. By the time she had made it back to the *Duchessa*, someone had had the bright idea of knocking-up a makeshift skull-and-crossbones, which was fluttering proudly from the ship's masthead.

Whether it was Appleyard or Lassen who first suggested it, the triumphant raiders had embraced the idea. Bed sheets had been retrieved from the ship's cabins, and with a pot of black paint a crude Jolly Roger had been splashed across them. But March-Phillipps wasn't best pleased. He was painfully aware of the vital importance of the next stage of the deception – that HMS *Violet* should approach the flotilla of ships, with all aboard bar her Captain believing them to be enemy vessels manned by mutinous Italian and German crews.

Flying a Jolly Roger didn't quite fit with the cover story. In a characteristic fit of anger, he ordered the flag be taken down and burned. But as always, his rage was short-lived. Under Appleyard's steadying hand the tow was got underway once more, sans Jolly Roger.

Understandably, London had insisted on absolute radio silence for the duration of Operation Postmaster. If the enemy managed to intercept just one message from the raiders it could blow the all-important aspect of deniability wide open. Which is how the *Vulcan* came to be steaming hell-for-leather for her rendez-vous, not knowing that there was no way on earth that HMS *Violet* could get there.

Somehow, the British destroyer had managed to run herself aground while en route to the meeting point. HMS *Violet* was stuck fast around the mouth of the mighty Niger River, which disgorges into the Gulf of Guinea via a vast delta, creating treacherous shoals and sandbanks far out to sea.

With HMS *Violet* stuck fast no British warship was about to make the rendezvous with the Operation Postmaster raiding force anytime soon. Worse still, no radio warnings could be issued in either direction – to either the flotilla of ships under the command of March-Phillipps, or to those waiting anxiously for news of the raid in London.

Unsurprisingly, as dawn broke across the Gulf of Guinea the atmosphere in Santa Isabel was somewhat frantic. The German Consul on Fernando Po, plus the Spanish Governor had both sent long, coded telegrams to their respective governments, decrying the raid. Acting Captain Umberto Valle, the *Duchessa's* commander, had radioed a report to the Italian authorities, declaring that his ship had been seized by a large tugboat of 'unknown nationality', complete with all 28 crew.

Those reports, together with further radio intercepts, would give London the first hints that Operation Postmaster had been successful. But Santa Isabel town itself remained awash with intrigue and unsubstantiated rumour. Every party imaginable seemed to have fallen under suspicion for the raid. To the Free

French and the British – the obvious suspects – had now been added the Americans, and even a party of mysterious anti-Fascist Spanish 'rebel pirates' led by Zorilla.

'Wild rumours were rife,' remarked agent Lippett, of the morning after the raid, 'especially when it became clear that Zorilla was not to be found . . .' Reports were that Zorilla had, '. . . slipped the moorings from the D. de A [Duchessa d'Aosta] and went off with the ship . . . Some said it was the Free French, others Vichy French, from Dakar, others said it was the English. In fact no one knew anything, or no one saw anything.'

There were some among the local Spanish and African population who couldn't help but express their amazement at the skill and dash of the raid. Heinrich Luhr, husband of the ill-fated dinner party's 'host', even went so far as to suggest that only Germans could have executed such an accomplished attack, and that all who had done so would be awarded the Iron Cross.

But around the bay, now denuded of its Italian and German ships, the mood quickly darkened, and especially when the official investigation – led by Captain Binea, the Falangist commander of the Colonial Guard – got underway. The dinner party – particularly those who had organized and paid for it – became the key focus of the investigation.

By midday the first suspects were being arrested by Captain Binea's men and taken in for questioning, Herr and Frau Luhr foremost among them. The Spaniard Zorilla's absence had been conspicuous from the very start, and rumour had it that he had plied the dinner guests with so much drink that none had been able to react to the raid taking place in the harbour. In short order Zorilla's closest friends and colleagues were also rounded up for interrogation.

No one knew of course that it was a tiny dugout canoe piloted by a local fisherman that had spirited Zorilla across the sea to safety – all apart from Richard Lippett, and the SOE agent and mastermind of the Fernando Po deception was doing his best to keep his head well down. But Lippett soon found his Spanish friends deserting him, and he sensed that it was only a matter of time before Captain Binea's men would come for him.

In London, meanwhile, there was mounting consternation and concern. Apart from a short cable received from Vice Consul Lake, direct from the Santa Isabel Consulate – '*Duchessa d'Aosta* and *Likomba* sailed midnight 14th' – there had been little further news. The expected coded radio message from HMS *Violet* – *Postmaster successful*; the trigger for the next stage of the cover story to be launched – hadn't been received. It was well past the planned rendezvous time, and yet the airwaves remained stubbornly silent.

As the Spanish and Axis media began to bemoan a 'gross breach of neutrality', M, the War Cabinet and Winston Churchill himself felt unable to respond. If the full truth became known, it was all but inevitable that Spain would be forced into hostilities against Britain. The missing flotilla had to be found and the great deception maintained.

Unfortunately, March-Phillipps had reached the mid-ocean rendezvous point only to discover that HMS *Violet* was nowhere to be seen. He hadn't the faintest idea as to why the British warship had failed to appear, but there was little use in speculating on that now. March-Phillipps had to act, and he had to do so quickly and decisively. The longer the *Vulcan* and the *Duchessa d'Aosta* remained stationary at the rendezvous point, the more likely a roving enemy warship or aircraft would happen upon them.

His only option was to press onwards, west towards Lagos – the nearest British port. The problem was, the *Nuneaton* with her two German ships in tow was nowhere to be seen. Presumably, the smaller tugboat's engine trouble had persisted and she was somewhere to the east of them struggling to make headway.

But it didn't escape March-Phillipps' attention that her fate might be infinitely worse. The *Nuneaton* may have drifted closer to Fernando Po, and been re-taken by the Spanish authorities, aided by some very angry German and Italian ships' officers. And if that were so the great gamble would have turned decidedly sour, Operation Postmaster becoming a spectacular and costly failure.

Their detractors – waiting like hungry vultures – would have a juicy carcass to fight over.

Chapter Eight

It was 17 January 1942 – three days after the raid – when matters reached their lowest ebb. While the German and Spanish press were having a field day, London could say nothing. It was as if Britain was being forced to fight with one arm tied behind her back and while gagged, and it was a losing battle.

The German press was loudly proclaiming that a force of British warships had carried out the raid, and that the captured ships' crew had been executed. Even the supposedly neutral Swedish press was decrying the British aggression. There were angry street demonstrations in Spain, as the Falangist press accused the British of being responsible for an unprovoked assault. The Spanish newspaper *Arriba*'s report was typical. The raid was 'planned with the most revolting perfidy and embraced every form of cowardice and cruelty. It seems all members of the crew . . . were assassinated.'

Hour by hour, the pressure on the London architects of Postmaster kept growing.

Worse still, in Santa Isabel the inevitable had occurred: SOE agent Richard Lippett, the cool and consummate conductor of that end of the great deception, was taken in for questioning. Lippett had prepared for the coming interrogation with the utmost care, but still its rigour and aggression disconcerted even him, especially as it was carried out in what Lippett described as 'very Gestapo-like' conditions. At every turn the beak-nosed, sunken-eyed Captain Binea tried to pin something on him: his lavish gifts to all those involved; his funding of the fateful dinner parties; his close friendship – *his partnership* – with Zorilla.

Lippett dealt with the accusations the only way that he could, by deflecting them onto the absent Zorilla, his Spanish cohort, who by now was safely in Nigeria. Lippett was booked to leave Fernando Po in six days time, taking the regular steam ferry to the mainland. He knew that if he'd made his getaway at the same time as Zorilla, the case against the British would have been infinitely more damning. So he'd opted to stay, to help deflect suspicion away from the perpetrators of the raid. But the decision to do so was threatening to cost him dear.

Lippett's performance during his grilling was superlative. 'I was thankful that no younger man had gone through what I had,' Lippett wrote, 'as they may have broken him down.' In fact, his act had been almost too convincing. By the time Lippett was hauled in for a second session of questioning, Binea's atti-tude had changed completely. He seemed convinced that Lippett was what he claimed to be – the archetypal upstanding, incorruptible Englishman.

Captain Binea explained that he was intending to bring charges against those who were 'Zorrilla's closest collaborators', and that he would need Richard Lippett to give evidence in the trials against them. Lippett was to be one of Captain Binea's key prosecution witnesses, and accordingly he was refused an exit visa to leave the island.

Richard Lippett, SOE agent W.25, was trapped: Postmaster's great deception risked being blown wide open.

They say that the darkest hour is just before the dawn. The day after Lippett's second interrogation by Captain Binea, London secured its first piece of positive news. A message had finally reached British ears regarding the fortunes of the Operation Postmaster armada – or at least one half of it.

On 19 January HMS *Violet's* commander, Lieutenant Nicholas, had cabled a short communiqué: 'Have intercepted *Duchessa d'Aosta* in 003 degs 53' North 02' East steering westwards. Have placed prize crews aboard without opposition. Escorting to Lagos unless otherwise ordered.' The message absolutely fitted the needs of the deception. Behind it lay the wider story: the British destroyer had finally managed to shake herself free of the sandbank and go to the British raiders' aid.

In theory, March-Phillipps, Appleyard, Lassen and their raider cohorts were now formally 'under arrest', as were the 'mutinous' Italian crew. But of Graham Hayes and the others aboard the *Nuneaton*, the *Likomba* and the *Bibundi* there had been no further sign. Ever since March-Phillipps had made the agonizing decision to leave the three ships wallowing in the lea of Fernando Po, there had been no further sighting of them.

To all intents and purposes they had disappeared.

Still, the cable of the 19th from HMS *Violet* was seen by London as being enough to warrant a response to the accusations being pumped out by the Axis media, and that of her supposedly neutral allies.

That very day the Admiralty issued the first counter communiqué:

> In view of the German allegations that Allied naval forces have executed a cutting out operation against Axis ships in the Spanish port of Santa Isabel, Fernando Po, the British Admiralty consider it necessary to state that no British or Allied warship was in the vicinity of Fernando Po at the time of the alleged incident. As a result, however, of the information obtained from German broadcasts, the British Commander in Chief dispatched reconnaissance patrols to cover the area. A report has now been received that a large unidentified vessel has been sighted and British naval vessels are proceeding to the spot to investigate.

The statement was a masterpiece of double-speak and deception – one deliberately designed to suggest that the Germans, by means of their wild accusations, had brought the subsequent misfortune upon themselves.

Curt instructions were issued to the SOE head of operations in Lagos: long before any of the ships reached harbour, the raider crews were to be spirited away and kept hidden. As far as M and the wider SOE were concerned, no one bar the *Maid Honour*'s crew and a small circle of insiders should ever know that this clandestine force had existed. The Italian prisoners were to be transported up country, and incarcerated in a POW facility far away from curious eyes or ears.

It wasn't until Wednesday 21st January that the *Vulcan* and the *Duchessa d'Aosta* finally reached Lagos, under escort of *HMS Violet*. As chance would have it, the *Nuneaton* and her two charges would also materialize at around about the same time. Despairing of locating an escort, Hayes and crew had been forced to make do and mend with the *Nuneaton's* engines and, dodging potentially hostile vessels and warplanes en route, their little armada had limped into the nearest British port more or less unaided.

Gus March-Phillipps was finally able to send a telegram to London, informing M and his political masters of the success of his mission: 'Casualties our party absolutely nil. Casualties enemy nil, apart from a few sore heads. Prisoners: Germans nil, Italians: men 27, women 1, natives 1.'

Congratulatory telegrams were sent by return, both from M and from the British Prime Minister himself. Now the challenge was to keep the role played by Churchill's secret raiders in Operation Postmaster hidden for the duration of the war.

Three days after the five ships had made it safely into Lagos, the Spanish government issued its first note of 'most energetic protest' about the attack. All the facts led the authorities in Madrid to deduce that 'the act of aggression was carried out by ships and elements in the service of British interests or direct collaborators with the British forces operating on the coast of West Africa.'

Behind the diplomatic angst and aggrieved language lay a simple truth: ten days after the attack the Spanish still didn't have a clear sense as to who exactly was responsible for the raid. They strongly suspected British connivance, but that was about as far as they could go. That in turn meant the most important aspect of Operation Postmaster – its deniability – had been sustained.

In a 'MOST SECRET' report submitted to M and others, five days after March-Phillipps' flotilla reached Lagos harbour, 'CAESAR' – Lieutenant-Colonel Julius Hanau, M's deputy at the SOE – sounded an exultant note of triumph:

Now that <u>POSTMASTER</u> is in the bag, I feel you may care to have the enclosed record of its romantic and dramatic career set out chronologically from its early days until the climax was reached.

In that report, CAESAR reveals that the *Nuneaton* – together with the *Likomba* and *Bibundi* – actually ran aground on the night of the raid, after the tugboat's engines failed. Fortunately for Operation Postmaster, she was refloated and managed to make her getaway with her prizes in tow. CAESAR goes on to praise the dash and daring of the raiders, and to lament bitterly those who stood in Postmaster's way:

The operation not only achieved more than its material object, but it achieved it in such a way that the task of the Foreign Office and the Admiralty in meeting the political and legal aftermath has been reduced to a minimum. We hope that SOE will be permitted to demonstrate that what was possible in Fernando Po is possible elsewhere: perhaps on the next occasion it will not be found necessary to preface twenty-five minutes compact and decisive action by over four months prolonged and desultory negotiations.

Caesar also stresses the value of POSTMASTER to the SOE, in terms of proving its modus operandi:

POSTMASTER was the first special operation of any scale to be undertaken by S.O.E. in a neutral port, and was therefore something of a test case – nor is it the easiest task to spirit away on a dark night an 8,000-tonne liner moored close into shore without leaving any trace of one's visit. No reports from any sources have indicated that any tangible evidence of British complicity was left behind.

But in a sense, CAESAR had spoken too soon. He'd forgotten one crucial element: Richard Lippett.

Agent Lippett's fortunes were looking decidedly dark. He feared that if he were forced to give 'evidence' against his Spanish friends in what amounted to a court martial, he would crack. While all SOE agents were sworn to wage total war with no holds barred – putting normal moral objections aside in time of war – this was a step too far. If found guilty, his Spanish friends would face a long period of imprisonment and possibly even execution.

By now London had issued several formal statements claiming that the Italian and German vessels had been seized fair and square on the high seas. If Lippett broke during the court martial, the British government would be exposed at the very highest level. *He had to be spirited away.*

All options were explored to get Lippett off the island, but every which way seemed to be blocked. Captain Binea was determined to keep his prime witness close at hand, so the Spanish certainly weren't going to grant Lippett permission to leave. Alternately, if the British Consulate were to organize some form of escape and their involvement was discovered, Britain's role at the heart of the Postmaster deception would be revealed.

Eventually Lippett – suffering intense fevers due to a bout of malaria – decided that he had no option but to follow in Zorilla's footsteps and engage a native fisherman to paddle him across the water to Nigeria. He had many friends among the Nigerians resident on the island – most of whom were strongly pro-British – and he made arrangements with one of them to help execute his escape.

On 25 February 1942 – six weeks after the raid – Lippett made a break for it. He travelled overland to a remote coastal village. But while waiting for the fisherman to collect him, word reached Lippett that a contingent of Spanish police had arrived seeking his arrest. With the native canoeist failing to appear, Lippett did the only thing he could: he made a solo break for it.

Hurrying down to the shore to steal a native canoe, Lippett ran into a Spanish Colonial police officer. In his younger years Lippett had been something of a heavyweight boxing champion. Despite being weakened by malaria, he punched the living daylights out of the Spanish policeman and laid him out unconscious. As he neared the beach he had to do the same to a second police officer, before he was finally able to grab a dugout and push it into the foaming surf.

Unfortunately, he'd broken his thumb during the melee, and he was in agony as he started to paddle. Ahead of a man already racked by malaria lay a forty-mile journey across often intemperate seas. But Lippett had little choice. It took him fifteen exhausting and painful hours to complete the crossing, before finally he made the Nigerian shoreline.

In a cable from the British Consulate in Fernando Po, shortly after Lippett's escape, his dire predicament is made clear: 'W.25 was in a highly nervous state when he left Fernando Po and we are of the opinion that . . . if he had remained for the Courtmartial, under pressure from cross examination he would most likely have confessed his complicity in the affair.'

Lippett had escaped by the skin of his teeth, as – arguably – had the grand deception behind Operation Postmaster. With the crucial witness having disappeared, Captain Binea's case against the Spaniards fell apart. None were ever found guilty. Instead, the focus of inquiries shifted onto Heinrich Luhr, who was seemingly the paymaster for the dinner parties, and he was to face accusations of being a British spy.

In a delicious irony, responsibility for SOE's Operation Postmaster was laid at the door of a German.

With Postmaster's success the SOE had pulled off its most daring coup of the war so far. Postmaster was an accomplishment that few in the know could afford to ignore. Much of the

Regular Armed Services – the Army, Navy and Air Force – still resented these lawless agent-commandos, but grudging respect did have to be paid for a mission that was so utterly remarkable.

March-Phillipps recommended Appleyard – 'a great gift for organization and command' – and Graham Hayes – 'a most accomplished all around fighting soldier' – for promotion. M rubber-stamped both their promotions to Captain. As for Private Anders Lassen – in March-Phillipps' words 'the most outstanding in the operation on the *Duchessa*' – he received his formal officer's commission.

In his diary Lassen wrote of the cut-out operation and his promotion – which March-Phillipps had bestowed upon him informally, as they sailed away from Fernando Po with their prizes – with lighthearted understatement. 'Went straight into a foreign harbour. Snatched a big ship and sailed off with it. The Jerries and the Italians made a hell of a row. Was promoted officer on the bridge by Captain March-Phillipps.'

In the SOE's signature way, without requiring any officer's training whatsoever, Lassen was directly appointed a Second Lieutenant, the pips simply sewn onto his uniform. 'They just gave the pips to me,' Lassen explained laughingly, to one of his fellow raiders. To another, Tom Winter, who along with Hayes had seized the *Likomba*, he confided: 'The greatest promotion I ever had before this was being made up to able seaman!'

Before his departure from Africa, Lassen had again gone up-country to help train the guerilla forces at Olokomeji – where the raiders had trialled their anchor-chain charges, prior to the attack. There he'd fallen for a young and decidedly lissom African girl.

Lassen had just completed negotiations with her father to buy her for £10 and two bottles of gin, when he was recalled to London to receive his promotion. As he commented in his diary: 'Unfortunately had to leave Africa when I was just completing negotiations to buy an exceedingly pretty wife . . . A great pity for that and other reasons I was recalled.'

One other comely maid was to be left behind by the raiders in West Africa – the *Maid Honour* herself. Stripped of her hidden weaponry, the ever-faithful Q Ship reverted to being a simple fishing trawler, and she was sold off for civilian use. She had served her purpose and had not been found wanting, and she would hold a special place in the hearts of the raiders long after the unit whose name she shared had ceased to exist – for the *Maid Honour* Force's days were numbered.

Operation Postmaster had raised March-Phillipps' stock to new heights, and his agent-commandos were moving on to bigger and better things.

Back in England, marriage seemed to be generally in the air, in spite of Lassen's failure to bag his African bride. March-Phillipps – now promoted to Major – had met and fallen in love with Marjorie Stewart, a striking-looking actress who had signed up as an agent in the SOE. Barely two months after his return from Operation Postmaster, March-Phillipps married his lovely agent-bride. M attended the wedding, as did Appleyard, Hayes and Lassen, and most of the *Maid Honour* Force regulars.

A cascade of honours followed Op Postmaster's success: a Distinguished Service Order (DSO) for March-Phillipps; a Military Cross (MC) for Graham Hayes and a bar to Appleyard's already existing Military Cross. The citations for these decorations talk euphemistically of being in 'recognition of services while employed on secret operations.' Anders Lassen was also written up for an honour, but it was yet to be bestowed upon him.

Churchill was known to be delighted at the raid's outcome. A buccaneer at heart, he'd been the driving force behind Postmaster from the start – and the high stakes only seemed to quicken his appetite for such undertakings. While there was widespread dismay expressed by rival politicians and amongst the top brass at the 'piratical' and decidedly 'un-British' nature of the operation, Churchill was unrepentant.

As to the three ships seized in the iconic mission, the foremost prize, the *Duchessa d'Aosta* was sailed back to Britain with a Royal Navy prize crew aboard. She was re-named the *Empire Yukon*, and used as a troop transport until the end of the war. Together with her cargo, she was valued at some £300,000 for requisitioning purposes, a significant amount when considering that 23 Spitfires could then be built for such a sum. The two German ships were also renamed, and they remained at work in British West Africa until the war's end.

The Italian prisoners seized during the raid were sent to South Africa, for interrogation, and to be kept well out of the public eye. Yet as late as January 1944, the powers that be were still considering mounting a second mission to Fernando Po, to seize the Italian ship's officers who had escaped capture. Whatever secrets the *Duchessa d'Aosta* had harboured, the British Government seemed determined to discover them in their entirety.

After March-Phillipps' nuptials there was much work to be done. March-Phillipps – *Maid Honour* Force's guru, master and commander – was older than most of his men, and he was also highly intelligent and idealistic in the sense that he would stop at almost nothing to further his ideals. In Anders Lassen he had found a very different individual, but each was drawn to the other irresistibly. Upon joining the SOE Lassen had been found too ill-disciplined to learn any drill, and too aggressive to perfect his spycraft, but by now March-Phillipps knew him to be perfect for 'leading a boarding party,' and for the kind of missions that he had in mind.

Together with Appleyard and Hayes – the calming, steadying influence to March-Phillip's fiery vision – these men formed the corners of a immensely strong pyramid, and the base of a new unit that was to rise out of the ashes of the *Maid Honour* Force. *Maid Honour* was sacrificed on the altar of deniability: it was the unit that never was. In its place rose phoenix-like the Small Scale Raiding Force (SSRF). Equally secretive, the SSRF was the means by which March-Phillipps would realize stage two of his grand plan.

Using similar tactics to those they'd employed in Fernando Po, his men would strike fear and terror into the German enemy where they least expected it – on the French beaches from where British forces had only months earlier fled before the might of the German blitzkrieg.

When Lassen had first signed up as a Special Duty volunteer, he had done so simply in the name 'A. Lassen'. In reality, his full name was Anders Frederik Emil Victor Schau Lassen, and he hailed from a long line of Danish landed-gentry adventurers. Before the war his father was wont to visit London and summon their chauffeur-driven Rolls Royce from the steps of the Hyde Park Hotel with a blast of his hunting horn.

Throughout his unrivalled wartime career Lassen never once let on to his closest comrades about his highborn, moneyed background. All he ever wanted was to be known as 'Andy' and to be at one with the mixed band of fellow rebels and mavericks with whom he would wage war.

But all of that was to come. For now, the tiny unit that had become the SSRF was riding high on the success of the Fernando Po raid. A major recruitment drive ensued. One of the first new arrivals was Ian Warren, a British soldier 'recruited' into the force in Africa. During the *Maid Honour*'s stopover in West Africa March-Phillipps and Warren had got into a fight because Warren wouldn't stop singing along to the smash wartime hit, 'Stardust', as he played it over and over again on the gramophone. March-Phillipps had ordered him to cease his crooning, or he'd throw him out of the mess window. In spite of being a few inches shorter than March-Phillipps, stocky Warren had squared up to the *Maid Honour* commander, and thrown him out of the window instead.

March-Phillipps had climbed back in and told Warren, with typical sporting good grace: 'You bloody little man – you'd better come and join us!'

Warren would become one of Lassen's roommates, a position not without its risks to life and limb. Warren would return from one bit of training or the other, only to find a knife quivering in the wooden doorframe inches from where he stood, or to hear the thud of an arrow embedding itself in the leg of his bed. It was an occupational hazard of sharing a room with the Dane, who was forever honing his skills with the blade, and testing the mettle of his fellow operators.

From the original force of a dozen agent-commandos, their number grew to approaching sixty. It included John Gwynne, recruited to join them as the operations planner, but known to all simply as 'Killer'. Gwynne was a vegetarian and a teetotaler who shaved only in cold water, and he had an absolutely fanatical gleam in his eye.

Peter Kemp was another incurable war-seeker. He'd failed the British Army medical due to wounds he'd suffered while fighting in the Spanish Civil War. A mortar had exploded, injuring both his hands and shattering his jaw. But Kemp's being 'unfit for military service' didn't stop March-Phillipps from taking him, especially as he had such a wealth of frontline experience.

Another combat veteran was Sergeant Jack Nicholson, a Distinguished Conduct Medal (DCM) winner. Nicholson, a Scot, had soldiered with No. 7 Commando, the unit in which March-Phillipps and Appleyard had originally served, as they'd suffered a series of defeats and were driven off the beaches of France.

For the majority of March-Phillipps' men a return to mainland Europe – albeit temporary – was long overdue.

Chapter Nine

In order to prepare for the coming cross-Channel sorties, the SSRF was assigned a new base. Previously, they'd been operating out of the *Maid Honour*, anchored at a Poole dockside. The SSRF's new headquarters was set in the fading grandeur of an SOE-requisitioned country house – Anderson Manor, lying on the banks of the Winterbourne River, in north Dorset.

Codenamed 'Fyfield' by the SOE, it was at Anderson that March-Phillipps forged his unit's unique *esprit de corps*. At Fyfield he imbued his new recruits with the same contempt that he felt for the petty rules and regulations that so often plagued the wider military. Rank was subordinate to a soldier's merit, and smartness and neatness of uniform – such that they wore – were secondary to a man's ability to wage the kind of warfare that was coming.

In truth that warfare – isolated, without back up or support, often deep behind enemy lines – left little chance for long-term survival. As Lassen explained to some fellow Danish recruits: 'I'll make it quite clear you have less than a 50 per cent chance of coming through alive.'

In spite of such warnings, all sixteen prospective Danish recruits signed up to join the SOE agent-commandos. To better prepare the newbies for facing such daunting odds, March-

Phillipps had them train with detonators stuck in potatoes, which they hurled at each other; you either ducked out of the way, or you risked being blown up and hurt.

From Anderson Manor March-Phillipps, Appleyard, Hayes, Lassen, Warren, Gwynne, Kemp, Nicholson and several dozen others began training among the many estuaries and rivers of the Dorset coastline. Perhaps unsurprisingly, these rough-looking men dressed in a motley collection of British and foreign uniforms aroused enormous suspicion among the locals, especially when they were spotted canoeing up the rivers in the dead of night.

Lassen in particular, with his white-blond hair and foreign accent, was forever being seized by the Home Guard as a suspected German spy. After a phone call to the SOE's head-quarters he would be verified as one of Churchill's Special Duty volunteers and released back to his unit.

In raiding the French coast March-Phillipps knew they would be going up against a far tougher enemy than those faced in Fernando Po. The German troops stationed in France had very likely fought across Europe. Accordingly, he devised a crash-training regime reminiscent of today's SAS Selection. It involved forced marches of up to sixty miles in length, prolonged night navigation, unarmed combat, hand-to-hand fighting, marksmanship, as well as movement by water.

Teams were dropped in the remote Dorset countryside at night, and told to find their way back to Fyfield, with no money nor even any idea where they might be. It was during such epic marches that the city slickers among them first introduced their fellow recruits to Benzedrine, an amphetamine then popular in London's glitzier nightclubs and known colloquially as 'bennies'.

With its euphoric stimulant effect, Benzedrine could keep an operator alert and clear-headed for long periods without any need to sleep.

There were the highly realistic simulated missions to penetrate an 'enemy headquarters', with hunter forces in pursuit and manning the supposed target. Throughout all of this Lassen's skill as a born fighter was to the fore. Under the heading 'Bow and Arrow Use in Modern Warfare' he petitioned the War Office to be allowed to develop it as the ultimate silent killing weapon.

'Having attended different training schools . . . I have no doubt that the bow and arrow would in many cases prove of great value,' he wrote to the War Office. 'I have considerable experience hunting with bow and arrow. I have shot everything from sparrows to stags, and although I have never attempted to shoot a man yet it is my opinion that the result would turn out just as well . . .'

He then listed its advantages:

1. The arrow is almost soundless.
2. The arrow kills without shock or pain, so it is unlikely that a man would scream or do anything like that.
3. A well-trained archer can shoot up to fifteen shots a minute.
4. The arrow is as deadly as an ordinary bullet.

In a typical fudge the War Office provided Lassen with two hunting bows complete with arrows, but not the permission to use them against the enemy, for in the age of the machine gun and the flame thrower the humble bow-and-arrow was somehow viewed as being an 'inhuman weapon'. That didn't stop Lassen from training with his newly acquired weaponry around the Dorset woodlands and meadows, where villagers started to speak of him as 'the Robin Hood Commando'.

By the summer of 1942 Anders Lassen was poised to justify his nickname.

The SSRF were about to launch Operation Dryad, their debut raid in Europe. They were allocated two Motor Torpedo Boats (MTBs), one of which was designed to present a particularly low profile when powering through the sea, making her difficult to detect from land. An 'experimental-type' boat made by the shipbuilders Thorneycroft, she'd been nicknamed 'Little Pisser' by the men of the SSRF, due to the continuous bubbling noise made by her submerged – and therefore largely silent – exhausts.

Little Pisser – formally MTB 344 – would become indispensable on the coming missions. She was a hotted-up MTB of diminutive size that had been stripped of all weaponry, bar a pair of machine guns, to boost her speed to some thirty knots. She boasted twin Thorneycroft engines and as long as the weather remained relatively calm there was little could catch her on the open sea. She was skippered by Lieutenant Freddie Bourne who would become a stalwart of SSRF operations.

The plan for Operation Dryad involved an SSRF team crossing the Channel in Little Pisser, kidnapping the Germans garrisoning Les Casquets – one of the most northerly points of the Channel Islands, and one of the German-occupied outposts closest to Britain – and leaving the place in total ruins. Les Casquets was used as a signal station for the German Navy, so this was a target of real strategic value.

The Channel Islands were the only part of the United Kingdom to have been taken by the Germans. They had been abandoned by British forces after the fall of France because they were seen as being indefensible. In range of the shore batteries stationed along the French coast, they could be pounded into oblivion and, after a raid by Heinkel bombers killed over forty islanders, they had surrendered in June 1940.

Les Casquets – a jagged line of humped rocks – forms part of a series of barren outcrops where an underwater sandstone ridge emerges from the waves. Blasted by the elements, they are devoid of vegetation. The name Les Casquets is thought to be a derivation of the French word 'cascade', alluding to the fierce tidal surges that swirl around the islands. The raiders' chief interests were the lighthouse built upon the rock's highest point, plus the all-important radio station and German garrison.

The sea around Les Casquets boasts a long and fearsome history of shipwrecks, making a successful approach challenge enough in itself. The raiders would only be in a position to scale the 90-foot rock and launch their attack once they'd navigated a series of treacherous shoals, through which the tidal race surges like the flushing of a giant toilet.

As with Fernando Po, March-Phillipps' plan of attack called for striking under cover of darkness, absolute secrecy, shock and surprise. Key to the raid's success was subduing the island's garrison before they were able to use their radio to call for help from the German forces sited on neighbouring islands.

Three attempts were made to execute the raid in July and August 1942, but each was foiled by a combination of bad weather and the unmanageable approach to the target. Yet such aborted runs weren't entirely wasted. They enabled close recces of the target to be carried out, and for a scale model of it to be built at Anderson Manor so the raiders could better plan their attack.

By the time of the fourth attempt, March-Phillipps had scaled down his plans, utilizing a more nimble, manageable force. Instead of using two MTBs, only Little Pisser would go, carrying a force of twelve. Crucially, two of those would be German speakers – a Polish Jew called Abram 'Orr' Opoczynski, and Patrick Dudgeon, a Briton who had learned enough of the language to get by at school. As with Fernando Po's 'friendly Spaniards', they would be placed in the vanguard, to shout confusing orders in German and confound the rocky outpost's defenders.

The morning of the raid – 2 September 1942 – dawned bright and clear. As March-Phillipps and his cohorts gathered around the scale model of Les Casquets for one final planning session, the decision was made not to go in on one of the three easier landing points – small rocky beaches formed at the base of the rocks. It stood to reason that those could be mined, or sentries set guarding their approach.

Instead, they would go for the most difficult landing, putting ashore at the base of a sheer, 80-foot rock face immediately beneath the lighthouse itself, with a view to scaling that and attacking with ultimate stealth and surprise. Laden down with weaponry – each would carry a Tommy Gun plus half-a-dozen magazines of ammo, Mills bombs, charges to blow their targets, plus the indispensable Fairbairn-Sykes fighting knife – it was going to be some climb.

After a day thick with nerves the men ate a last meal and dressed for the coming mission. Each wore dark combats, a black balaclava and silent, felt-soled boots, while any exposed skin was given the obligatory 'blackening-up' using British Army camo cream. Just before dusk the army lorry set out from Anderson Manor, the raiders singing softly to themselves as it bumped along the Dorset lanes and they psyched themselves up for what was coming.

At Portland Harbour, lying just off the coast at Weymouth, Freddie Bourne was ready and waiting with Little Pisser. Under the cloak of darkness Bourne powered up the low-lying MTB and set a course for the Channel Islands. Bar March-Phillipps and Appleyard, who remained with Bourne on the bridge, all the raiders went below decks. Like most MTBs Little Pisser had a habit of smashing her way through the waves like a battering ram, lurching from one to the next with bone-shaking impacts, plus the noise from her twin engines was as if a Spitfire was taking off to either side of her hull.

She was showing no lights, and the men made the best of the journey they could, getting their eyesight adjusted to the darkness in readiness for the assault.

At 2245 the faint silhouette of Les Casquets – a sea-serpent's humped back rearing out of the night-dark waters – came into view, with the knife-thin form of the lighthouse stabbing above it. With Appleyard helping navigate, Bourne steered the MTB as close as he could to the northern side of the rocks, where the raiders would attempt to make their ascent.

As she made her final approach, Little Pisser was switched to silent-operation mode. In addition to her powerful twin Thorneycroft engines, she was fitted with a more sedate, auxiliary Ford V8, for sneaking in close to enemy targets. She puttered in quietly to within 800 yards of the rocks and dropped anchor; it was now all up to March-Phillipps and his crew.

For tonight's operation the chosen close assault craft was a Goatley, a collapsible, wooden-bottomed rowing-boat-cum-canoe with canvas sides. Some 1,000 Goatleys would be ordered by the War Office by the war's end, but at this stage in proceedings their use was restricted largely to unconventional raiding forces.

March-Phillipps gave the order for the off. Appleyard knelt in the prow, signalling directions to left and right, as the four men on either side paddled for all they were worth. A powerful current was trying to force the craft north-eastwards, threatening to sweep them past the eastern edge of the rocks and into the open sea. With the Goatley's canvas prow set into the teeth of the tide, backs bent to their task, sweat pouring down blackened faces despite the cool of the night.

Some fifteen minutes later the low-lying craft crept into the lee of the dark, uninviting island. Appleyard had detected a slab-sided, sloping rock lying directly below the engine house tower that he figured they might just use as a makeshift landing-platform. With the crashing of the sea masking the noise of their approach, the Goatley was brought in as close as he dared, lest her flimsy sides be dashed against the cliff and holed. The kedge anchor – a light anchor used to help a craft manoeuvre in narrow, treacherous spaces – was released. The Goatley was now fixed at the stern.

Appleyard took a line from the bows and prepared to make the jump. Timing it to perfection, he leapt across to the slimy, seaweed encrusted rock, and made the bowline fast. The Goatley was now secured in place from both ends, which made it slightly easier for the remainder of the heavily-laden raiders to follow him.

Graham Hayes – the hero of the cutting-out of the *Likomba* – plus one other remained in the Goatley, to safeguard her both from the sea and rocks, and from enemy discovery. The ten remaining men scrambled across to their slippery landing and onto enemy territory.

The night was clear and star-bright, with just the faintest sliver of a moon. The men surveyed the route ahead. The first half of the rock face was stained almost black from the constant pounding of the sea. Above that, the humped folds of sandstone took on a greyer hue, with here and there a slash of brighter yellow reflected in the moonlight, showing where stubborn lichens clung to cracks and crevices.

Ten men hauled themselves up the rock face, the noise of their climb being inaudible among the heavy booming of the sea in the chasms and gulleys. Fortunately, the cliff offered plenty of generous – if at first slimy – handholds. As they neared the top the raiders hit their first obstacle – coils of barbed wire, forming a defensive perimeter. With his body hugging the earth to keep well hidden, the lead man cut through the wire, the roaring of the surf below drowning out the sharp clips of his snipping.

With muscles burning from the long paddle across the sea, plus the climb under heavy loads, it was now that the rigours of their Dorset training really stood the raiders in good stead. No sentries were visible, but the base of the lighthouse tower was a mass of barbed-wire entanglements, concrete bunkers and blockhouses, with a shoulder-high wall encircling the lot. A 20mm Oerlikon cannon was positioned against one wall, which could put down devastating fire onto the raiders.

It was shortly after midnight when March-Phillipps led his men over the western perimeter wall. It was thankfully free of wire, and nowhere near as high as the one on the Anderson Manor assault course. As they landed soft-soled in the interior of the compound, they knew time was against them. They had just seconds until they were discovered, and they had to strike fast while the enemy were still off-guard.

March-Phillipps split his men into four groups – signalling one to take the lighthouse tower, another to hit the accommodation block, a third to secure the engine building, and the last to hit the all-important radio room. March-Phillipps led the assault on the accommodation block. He kicked open the main door and burst into the central room, Tommy Gun at the ready. The first thing he saw were two German soldiers on sentry, an open box of stick grenades lying at their side.

Menaced by the barrels of four Trench Sweepers wielded by a murderous-looking adversary, and taken by utter surprise, the Germans opted not to reach for their grenades. They were taken prisoner, and left in no doubt that one word of alarm from them would be fatal. That done, March-Phillipps ordered his men to move further into the building. Sleeping quarters branched off a main corridor. Presumably, the rest of the garrison was in there, relying on their two comrades on watch to raise the alarm should there be any sign of trouble.

Outside, two raiders stormed through the door to the radio room, where a light could be seen burning the midnight oil. For some reason the place had been temporarily vacated, the wireless operator perhaps heading out to use the bathroom. Either way, it was an absolute Aladdin's cave. Scattered across the desk were a treasure trove of German codebooks, note-books full of scribbled information and instructions, plus signal pads used for compiling messages, wireless diaries and logs. It was exactly this kind of material – hard, usable intelligence – that the raiders had come for.

It was around 0100 by now. In the accommodation block Patrick Dudgeon surprised two German telegraphers, those who had just vacated the radio room. They were in the process of preparing for bed when he slammed open their door and the gaping barrel of his Tommy Gun swept the room. Dudgeon was a fearsome figure of a man, nicknamed 'Toomai, the Elephant Boy' by his raider-mates, after the 1937 British adventure film. He started snarling questions at the telegraphers in his schoolboy German, demanding to know where the rest of their comrades were located, and how heavily armed they might be.

Almost before the bewildered radio operators could answer, March-Phillipps and his men were at work further down the corridor. They booted open the door to a final room, and discovered three figures still asleep. Dragging two out of their beds, March-Phillipps objected to the third being seized, because the figure that was lying there was wearing a hairnet.

'You can't t-t-take that!' he cried out. 'It's a w-w-w-woman.'

It soon transpired that all three Germans had been sleeping in hairnets, and so the one mistaken for a woman was seized as well! One of them had actually fainted upon seeing the fierce, staring eyes of the raiders appear from out of the night. The scramble down the cliff to the sea would surely revive him.

By the time all the garrison had been rounded up, the raiders had netted four Navy men – three of whom were Leading Telegraphists – under the command of Chief Petty Officer Mundt, plus three Army men who were there to stand guard over the remote outpost. Position secured, March-Phillipps ordered a thorough search and anything of intelligence value to be taken. Ration books, identity cards, the station and light log, plus personal letters and photos – everything was loaded up as the raiders prepared to make their getaway.

In the radio room they gathered up a final hoard of documents, after which came the moment that gave them greatest pleasure – smashing apart the German radio sets with an axe.

The only challenge now remained how to get seven prisoners down the slippery rock face and into the waiting Goatley. March-Phillipps had also seized the Germans's weaponry – so his men were laden with the 20mm Oerlikon, boxes of grenades, several long Steyr rifles, as well as helmets and other items of German uniform. Trying to get off again with this lot aboard the Goatley would risk sinking her.

March-Phillipps ended up with seventeen shadowy figures crouched on the slimy rock slab, waves sweeping back and forth and eager to pluck both raiders and their captives into their icy clutches. There was clearly no room in the boat for the purloined weaponry, so it was tossed unceremoniously into the depths.

The only way into the waiting Goatley – for prisoners as well as raiders – was to slide down the 45-degree angle of the rock slab, and leap across the water into the fragile craft. Two raiders were injured doing so, the second being Appleyard. He was last man off, jumping with the rope into the crowded vessel's bows. He landed awkwardly, hearing a sharp crack from his lower leg, followed by a jab of pain at shin level. There was little time to investigate his 'crocked ankle', as every man had to paddle like hell for the waiting ship.

With bare inches of her canvas hull protruding above the waves, the Goatley made it back to the waiting MTB, under the power of her exhausted but exultant raider-crew. Upon rendez-vousing with Little Pisser the prisoners were herded into the front of the boat, where they could be covered by a couple of Tommy Guns. As the MTB crept silently away from Les Casquets, the quizzing of the German captives had already begun.

March-Phillipps and his men had just abducted the entire garrison of Les Casquets – an important German naval signal station – wrecking the wireless room and dumping all their weaponry in the sea, and they had secured a bonanza of intelligence materials to boot. After the success of Operation Postmaster, Operation Dryad was as fitting a follow-up as they could have wished for.

The raiders had a two-hour crossing ahead of them, and by the time Little Pisser rounded Portland Bill, the jubilant raiders

126

had dressed themselves in assorted items of captured German uniform, including the enemy soldiers' distinctive helmets.

They were greeted by their fellow SSRF brothers with cries of 'You look like the bleedin' Hun!' and 'Here comes Jerry!'

The words were uttered in jest, of course, but a seed had been planted in the minds of several of the raiders, Lassen first and foremost. If they could lay their hands on enough German kit, surely they could go about their raiding business posing as the enemy? With Lassen and his Danish and Polish comrades fluent in German, surely they could do so convincingly? The idea would take some finessing, but it was one that the Danish Viking was determined to make a reality.

At 0400 hours the prisoners were handed direct to Military Intelligence (M19), along with all the documentation the raiders had secured. The telegraphists among them – first and foremost Chief Petty Officer Mundt, a forty-one-year-old veteran of the First World War – would prove remarkably talkative. They were able to furnish accounts of enemy positions along a vast sweep of the French coastline from Calais in the east through the Cherbourg Peninsula in the west, and across the expanse of the Channel Islands – intelligence that would prove invaluable to the SSRF on future raids.

In some aspects their accounts were incredibly detailed. They recalled a carrier pigeon that had been driven into Les Casquets during that August's storms. The exhausted bird had settled under the lighthouse and been caught in a snare. Attached to the bird's leg was a tiny green canister containing a roll of paper and a message in pencil. It was in French, and began with the words 'Pigeon 28/8/42 15 hours'. The message spoke about locations at Bologne, Dieppe, Avions and Hangars. The pigeon and its message – presumably linked to the French resistance – had been handed over to German intelligence.

It took twenty-four hours for the Germans to discover why their naval signal station on Les Casquets had fallen silent. The unit sent to investigate discovered a veritable ghost-station. There were no signs of resistance: no blood or bullet holes. Some of the missing, seized as they were in their pyjamas, had even left their uniforms behind.

Hitler's initial reaction upon hearing the news was to declare Les Casquets indefensible, but the German Navy argued that it was too vital to lose. When Les Casquets was reoccupied by the Germans the garrison was increased five-fold, and the outpost's defences significantly strengthened.

March-Phillipps' own report on the mission expressed a quiet satisfaction in a job well done. 'Great credit is due to Lieut. Bourne for his handling of his ship . . . [in] hazardous and difficult undertakings in close proximity to reefs and sunken rocks, and to Captain Appleyard, whose navigation made them possible. Also, to Private Orr, a German speaker, who marshalled the prisoners and did much to make the search successful.'

As much as anything, Operation Dryad proved a major propaganda victory for a British military still to set foot again in any significant numbers upon European soil. Churchill's subsequent words of praise for the mission – and similar cross-Channel raids – were telling: 'There comes out of the sea from time to time a hand of steel which plucks the German sentries from their posts with growing efficiency.'

Shortly after Operation Dryad Anders Lassen was back wielding Churchill's 'hand of steel', as he led a six-man team onto the island of Burhou, a rocky outcrop at the eastern end of the sandstone ridge that forms Les Casquets.

His was a reconnaissance mission designed to see if light artillery could be landed on Burhou, with which to launch a lightning strike against the German positions across the water on the Channel Island of Alderney. Burhou proved to be another bare and windswept outpost, which the Germans were using solely for target practice.

The raid yielded useful intelligence, and March-Phillipps was able to recommend that a force equipped with mortars and pack-artillery – man-portable guns – could land on Burhou and put down barrages onto the enemy, before melting away into the night.

Lord Louis Mountbatten – Commodore and later Admiral of the Fleet – was then Britain's Chief of Combined Operations. Strictly speaking SOE agent-commandos like March-Phillipps and his men didn't fall under Mountbatten's area of responsibility, but after Operations Postmaster and Dryad he was well aware of their actions.

Mountbatten decreed there should be a minimum of one cross-Channel raid every two weeks, to keep the German coastal forces on their toes, and to demoralize and terrorize them. At the same time, the raiding forces were to gather intelligence for any forthcoming invasion fleet heading towards the French beaches.

The SSRF was involved in several other cross-Channel missions – including some vicious night-time skirmishes with the enemy, as well as clandestine probing of their defences. But it was now that March-Phillipps, Appleyard, Lassen and the other veteran raiders began preparing for the mission that would truly cross the line.

In the forthcoming Operation Aquatint they planned to target mainland France, landing on the coastline from where months before British forces had been driven into the sea by the German blitzkrieg. They planned to put ashore at the village of St Laurent-sur-Mer, at the eastern end of what was to become known, in the D-Day landings to come, as 'Omaha Beach'.

As always with such raids, Operation Aquatint was heavily weather-dependent. It finally got the go ahead on a Saturday in September 1942 when Anders Lassen was off on a rare weekend's leave, most probably with a lady friend.

On that fateful night March-Phillipps would feel the absence of his Viking raider as never before.

Chapter Ten

On the night of 12/13 September 1942 Operation Aquatint went ahead without Lassen. It turned into an unmitigated disaster. Little Pisser took the raiders to the French coast, yet they failed to find the cliff they had planned to scale. Instead, they emerged from their Goatley boat onto a stretch of open sand.

The night was as black as pitch but luck was against them. A heavily-armed German patrol was moving on to the beach, and it stumbled into the British raiding force. In the bloody firefight that ensued one raider was so badly injured that he had to be left behind, as the others retraced their path to the waiting Goatley, all the while putting down fire on the enemy in pursuit.

The remaining ten made it back to their canvas-sided boat, but the Germans used machine guns mounted on the beach to rake the Goatley with fire. It was torn to pieces. Little Pisser tried to sneak in to pluck the survivors from the water, but she was forced out to sea again under heavy bombardment from German shore batteries.

Eleven men had gone ashore on 'Omaha' beach. None would return. Three were dead, four were on the run, and the rest – many badly injured – were captured by the enemy.

Among those who had evaded capture was Captain Graham Hayes – the *Maid Honour* original who had led the cut-out mission against the German vessel, the *Likomba*. He would make it as far as supposedly neutral Spain, only to be betrayed by the Spanish – and possibly elements of the French resistance who had been infiltrated by the Gestapo – and handed back to the Germans.

By then Hayes's three fellow escapees had already been captured. The two 'foreign' – i.e. non-British – men among them, the Pole 'Orr' Opoczynski and a Dutchman, Jan Hellings, were sent to the notorious prison camps Stalag 133 and Luft Dulag. At some stage they either died in those camps, or were executed. Hitler had already decreed that any man from occupied Europe found fighting with the Allies would be shot: that may well have been their fate.

As for Graham Hayes, he was incarcerated in the infamous fortress-prison of Fresnes, south of Paris, in solitary confinement. The only break from the loneliness and abject squalor of his cell were the regular visits to the Gestapo headquarters, for interrogations that were supplemented by savage beatings, semi-drowning in icy baths, and whipping by ox-gut lashes stiffened with steel rods.

Hayes never broke nor gave anyone away – including those in the French resistance who had genuinely done so much to try to help him escape.

Among those who lost their lives on the beach at St Laurent-sur-Mer was Major Gus March-Phillipps DSO, the founder and visionary leader of the *Maid Honour* Force and the SSRF. He died in the water as he tried to swim ashore from the bullet-ridden Goatley.

In a poem penned in Africa shortly before Operation Postmaster had gone ahead, March-Phillipps had written of a bloody but noble end to a short life lived as a warrior.

Let me be brave and gay again
Oh Lord, when my time is near.
Let the god in me rise up and break
The stranglehold of fear.
Say that I die for Thee and the King,
And what I hold most dear.

It seems as if March-Phillipps had foreseen his own death while in the steamy tropics of West Africa.

As for the unit that he had founded and nurtured, the Small Scale Raiding Force suddenly had lost its irreplaceable figure-head. Along with Graham Hayes and Orr Opoczynski, the Free Frenchman Desgranges – he of the loincloth and piratical headscarf worn during Operation Postmaster – was also gone, as were many others. Leaderless, rudderless and deprived of those who had shaped it and made it what it was, this was the unit's darkest hour.

Fortunately, Appleyard had remained on Little Pisser during the mission, for it had been his duty to oversee the rendezvous with the Goatley once some German prisoners had been snatched for interrogation purposes. Due to his broken ankle he wasn't even supposed to be on active operations. It was only Appleyard's stubborn sense of duty that had taken him as far as he had gone on the fateful Operation Aquatint.

Even before the raiders had reached landfall Lassen had sensed that disaster was upon his brothers-in-arms. The night of Operation Aquatint he'd paced the bedroom where he was staying, restless and unable to settle. In the middle of the night he awoke in a cold sweat, yelling out in fear and shock. He was convinced that March-Phillipps was dead, killed during the raid.

He couldn't rest, and early the next morning he headed over to Anderson Manor, only to learn that none of those manning the Goatley had returned. It wasn't until the following day, 14 September, that the Germans issued an official communiqué concerning the force that March-Phillipps had led to the French coast:

> Their approach was immediately detected by the defence. Fire was opened upon them and the landing craft was sunk by direct hits. Three English officers and a de Gaullist naval officer were taken prisoner. A Major, a Company Sergeant Major and a Private were brought to land dead.

Though he rarely spoke of it, Lassen would blame himself for the failure of Operation Aquatint and for losing March-Phillipps, his close friend, mentor and guide. March-Phillipps had been blessed with a rare quixotic genius, making him the ideal figurehead for a unit such as the *Maid Honour* Force/the SSRF. His loss lay heavily upon all.

Lassen wrote poignantly in his diary about the death of a man he had idealized and tried to emulate, and to whom he was described by many as being 'devoted'. 'Major March-Phillipps is dead now,' he noted. 'The only man I sincerely liked and respected, he died in battle leading his men, a death worthy of him. At times I wish I'd been with him when things went wrong. At all the other times we fought together, but not the last.'

The resulting guilt and anger would drive Lassen to the limits in the missions to come, as he sought to avenge March-Phillipps' death and that of the others. But right now eleven men – the SSRF's commander first and foremost – were gone, and the unit was in danger of losing its way and its very purpose. Command of the SSRF now fell to Appleyard, and it was chiefly due to his refusal to let grief overcome the raiders' sense of mission that the unit survived its near-catastrophic loss.

In a War Office cable stamped '*Most Secret*', the change in command is reported in the driest possible terms: 'Major March-Phillipps, the former Commander of the raiding force . . . is unfortunately missing, and we wish to appoint in his place W/S Lieutenant J. G. Appleyard, MC . . . Captain Appleyard is 26, an officer since the War began . . . and recently won a bar to his Military Cross.'

In the aftermath of the fateful Operation Aquatint M visited Anderson Manor, and spent time among his agent-commandos in an effort to bolster morale. A true leader of men, he had been close to March-Phillipps – one of the earliest believers in M's vision for the agent-commandos – and he felt his loss and that of the others as keenly as anyone.

It was their anger and their thirst for revenge that drove M, Appleyard, Lassen and the others on. And as luck would have it, their very next mission would take these men to new levels of daring, notoriety and opprobrium.

Barely two weeks after Aquatint the raiders prepared to go into action again, on Operation Basalt. It was the night of 3 October when Appleyard, Lassen, Patrick Dudgeon – Toomai, the Elephant Boy, the German speaker who had interrogated the prisoners on Les Casquets – and nine others prepared to set sail once more in Little Pisser, their faithful ship being one of the few that had survived the disastrous raid on the French coast.

Nerves were stretched to breaking point for Operation Basalt. This was the unit's chance to prove that, despite their horrendous losses, they remained an effective fighting force. It was also a golden opportunity to seek revenge for those who had died, or perhaps worse still, like Graham Hayes, been taken captive.

Tonight's raid would take the men back to their old stalking ground – the Channel Islands. The target was Sark, a relatively small but heavily populated – and heavily garrisoned – land-mass, one menaced by barbed-wire entanglements, and with machine-gun nests and minefields covering just about every conceivable avenue of approach.

Just 2.1 square miles in area, Sark lies to the far south of Les Casquets and east of the main Channel Island of Guernsey. In the autumn of 1942 Sark was under the rule of Kommandant Major Albrecht Lanz, the German force commander based upon Guernsey. According to the prisoners seized from the earlier raid on Les Casquets, the garrison on Sark consisted of around 200–300 men, equipped with small arms, grenades, light machine guns and artillery pieces.

More worryingly still, there were some twenty minefields dotted around the island. These were armed with the dreaded S-mines, the so-called 'Bouncing Bettys', which when triggered sprang up to knee height, exploding in a hail of ball bearings. There were also fixed flamethrowers and anti-tank guns to deter any would-be aggressors. As if that wasn't enough, the civilian population was under a night-time curfew enforced by roving German patrols, which meant that anyone spotted during the hours of darkness would be assumed hostile.

The German garrison on Sark was in the process of reinforcing its defences still further. The SSRF's mission was to somehow infiltrate those defences, raid an enemy billet and seize as many prisoners as possible. Spiriting enemy soldiers away in the night was seen as being the means to spread ultimate terror among the German ranks – even more so than taking lives.

The twelve chosen men were told they could have their pick of weaponry for the coming raid. Lassen deliberated long and hard about taking his bow-and-arrows. In the end he decided against it – most probably because the War Office had proscribed its use in battle – settling instead for his Fairbairn-Sykes fighting knife.

Little Pisser ploughed through the darkened seas, each wave seeming half to swamp her, as her low-lying hull cut a path ahead. Salt spray whipped and stung the faces of those standing on the open deck. Appleyard and Lassen were in the wheelhouse, legs planted wide against the thumping impacts, and bracing themselves for what they knew was coming: *revenge*.

At shortly before 2300 hours she rounded Les Casquets, and struck a southerly bearing towards Sark. As always, Lieutenant Freddie Bourne was at the MTB's wheel, and as they neared their target he dropped their speed to around 10 knots, to dampen the earsplitting howl of the engines. Shortly, the craggy form of Sark took shape, cliffs washed a silver-grey in the moonlight.

Bourne brought the force in from the south-east, making for a semi-circular natural harbour scooped out of the island's south-eastern corner. On silent-engine mode the MTB puttered closer to the shoreline. From his charts Bourne knew that the water beneath his keel would remain deep and navigable almost to landfall. Making no more than one or two knots he crept under the lee of the cliffs, dropped anchor and cut the auxiliary engine.

Before them lay two apparently easy landing points – gently shelving shingle and sand beaches, with a simple scramble leading to the island's flatter level above. But fearing that each would be mined, the raiders intended to take a far more challenging approach. Between the bays lay a snub-nosed headland known as the Hog's Back. Mounted atop this feature was what aerial reconnaissance suggested was a German machine-gun post with clear fields of fire into both the bays below.

Mindful of the fate of the Operation Aquatint raiding force – whose Goatley had been machine-gunned in the water – Appleyard had decided it was crucial to make landfall unseen by the enemy manning that machine-gun post. The only way to do so was to head directly to the Hog's Back, and to put ashore where its furthest point plummeted into the sea.

During preparations for the mission Appleyard had discovered an old Sark guidebook – the Channel Islands being a popular tourist destination before the war – which mentioned the existence of a path leading directly from the Hog's Back to the sea. There were caves at the shoreline, and it was likely that the path had been used by smugglers in the past. Whether it still existed and was navigable remained to be seen.

With Lassen acting as bowman, the Goatley made its final approach to shore. Paddles kissed the water as the Dane brought them in close to the rocks. It had fallen to Lassen to be the first to scale the cliff ahead of them and deal with the German gun post above.

Shortly before midnight the canvas-sided craft nudged against the rocks and Lassen leapt ashore. Within seconds he was swallowed by the darkness. Like a mountain goat, he trotted up the near-vertical cliff and was gone. Ten other ghostly figures followed, moving at a more cautious pace with Appleyard in the lead. Behind them, one man was left to guard the Goatley.

As the guidebook had intimated, the start of the climb was steep and treacherous, the cliff face being sodden and weather-worn from where the sea repeatedly smashed against it, and plagued by patches of wet, loose shale. After a good hundred feet or more of scrabbling on all fours, the gradient gradually lessened. Appleyard found himself on a steep, winding path, leading to the summit of the Hog's Back. It switchbacked through sharp gullies lined with thick bracken and gorse, but it was easy going compared to what had gone before.

Appleyard pushed on, keen to link up with the often recklessly brave Dane. Ahead of him Lassen had already made the summit. Lying with his face pressed into the earth he surveyed the cliff-top position. It was surrounded by rolls of freshly-laid barbed wire and there was indeed a gun there. Fortunately for the raiders it was an old, disused one – something that it hadn't been possible to ascertain from studying the aerial photos alone.

For several seconds the stillness of the night was broken by the sharp snip of wire being cut. Lassen wormed through the crawl-hole that he'd made, and flitted into the shadows, scouting the terrain ahead as far as it seemed sensible to go. Finding it clear of the enemy, he hurried back to brief Appleyard. The raiders rendezvoused at the V-shaped summit of the Hog's Back, then moved inland along its ridge, making for a group of houses at a hamlet called Petit Dixcart, where the nearest enemy troops were supposedly billeted.

En route the silent force came across what appeared to be a German radio post, complete with sentries. Appleyard and Lassen crept forward, hoping for a repeat of Les Casquets – the chance to seize priceless intelligence and prisoners, and to vanish before the enemy even knew they were there. But there was something decidedly spooky about the still, moonlit scene: the sentries were impossibly quiet and immobile in the darkness.

They turned out to be dummies, the entire set-up being a firing range where the German occupiers had been honing their gunnery skills. It was ominous. The garrison on Sark was clearly made up of businesslike and professional soldiers who outnumbered the raiders some 20–1.

They evaded a first enemy patrol by lying motionless in the thick vegetation at the edge of the path. Minutes later the raiders found themselves approaching their target – Las Jespellaire, a large detached house said to be the billet of several German troops. They surrounded the building and burst in through the French windows, but the only occupant turned out to be a lady in her forties asleep in an upstairs bedroom.

Mrs Frances Pittard reacted remarkably well to the fearsome-looking raiders storming into her room. She announced that she was English, the daughter of a Royal Navy commander living in England, and asked what she might do to help. While Lassen organized a guard force to keep watch for the enemy, Appleyard quizzed Mrs Pittard on enemy strengths and their positions all around the island.

Time was against Appleyard and his raiders now. What with the cliff climb, the stealthy stalking of what turned out to be a firing range, hiding from a passing enemy patrol and now their abortive attack, it was approaching 0200 hours. They'd been in German-occupied territory for well over two hours.

Mrs Pittard gathered together some local newspapers plus a map of Sark, and gave Appleyard an invaluable off-the-cuff briefing. She showed him where the key enemy positions were, and confirmed that both the beaches that Appleyard had chosen not to land on were indeed mined. Disturbingly, the newspapers revealed that the Germans had ordered hundreds of able-bodied men to be deported from the Channel Islands, and that they were destined for the German labour camps.

Many had already gone.

The obvious place to target was the annex to the Dixcart Hotel, Mrs Pittard explained. It had a separate entrance, and there were some half-a-dozen Germans billeted there. As long as the raiders could execute their attack with silence and surprise they should be able to spirit away their prisoners undetected. But if they were discovered, the nearby Dixcart Hotel was packed with enemy troops. In no time the island would be swarming with German soldiers hunting for the tiny British force.

Before leaving, Appleyard offered Mrs Pittard a safe passage to England aboard Little Pisser, for it was obvious she might be a target for German reprisals. She refused. She had lived in the Channel Islands all her life and she wasn't about to leave now.

Just a few hundred yards lay between their present position and the Dixcart Valley, the location of their new target. Appleyard set a rendezvous for his men beneath a distinctive yew tree at the edge of the hotel grounds. Once the raiders had snatched their prisoners they would regroup there, before heading directly along the valley bottom to the Hog's Back and down to the Goatley waiting below.

With barely a sound Appleyard's force slipped off the higher ground of Petit Dixcart and into the wooded valley below, flitting between the trees towards the hotel grounds. Once there, Appleyard sent Lassen plus one forward, to check out the lie of the land and to search for any sentries. One was spotted, pacing backwards and forwards in a clearing. Having observed his progress for several minutes, the two raiders returned to Appleyard.

'Apple, I should have brought my bow-and-arrow, after all,' Lassen whispered, his eyes glinting in the moonlight.

Lassen volunteered to go in and take out the lone sentry, after which the main body of men would be called forward. He wormed his way back through the undergrowth until he was close enough to the unsuspecting German to hear his footfalls. Otherwise, all was silence and stillness, but there was now a noticeably sinister edge to the quiet that sent a shiver up the spine.

That peace was broken by an agonized groan, which carried clearly to the waiting raiders. As Lassen lowered the dead German to the earth, he yanked his knife out, the blade glistening a sickly red in the silvery light.

For a moment he hesitated. Knifing a man to death – even one of the reviled enemy – had been very different from killing a wild animal. The intimacy of what he'd just done, juxtaposed to the savagery, chilled Lassen to the bone.

He shook himself out of his stupor.

Signalling the others forward they moved swiftly as one body, surging across the mown lawn of the hotel grounds. Bursting through the main door to the annex, they found the lights on in the room before them, but it was deserted. A door opened off the far end. Lassen slipped through it, finding a corridor with several further doors – leading into what had to be bedrooms.

Appleyard mustered his men. On a word of command they kicked open the doors in unison, discovering five Germans sound asleep in their beds. The shock and surprise were total. One of the comatose figures had to be cracked across the jaw with a knuckleduster, just to show him that the raiders were for real and not some nightmare apparition.

Appleyard decided they could manage all five captives. After all it was two fewer than they'd seized on Les Casquets. But between them and the Goatley lay a trek of several hundred yards through a dark and wooded valley, and to all sides there were German positions plus, very possibly, mobile patrols. As a precaution he ordered the prisoners' hands to be tied, the better to keep them under control as they were stolen away.

During the process one or two of the prisoners had to be duffed up a little, to keep them docile and cooperative. All five were engineers working on the nearby harbour defences. They hailed from the Pioneer Corps Engineer Unit, and like engineers everywhere they were strapping fellows. *Obergefreiter* Weinrich – the equivalent of a lance-corporal and the group's commander – seemed a passive enough individual. But one or two of the *Gefreiters* (privates) were giants, and they dwarfed several of the wiry raiders.

The quarters were searched, all useful documents gathered up and the prisoners frogmarched outside. Almost as soon as they reached the rendezvous under the yew tree, one of the *Gefreiters*, who must have realized how few raiders there were, made a break for it. He was immediately rugby-tackled by his guard, but a fight broke out, and amid the cries and the blows the German soldier could be heard yelling for help.

'Keep the prisoner quiet!' Appleyard cried.

Chaotic scenes unfolded, as Lassen tried to gag the captives to prevent them yelling out. The three remaining *Gefreiters* followed their fellow's lead and made a bid to escape. A shot rang out, one of the fleeing prisoners crashing to the ground. More shots split the darkness, as the *Gefreiters* tried to fight their way free and the raiders sought to stop them.

Only Lassen kept a firm hold of his man, the bloodied blade of his knife convincing *Obergefreiter* Weinrich of the futility of trying to run. But the alarm had well and truly been raised. There were the bangs and crashes of doors being thrown open from the direction of the main hotel, as sharp cries and orders rang out in German.

Thinking like a true butcher-and-bolt raider, Lassen saw an opportunity here to spread real mayhem and terror. He grabbed a couple of grenades, and turning to Appleyard explained in hurried tones what he had in mind. The main hotel building was even now a seething mass of German soldiers, readying themselves for battle.

Lassen was going to dash forward and hurl a grenade through each of the windows, sowing bloody chaos among the lot of them.

Chapter Eleven

For a long moment Appleyard – as calm and unflappable as ever – considered Lassen's proposal. The grenades would certainly wreak carnage among the German soldiers. But Appleyard's priority had to be to get his men back to the boat, together with their one prisoner and the documents they had seized, which he hoped would yield vital intelligence.

'Keep the grenades,' Appleyard told Lassen. 'We might need them later.'

He signalled his force to move out. As they hurried through the trees – running for the Hog's Back, the Goatley and relative safety – they kept to an open patrol-formation, Lassen bringing up the rear with the precious grenades in hand. Lassen was a natural with the Mills bomb. Few could match him in terms of strength of throw or accuracy. Should an enemy patrol come doubling after them, he would transform the ground to their rear into a whirlwind of deadly blast and shrapnel.

The escape was all about speed and stealth now. With the petrified *Obergefreiter* Weinrich in their midst, they kept to the cover of the thick gorse and bracken, avoiding the main paths – for those were the most likely route for the enemy hunter patrols to take. They made the ridge of the Hog's Back with the shouts of German forces echoing in their ears from all sides.

Out to sea, Freddie Bourne, the captain of Little Pisser had heard all the shooting and commotion ashore. Though the raiding force was well overdue, he was determined not to leave them. With the memory of Operation Aquatint still raw and fresh in his mind, he was going to keep his little boat on station for as long as she was still afloat.

Closer to shore, the lone raider manning the Goatley was equally determined to hold his position and await his fellows' return.

Back at the Dixcart Hotel, one at least of the *Gefreiters* who had escaped from the raiders' clutches was uninjured. He was able to brief the German commander on Sark, *Oberleutnant* Herdt, on all that he knew. A patrol was sent to search the Hog's Back, all defensive batteries around the island were alerted by field telephone, and a boat armed with a machine gun was sent to search for a landing craft in the bays to the south of the island. The hunt was well and truly on now.

Meanwhile Appleyard led his men – plus their one prisoner – in a helter-skelter descent of the cliff, arriving on the shoreline at around about 0300 hours. Thankfully, the Goatley was waiting for them, and they were able to bundle *Obergefreiter* Weinrich and themselves aboard. With thirteen men crammed into the little boat they began to paddle furiously, all the while fearing that the cliff tops behind them or the sea to either side would become alive with the enemy, and tensing for the burst of bullets in their backs.

The thin sliver of the moon was now high in the sky, and by its faint light the low-lying form of Little Pisser was clearly visible. This moment – paddling through the open, silvery water in their flimsy craft – was when they were at their most vulnerable. But tonight luck was on their side. Appleyard's raiders made it to the comparative safety of the MTB without a shot being fired, and they were able to clamber aboard. The Goatley was instantly collapsed and stowed aft, whereupon a much-relieved Bourne slipped anchor and made haste for the open sea.

Three hours later Little Pisser docked at Portland, the lone prisoner was handed over to MI9 for interrogation, and the twelve raiders headed back to Anderson Manor. They were in jubilant mood, each man looking forward to a large plate of fried eggs and bacon. The raid was seen by all as being an immense success. They'd grabbed a German captive, plus bundles of intelligence materials; they'd killed maybe half-a-dozen of the enemy and not one of them had suffered the slightest injury.

But more importantly, in spite of the recent loss of March-Phillipps, Hayes and the others, tonight on Sark they had proved themselves still a potent fighting force. As a unit, they were very much back in business.

Lassen returned to his room at Anderson Manor and produced his Fairbairn-Sykes fighting knife with a flourish. He ran it under the noses of those who hadn't been on the Sark raid.

'Look: blood.'

Yet the aftermath of Operation Basalt would also leave the German hierarchy thirsting for blood. Although the damage wrought on Sark had been relatively light, the rage of the German High Command knew no bounds. Two days after the attack the headlines in the *Guernsey Evening Star* set the tone for what was to come: 'British Attack and Bind German Troops in Sark. Immediate Reprisals for Disgraceful Episode.'

Hitler was said to be apoplectic, and the line of the article came direct from the Führer himself. Sark spawned a propaganda war that would eclipse the achievements of the raid, and forever cement the notoriety of the SOE and its agent-commandos. First strike went to the Germans, when three days after the raid Hitler declared the following, as a direct response to the Sark raiders having bound the German prisoners' hands.

From noon on October 8th all British officers and men taken prisoner at Dieppe will be bound . . . In future all territorial and sabotage parties of the British and their confederates, who do not act like soldiers but act like bandits, will be treated by the German soldiers as such and wherever they are encountered they will be ruthlessly wiped out.

Ruthlessly wiped out: the phrase was deliberately unambiguous. In the aftermath of Sark, any raiders caught by the enemy could expect no mercy. The raid on Dieppe had been an attack in August on the German-occupied French port of Dieppe. In contrast to the tactics being refined by the SSRF, the Dieppe operation had involved landing a force of some 6,000 soldiers, the vast majority of whom were Canadian infantry, with British and American commandos in support, plus armour, warships and warplanes. In short, Dieppe had been no small-scale, clandestine operation striking by surprise.

The main objective of the operation had been to seize and hold the port of Dieppe, before blowing up the main facilities and withdrawing. The force had put ashore at 0500 and just five hours later their commanders had been forced to order a retreat, with none of the objectives having been achieved. Pinned down on the beach, over 3,000 troops had been killed, wounded or captured.

Now, in the aftermath of the Sark raid all prisoners from Dieppe were to be held in chains, on Hitler's orders. The Allies reacted by ordering a similar number of German prisoners to be likewise held in shackles.

The British media then took up the fight. On the day after Hitler's proclamation of 8 October, the *Daily Telegraph* headline ran: 'Germans Deport Channel Island Britons – Sark Raids Reveals Labour Camp Round-up.' The *Daily Mirror* reported how hundreds of males between the ages of 16 and 70 were being deported to Germany with their families. It added that the German prisoner who had been seized during the Sark raid had confirmed that these deportations were for forced labour.

The war of words continued to escalate. In retaliation for the 'cold-blooded execution of bound prisoners', as the German press portrayed the Sark incident, Hitler went on to draft his infamous *Sonderbehandlung* – what became known among Allied troops as his 'Commando Order'. In this order all raiding forces captured were to be singled out for 'special treatment', a euphemism for cold-blooded execution.

In that top-secret order – which was marked 'In no circumstances to fall into enemy hands' – the Nazi leader spoke of raiders behaving in a 'particularly brutal and underhand manner', and of the British military deliberately recruiting 'criminals' and 'convicts'. Hitler decreed that henceforth raiding forces were to be 'annihilated to the last man, whether in uniform or not . . . whether in combat or in flight'.

Any raiders captured were to be handed over to the feared SD – the *Sicherheitsdienst*, the Security Service of the SS and the Nazi Party, from whom nothing could be expected but an agonizing death under torture. Any German commander who failed to abide by the *Sonderbehandlung* would be summoned before a war tribunal. The execution of captured commandos was at all times to be kept secret, and they were to be buried in unmarked graves.

On Sark itself, fortifications were strengthened still further. Some 13,000 extra mines were laid, beaches and cliffs were closed to residents and the curfew extended. The local German commander, *Oberleutnant* Herdt, was court-martialled on a charge of allowing his men to sleep in 'undefended quarters'. Mrs Pittard – the courageous English lady who had provided such vital intelligence to the raiders – was sent away for questioning. Eventually, she was deported to the labour camps, along with some twenty other Sark residents who were seen as being 'unreliable elements capable of giving information to British Commandos'.

Sark, then, had sparked a murderous reaction from the Nazi hierarchy, one entirely out of proportion to the impact of the raid. It had yielded just a single prisoner, had caused barely a handful of casualties and had done no lasting damage. Yet Hitler's reaction to Operation Basalt reflected how the ability of British forces to emerge from the night and strike at German positions seemingly at will had shaken the enemy, exactly as Churchill had envisaged.

In the British Parliament there were those who railed against the lawlessness and anarchic actions of the raiders, especially as evidenced on Sark. But when he was challenged by one of his political detractors to rein in his clandestine raiding forces, Churchill gave no quarter in defending their actions.

In the aftermath of Sark, he invited Appleyard for a private audience in his chambers in the House of Commons, as a special gesture of appreciation. He congratulated Apple on his inaugural raid as the SRRF's new commander, and for furthering the concept of butcher-and-bolt raids. Clearly, their most recent operation had Hitler seriously rattled.

Churchill went on to taunt Hitler personally: 'The British raids along the coast, although only the forerunner of what are to come, inspire the author of so many crimes and miseries with a lively anxiety.'

Honours for the Sark raid followed in good measure. Appleyard received a DSO and Patrick Dudgeon an MC, as did Anders Lassen. Lassen's decoration was in recognition of his role in the still top-secret Operation Postmaster, plus the Channel Island raids that had followed.

The citation, signed off by Mountbatten, was marked 'on no account to be published'. It described Lassen as 'An inspiring leader . . . and brilliant seaman possessed of sound judgment and quick decisions.' Mountbatten sent a personal letter of congratulations to the Danish Viking.

Dear Lassen,
I was delighted to see the announcement of your MC and send you my heartiest congratulations. Any decoration won with the Small Scale Raiding Forces is thoroughly well deserved. Good luck with your future ventures.
Yours sincerely,
Louis Mountbatten

In spite of such honours, even Lassen had found some elements of the Sark raid disquieting. In contrast to his Anderson Manor bravado with the bloodstained blade, it was in his diary that Lassen confided most candidly his feelings upon first knifing to death a fellow human being: 'The hardest and most difficult job I have ever done – used my knife for the first time.'

Lassen had always intended that his diary go to his mother if he were killed in action. He'd clearly found that silent killing at close quarters troubling: the reference to using the knife is his last diary entry; the remaining pages are left blank.

Lassen's hunger to fight and to kill the enemy was self-evident, but it wasn't based upon a hatred of the German people per se. Many of his cousins and second cousins were German, and a number of them were fighting in Germany's cause. What he hated was that the Germans had invaded and subjugated his homeland – he would have fought any invader of his native Denmark just as fiercely.

But more than that Lassen despised the Nazis' elitism, their cruelty and their warped concept of world-domination, not to mention their misguided belief in themselves as a master race. Anders Lassen MC was desperate to fight back against their deluded ideology, and he was about to be given a golden opportunity to do just that.

In the North-African desert another elite unit of raiders had also been scoring a string of spectacular victories. The highly mobile jeep-borne raiding operations of David Stirling's Special Air Service (SAS) had been credited with helping turn the fortunes of the war in North Africa, aided by their sister unit, the Long Range Desert Group (LRDG). But with the conflict there all but won, a new role needed to be found for the SAS, one not solely predicated upon desert operations.

The next stage of the Allied offensive would involve seaborne sorties striking into the soft underbelly of Europe – Italy, Greece, Crete and the Aegean Islands, butting up close to Turkey's western coastline. As the SAS had little amphibious experience, officers would have to be drafted in from other units to help train and lead them in their intended missions – most notably from the Small Scale Raiding Force.

A cable of 20 January 1943 marked 'HUSH – MOST SECRET' sets the scene for what is to come: 'Agreement reached for dispatch of special force of 200 all ranks . . . Please dispatch earliest possible by air to Cairo two officers with experience of amphibious operations small scale raiding force to assist SAS amphibious training and operations.'

Stirling's Special Air Service – in which every man was parachute-trained – consisted of four Squadrons: A, B, C and D. D Squadron was to form the new seaborne element of Special Forces. Earl George Jellicoe – the son of the famous World War One sea admiral – would command this new amphibious raiding force, and he personally requested Lassen's transfer to his unit. He and Lassen had met by chance in London shortly after the Sark raid, and Jellicoe was convinced that he needed the Dane to help shape his new force.

On 8 February 1943 Lassen flew out to Cairo in an American-made Liberator long-range bomber, to join the 1st SAS Regiment, as it was formally known. He was to be the vanguard of the main body of SSRF operators, who were mostly now to be taken into Special Forces. Shortly after Lassen's arrival Appleyard was ordered to follow on by sea, bringing with him some fifty of the remaining SSRF men. A small rump was to be left at Anderson Manor, as the unit was effectively subsumed into the SAS.

With Allied forces gearing up for the coming D-Day land-ings, the centre of gravity of small-scale amphibious raiding operations had shifted to the Mediterranean. It was there that Churchill's butcher-and-bolt raiders were to be massively expanded in number, and where their unorthodox means of waging war was truly to come of age.

Even then, in its formative years, the SAS was a unit with a certain distinctive dash. Nourished by success and prestige, and unconstrained by SOE-levels of secrecy, it carried an air of romantic mystery. By nature of their clandestine status the

Maid Honour Force and the SSRF had had no specific insignia, while the SAS possessed its own, unmistakeable cap badge, one designed by David Stirling himself. It showed a white dagger, somewhat reminiscent of a Fairbairn-Sykes fighting knife, with the words 'Who Dares Wins' superimposed beneath it. The badge was worn with the distinctive set of parachutist's wings, which together would become the famous winged dagger.

When Stirling had first bumped into General Claude Auchinleck – then Commander-in-Chief of the Middle East Theatre – after adopting that early cap badge design, the General had stared at it for a long moment, before announcing: 'Good heavens, Stirling, what's that you have on your shirt?'

'Our operational wings, sir,' Stirling replied, smartly.

'Well, well,' Auchinleck murmured, 'and very nice too . . . Very nice too.'

The soon-to-be famous SAS insignia had just got its formal blessing.

Sadly, David Stirling hardly got to wear the iconic badge for long. In January 1943 – just weeks prior to Lassen and the larger SSRF contingent joining his unit – Stirling was captured during a raid in North Africa. He was to spend the rest of the war in captivity, and would end up being incarcerated in Colditz, in an effort to try to foil his repeated escape attempts.

Thus Stirling and Lassen – two of the foremost pioneers of British Special Forces soldiering – would never get to meet, but in any case, in Earl Jellicoe, Lassen had a superlative commander under whom to operate. With Stirling in captivity, Jellicoe became the overall commander of the amphibious element of Special Forces, while the land-based arm of the SAS fell under the command of another towering Special Forces legend, Robert Blair Mayne, better known to all simply as 'Paddy'.

The two men could hardly have been more different. Earl Jellicoe, then just twenty-three years of age, was blessed with pronounced features beneath a shock of curly dark hair and a biting wit. The son of the 1st Earl Jellicoe, former Admiral of the Fleet, he listed a string of royals and former top military commanders as his godparents. Educated at a Broadstairs, Kent, preparatory school, Winchester College and then Trinity College, Cambridge, George Jellicoe could hardly have hailed from a more privileged and genteel English background.

His sang-froid and irony were characterized by the way he greeted one of his returning operators, who'd escaped from German clutches after 134 days in captivity.

'Ah, you're back,' Jellicoe remarked. 'Damned slow about it, weren't you?'

By contrast, Blair Paddy Mayne was a red-haired giant of an Ulsterman, and both an Ireland international rugby player and a heavyweight-boxing champion. When Stirling had invited Mayne to become one of his six founding SAS officers, Mayne had little other choice. It was either that or face a court martial, for he was under close arrest after knocking out his commanding officer.

Lassen was likewise known to be quick to anger and quick with his fists. In time, he'd flatten his new commanding officer, Earl Jellicoe, throwing a punch utterly from out of the blue in a Tel Aviv bar.

'I think I must have said something that annoyed him,' Jellicoe explained. 'I wasn't aware of it, except the next thing I was aware of I was flat on my back on this bar floor, and I must have been out for quite a bit. He carried quite a big punch if he wanted to punch. I said: "Well, I don't know what on earth this is all about, Andy" . . . And in any case we had a few more drinks and drove back to my camp. He was too valuable a person for me to make too much of a fuss about it.'

Fortunately for Lassen, Jellicoe had by then developed a soft spot for the Dane, not to mention a keen appreciation of his abilities as a piratical raider par excellence, and he chose to let the matter drop.

Another commander who would come to love and cherish the wayward Dane was David Sutherland, Jellicoe's second-in-command. Slender, sandy-haired and with a light, freckled complexion, Sutherland was a still-waters-run-deep type. He spoke only when he had something to say, and as a result he was listened to. Sutherland was known to all as 'Dinky', for he seemed able to sleep in a ditch for a week and still come out looking freshly shaven and well groomed. In time, Sutherland would nickname Lassen 'The Viking'.

'Anders Lassen was the master Viking,' Sutherland remarked. 'He was true to the trait. He had all the tricks and the tradecraft of the Viking raider; all the seamanship, the mastery of weapons and everything else.'

Lassen's reputation preceded him – and most notably concerning Sark. The outrage in Germany over Operation Basalt continued, as did the tit-for-tat reprisals against Britain. Indeed, Lassen quickly became known for his tongue-in-cheek refutation of the most damning accusations made against him and his fellow raiders – that they had stuffed the German prisoners' mouths with mud, to gag them and keep them quiet.

'It is not true that we stuffed the mouths of the prisoners with mud,' he would declare, with mock imperious outrage. 'We stuffed their mouths with grass!'

When Lassen was appointed commander of one of the D Squadron patrols, it was at first with some degree of trepidation on the part of his commanding officers. Sutherland called Sergeant Jack Nicholson – the SSRF veteran, and like Lassen only a recent recruit to Jellicoe's amphibious raiding unit – to his tent to have words.

'I'm putting Lieutenant Lassen in charge of your section,' Sutherland announced, quietly.

'Very good, sir,' Nicholson replied.

'Lieutenant Lassen needs watching,' Sutherland added, somewhat cryptically. 'He's been in trouble. Something about killing a prisoner in a raid on France. I want you to keep an eye on him. Restrain him.'

Nicholson was somewhat taken aback. He'd rarely had such an unusual introduction to a new section commander. More to the point, from what he knew of Lassen, Nicholson suspected the admonition would very likely prove impossible to observe. While he was an inspired leader of men, Lassen was, more than anything, a force of nature – wild and unstoppable.

In the very first coming raid, he was to prove his destructive powers as if a hurricane had been unleashed upon the enemy.

Chapter Twelve

Geoffrey Appleyard arrived in North Africa shortly after Lassen. Sadly, this signalled the end of Appleyard's long-lived and highly effective partnership with the Dane. While Lassen was sucked into Jellicoe's outfit, the much-sought-after Appleyard was claimed by the mainstream SAS, as was Patrick Dudgeon – 'Toomai, the Elephant Boy' to his raider mates.

With March-Phillipps dead, Graham Hayes incarcerated under the Gestapo, and Appleyard and Lassen going their separate ways, the *Maid Honour* founding originals had ceased to exist as a fighting force – but their legacy would drive amphibious raiding operations to new heights of daring and glory across the Mediterranean.

Appleyard, Lassen *et al.* remained under SOE auspices for the time being, but M was rapidly losing sway over his agent-commandos. Claimed by Special Forces, they arguably had little need for the kind of deniability and ultra-secrecy that SOE-agent status had allowed them. Before them lay the spectre of Operation Husky, part of the Allied grand invasion plan for Europe – and that would require their skills as fast-evolving raiding forces, not as agents of high-level deception.

Operation Husky was masterminded by the Allied High Command as a means to penetrate Europe via her southern 'underbelly', and to thrust north towards Berlin. The stepping-stone into Southern Europe was to be Sicily, and in order to take Sicily, Crete – the largest of the Greek Islands – needed to be wrested from German and Italian control, or at the very least the warplanes stationed at her airbases had to be put out of action.

It was from Crete's dusty airstrips that the Axis powers were able to dominate the skies over the eastern Mediterranean. En route to Sicily the Husky invasion convoys would pass close to the Crete coast, making them doubly vulnerable to warplanes based on the island. If Jellicoe's raiders could go in behind enemy lines and sabotage those airbases, then the 8th Army could move on Sicily largely without fear of such attack. If Sicily fell, Italy would follow, and if Rome were taken so Berlin would fall. That, at least, was the theory.

Whether Husky was actually conceived as a master plan or as a grand deception remains unclear. It was most likely a belt and braces approach. If the Axis powers could be convinced that the liberation of Europe would be driven from the south, then the Normandy landings would stand a far greater chance of success. On the other hand if the drive through Italy proved wildly successful, then the liberation of Europe might well be achieved from there.

Either way, to set the stage for Operation Husky a small group of very determined men needed to land on Crete, trek through the mountains, evade the numerous enemy forces stationed there and blow up the German and Italian warplanes and airbases. It was just the kind of mission that Lieutenant Anders Lassen MC, and his fellow former SSRF raiders lived and breathed for.

In a cypher message marked 'MOST SECRET' – most radio messages were sent doubly encoded and in Morse; in 'cypher'– Allied High Command laid out what was expected of Jellicoe's men: 'Attacks on enemy aerodromes by small parties of saboteurs on the lines of the S.A.S. Regiment in the Western Desert . . . Small scale raids against selected airfields in Crete to diminish enemy air effort against HUSKY convoys.'

In light of such a directive, Lassen gathered a core group of fighters around him. He was due to be given command of the Irish Patrol, described by many as 'an incredible collection of hoodlums'. They included Sean O'Reilly, Sidney Greaves, Les Stephenson, Dick Holmes, Douggie Pomford, Ray Jones, Hank Hancock, Douggie Wright, Fred Green, Gippo Conby and Patsy Henderson. Lassen would have no shortage of volunteers for the coming raids – but first, the training.

The base for Jellicoe's new amphibious raiding force was at Athlit, in what was then Palestine (in the far north of modern-day Israel). Athlit Bay consists of little more than a crescent shaped stretch of golden sand fringed by azure sea. To the north the dramatic ruins of a thirteenth-century Crusader castle – Château Pèlerin, once a famed seat of the Knights Templar – perch on a promontory, which juts out into the waters of the Mediterranean.

Jellicoe established his training camp under a cluster of canvas tents, pitched on the flower meadow to the rear of the beach. Rising steeply behind lie the Carmel hills, a range of mountains reaching to just short of 2,000 feet in height. Carpeted in expanses of olive groves, oak and laurel forest, scrub and grassland, the Carmel hills provided the perfect terrain in which to practise one of the key skills that would be required of Jellicoe's raiders – long-range penetration on foot through dry, largely waterless terrain, to strike distant targets.

As training got underway Jellicoe had under his command some 130 officers and men, but his force would expand to several hundred strong as operations intensified.

In Lassen's section were several men who would grow close over the coming months. First and foremost was SSRF veteran Sergeant Jack Nicholson – he who had been cautioned to do the seemingly impossible and to 'keep an eye on' Lassen and 'restrain him'. Nicholson was a tall, taciturn Scot, without an inch of fat on his sparse frame. He possessed a shock of wild, dark hair atop slender features, and there was something distinctly calming about the man's look, which belied his ferocity in battle.

In the months that lay ahead Lassen and Nicholson were to become inseparable, especially as the tempo of raids, plus their audacity and daring grew exponentially. Another man that Lassen would form a close bond with was Southern Irishman Sean O'Reilly. At 41 years of age, O'Reilly was truly the grandfather among the raiders. An Irish Guards veteran, O'Reilly – like Lassen – was good with his fists, and was reputed to survive largely on women and beer, though he'd opt for the latter if he absolutely had to choose.

Over time O'Reilly would develop something close to a father-and-son relationship with Lassen, becoming the Dane's de facto bodyguard. It was somehow natural that Scousers like

Douggie Pomford, a Liverpool native, would also graduate to the Irish Patrol – the Irish homeland lying just across the water from that city where so many Irish immigrants had made their home. If anything, the 22-year-old Pomford was even more accomplished a scrapper than O'Reilly.

Pomford had won Britain's Golden Gloves amateur middle-weight boxing championship in the year before the war, winning five fights, including one in which he'd knocked out the Irish Guards' contender in the first round. He was refreshingly open about his misspent youth, describing himself as something of a rascal, one who'd ran away to the circus with only his dog for company. He'd taught his dog to do some tricks, while he stood in a boxing booth challenging all-comers to a bout.

Pomford had left the fairground at the start of the war to join the Lancashire Fusiliers. But the rigours of boxing had taught the young soldier traits that didn't particularly endear him to the regular armed forces: self-reliance, self-discipline and the ability to focus on an aim come what may. Of course, those were exactly the kind of qualities that Earl Jellicoe was looking for in the force that he was raising at Athlit. Like everyone else at Athlit, Pomford was a volunteer, and he was to prove himself a five-star SAS recruit.

'We wanted self-reliant men with initiative and self-discipline,' Jellicoe explained, 'not the imposed discipline of the barrack square. Above anything else I sought self-starters, men not dependent on an officer telling them what to do.'

Another accomplished boxer and self-starter was the 21-year-old Guards veteran Dick Holmes. Hailing from the

East End of London, Holmes was one of the few Englishmen tolerated in the Irish Patrol. Tall and broad shouldered, his ability to trek across the hills would become legendary. Holmes and Lassen, both strong characters, would sometimes clash in the coming months.

'Everything with him was instinct,' Holmes explained. 'And so if somebody argued with him or pointed out something that he was doing wrong he didn't like that, so he would immediately shout back at them, without considering the consequences of what he was saying.'

Holmes had volunteered for the SAS because in his parent unit he'd been spooked by the kind of nonsensical orders, as he saw it, that officers were sometimes wont to visit on their troops. He hated mindless discipline and having no sense of control over his own destiny, and it was hardly surprising that he'd ended up in the punishment block on several occasions. But in Jellicoe's outfit Holmes thrived.

'I felt that anything happening to me would be my own fault,' was how Holmes described the experience of joining the force now gathering at Athlit. 'I found my niche . . . I enjoyed it, I was good at it, and it was the war I wanted to be fighting.'

Then there was Gunner Ray Jones. Jones was a stocky, barrel-chested man, with an unruly mop of wild brown hair topping off a cheeky, but open and honest-looking face. He'd joined the SAS from the Royal Artillery, his aim being to get away from what he described as the bullshit rules and regulations of the regular armed forces. Jones spoke with a broad Birmingham accent, and like many a Brummie he was a salt-of-the-earth type. Jones would end up being willing to follow Anders Lassen to the ends of the earth.

The training regime at Athlit was a rerun of Anderson Manor, though it was even more relentless. Here the assault course came complete with sections that could be set aflame: somehow the recruits had to crawl through and over blazing walls of fire and clouds of choking smoke. The 60-mile treks now had to be completed in the heat of a burning Mediterranean early summer, and across terrain mercilessly devoid of water.

Athlit proved brutal on the recruits, and the dropout rate was high. Training was deliberately harsh, being designed to weed out those who lacked the physical and mental stamina for what was coming – extended periods spent behind enemy lines on sabotage missions. It sought to push men to the limit, and to find their breaking point. New recruits found themselves collapsing and even falling unconscious with exhaustion, but there was little sympathy for any who fell behind.

One of the youngest was 19-year-old wireless operator Jack Mann, originally of the Royal Corps of Signals. Brought up and schooled overseas, Jack Mann had a natural gift for languages, speaking French, Italian and some German, which made him a real asset for raiding operations. He'd come to Athlit fresh from the Long Range Desert Group (the British raiding unit that had distinguished itself alongside the SAS, in the North African deserts), but unlike most grizzled LRDG veterans he'd found it impossible to grow a proper beard – and everyone had one in the LRDG.

'Put some chicken shit on it,' one old LRDG hand had joked. 'It'll grow thick as a bush.'

Upon joining Jellicoe's unit Mann compensated for his lack of stubble by growing his hair 'as big as a bush'. Jellicoe himself led the fashion for longer hair, which was driven by practical needs as much as anything. 'We could be out on operations for weeks on end,' explained Mann, 'and of course we had no barbers.'

At Athlit, Mann had drummed into him the 'train hard – fight easy' mentality – something that would become a catch-phrase of the SAS. 'The harder and harsher the training, the more likelihood there was of beating the enemy,' Mann recounts. 'I realized that all the mountain trekking and swimming I used to do as a child with my mother – that gave me an edge. I learned the value of total self-reliance, plus the value of your fellow raiders – those who quickly became your closest mates.'

He also realized that in Jellicoe's outfit officers couldn't expect to lead simply by dint of rank alone; they had to earn the right to command. On one exercise Mann was climbing a cliff and his handhold gave way, a chunk of rock falling and punc-turing the wooden dinghy below. They had a brigadier's nephew in their patrol, an officer who was there pretty much to get a feel for the unit. The officer seemed to take a dim view of Mann's 'damaging Army equipment'.

Later, Mann was cooking up an evening meal – an 'all-in': several tins of food emptied into a billie and boiled up together – and the officer ordered Mann to serve him.

'Oh no, not in this outfit,' Mann countered. 'In this outfit, you get your own.'

By the time they were back at base camp Mann had been put on a charge by the officer. He was relieved of his gun and his fighting knife and locked in the military gaol. For sheer devilment as much as anything Mann had recorded his religion on his Army papers as 'Russian Orthodox'. He spoke English with a foreign accent, so he figured he could pass as Russian anyway. He called the head gaoler and demanded to see the Russian Ambassador, claiming he was a Russian citizen seeking to complain about the conditions of his imprisonment.

'We had all sorts of nationalities in the unit, so the gaoler wasn't to know any different,' Mann explained. 'No one wanted trouble with the Russians, and within hours I was out of there. I got a riotous reception when I made it back to camp. They all wanted to know how I'd got myself out of gaol, what trick I'd pulled. But it just goes to show the kind of self-reliance the unit taught you, and of what an individual is truly capable when needs must.'

Weapons training had to encompass every type of arms imaginable – including the guns and the ammo of the enemy, which the raiders would be expected to scavenge and utilize as they saw fit. In nearby Jerusalem, Jellicoe's men had access to their very own equivalent of Experimental Station 6, the SOE's school for bloody mayhem, wherein Lassen had refined his skills of silent murder.

Dubbed the 'Killer School', the main aim of the Jerusalem establishment – situated in a former police station – was to prepare the new recruits for the physical and psychological rigours of what lay ahead, as small raiding forces went into battle against far larger formations of regular German and Italian troops.

Recruits went through the Killer School in batches of thirty, and they were left in no doubt as to what lay ahead. 'When you burst into a room full of enemy soldiers, you must remember . . .' an instructor cautioned. 'Shoot the first man who moves, hostile or not. His brain has recovered from the shock of seeing you there with a gun. Therefore he is dangerous. Next shoot the man nearest to you. He is in the best position to cause you trouble.'

Every day was spent working with weapons. The favourite of the raiders remained the Tommy Gun. It wasn't light, weighing in at around 12lbs loaded, but firing two .45 calibre bullets per second it truly packed a punch. As a bonus, its reliability was close to legendary. Drum magazines were frowned on, as they tended to jam. Clip magazines holding twenty rounds apiece were the norm, although the men were taught not to fire bursts, but to tap the trigger so as to fire fast, accurate, single round shots. On lengthy operations behind enemy lines ammo was too precious to spray off on automatic. They were taught to fire from a boxer's crouch, with the Tommy Gun held in whatever grasp came to hand, as long as the muzzle was on target.

From the legendary Leonard Grant-Taylor, a 49-year-old veteran of the First World War and an ace weapons instructor, they learned close-quarter shooting with either the .38 Smith & Wesson revolver, or the Colt 45. Grant-Taylor welcomed trainees with the following brief introduction, which left little to the imagination: 'This is a school for murder. Murder is my business. Not a vague shooting of people in combat, but the personal, individual killing of a man in cold blood. It is an art which you have to study, practise and perfect.'

And study, practise and perfect they did. They learned to shoot a pistol with either hand to accommodate whatever way a door might open. They were trained to use whatever enemy weaponry might come to hand. They were taught to handle the distinctive Maschinenpistole 40 submachine gun – often dubbed the 'Schmeisser' – and the Italian equivalent, the Beretta MAB 38. Plus they were introduced to the rugged reliability of the Luger P08 pistol, and the booby-trapping qualities of the Model 24 Stielhandgranate – the Germans' infamous stick grenades.

In the Killer School's passing-out test, each man had to fire ten rounds from whatever submachine gun he favoured, each of which had to nail a pop-up target. Those targets were entirely realistic, bearing in mind the kind of fighting that was coming: they sprang out unexpectedly from behind doors, cupboards or from darkened stairways. The passing-out test was undertaken only after each recruit was put over the school's obstacle course several times, so he was hot, sweaty and out of breath even before the start.

Jellicoe's men were left in no doubt as to the Killer School's credo, embodied in its informal slogan: 'Aim for his guts and he's surely dead.' The belly was the largest part of a man to shoot for and few ever recover from a stomach wound.

Winston Churchill had set great store by Jellicoe's men. He was convinced that it was time to 'play for high stakes' in the eastern Mediterranean, an area of vital strategic importance to the Allied cause. He described Jellicoe's force as 'composed of soldiers of the very highest quality', a fighting force that had been transformed from an SAS squadron into an 'amphibious unit resolved to recreate at sea the fame which it had won on the sands of the desert'.

In recreating that fame, no man would play a greater part than Anders Lassen.

It was June 1943 when the raid on the Cretan airbases – code-named Operation Albumen – got the final go-ahead. Command of Operation Albumen would fall to David Sutherland, Jellicoe's number two, who, in his quiet, calm manner had a touch of the Geoffrey Appleyard about him. The targets were three Cretan airbases: Timbaki, Heraklion and Kastelli. Each was to be hit by one group of raiders, and Sutherland split his force into A, B and C Patrols for that purpose.

Briefings issued to the force gathered at Athlit made the objective of the operation crystal clear: 'Primary tasks will be the destruction of as many aircraft as possible on the allotted airfields. Targets other than aircraft (e.g. petrol or bomb dumps) will only be attacked if it appears that this is the best way of destroying nearby aircraft . . . Ten Lewes bombs, with fuses and delays will be carried by each man.'

As with Operation Postmaster – the Fernado Po raid – Operation Albumen would be a multilayered undertaking. An information campaign would be wrapped around the raids, one orchestrated by the Political Warfare Executive (PWE) – a SOE spin-off involved with propaganda operations – working out of Cairo and London. The aim of the PWE was to win the information war by getting positive stories of the raid seeded into the British media at the earliest opportunity.

To that end the raiders were tasked to send a single-word signal – 'SUCCESS' – from the field, just as soon as they had hit their targets. That signal would trigger the PWE's media campaign, which was designed to steal a march on the German's propaganda machine. The speed of their operation is reflected in the PWE's briefing on Operation Albumen, marked 'MOST SECRET – OFFICER ONLY': 'It is hoped that D patrol signal will be received before first light. The reports from C and B patrols are unlikely to be received until 8 hours after the attacks . . . However, on receipt of the first success signal from one patrol the communiqué will be released . . . with the highest priority for handing immediately to the BBC.'

Indeed, the BBC had a crucial role to play on two levels. Apart from breaking news of the raid to British listeners, the BBC would also broadcast vital reports in Greek to the Cretan people. Those planning Operation Albumen fully expected the Germans to take reprisals against the locals, upon whose help the raiders would in large part rely. The broadcasts in Greek were to help soften the blow, and to deflect blame for the raids away from the islanders.

To that end each patrol was ordered to carry with them a decoy. 'A specially prepared flag will be left in the target area to indicate that the raid has been carried out by British troops.' That decoy should leave little room for any German misinterpretation: it was a Union Jack. It was to be reinforced by discarding 'certain articles of equipment (e.g. steel helmets, cartridge cases, etc.) . . . which will show that the raids have been carried out by British Army personnel'.

Sutherland appointed the 22-year-old Anders Lassen as the commander of C patrol, and selected 23-year-old Lieutenant Kenneth Lamonby to command B. Ken Lamonby had joined the Suffolk Regiment in December 1940, and as yet he was untried and untested in battle. His acceptance into Jellicoe's raider force was largely due to his excellent seafaring abilities, and he was the recruits' sea-training instructor at Athlit.

In the balmy waters off the coast Lassen, Nicholson, O'Reilly, Jones, Holmes and all underwent a new and testing form of instruction that would be crucial for the coming missions. Under Lamonby's watchful eye, they had to practise launching an inflatable rubber dinghy from a submarine's half-submerged upper surface. With the swell washing across the exposed deck the work was never easy. It was made even more challenging in that all such launches would have to be conducted at night with the crew having to paddle several miles navigating on a compass bearing, to land on enemy-held territory.

Perhaps due to their shared love of the sea, Lassen and Lamonby struck up a close friendship. Lamonby knew all about the Dane's fearsome reputation, and in Lamonby – a man seemingly forever with a pipe clamped between his teeth – Lassen was doubtless happy to have a fellow seafaring man in their number, especially as the coming raids would rely on seaborne access above all other means to strike at the enemy.

As Jellicoe's force prepared to penetrate deep into Crete, so Geoffrey Appleyard was readying himself for a series of airborne missions over Sicily – softening-up raids for the Operation Husky invasion force that would follow. With Appleyard serving with the main body of the SAS, based largely out of the Egyptian capital, Cairo, the two former brothers-in-arms had found little chance to meet since their deployment from Britain, some three months earlier.

Little did they know as they prepared for their respective missions that neither would ever get to see the other alive again.

At dawn on 17 June 1943 Jellicoe's raiders gathered at Athlit for their final mission briefing. The scene was fairly typical for this nascent force of pirate-desperadoes, though not one repeated much throughout the rest of His Majesty's Armed Forces. There were few signs among the gathered men of what would normally be defined as 'military discipline'. No saluting; no heel-clicking or stamping.

Indeed, most of the assembled throng appeared to be on first-name terms, regardless of rank, and many were addressed by – often seemingly illogical – nicknames. Lassen's was easy enough: 'Andy'. So was Jellicoe's: 'The Lord'. But Dick Holmes had somehow become known as 'Jeff', while one rock-hard Scottish operator seemed only to answer to his sweetheart's name, 'Myrtle'.

As to their dress, it was largely up to personal taste and tended toward the idiosyncratic. Dick Holmes sported a pair of giant Canadian paratrooper's boots, which reached almost to his knees, above which he wore a pair of baggy khaki shorts. The overall effect was almost comical: that was until you saw the steel in the man's eyes. Others wore South African military leather boots, with baggy, sandy-coloured parachute smocks above them, their hoods drawn close against the early morning chill.

'There was no bullshit, no saluting,' as 'Jeff' Holmes described it. 'Best of all you were among like-minded fellows who also hated spit and polish . . . I told myself I was fighting men who hadn't done the training I had. They hadn't jumped out of airplanes or marched for miles on end. In my mind I was better than them and that gave me – and I think the rest of the boys – a tremendous advantage . . . We were superior not only physically, but psychologically.'

The assembled force bristled with weapons. Among the ubiquitous Tommy Guns were a couple of Schmeissers, plus an American M1 Carbine, which could double as a passable sniper rifle. From somewhere the men had got their hands on a consignment of Italian grenades – nicknamed 'Red Devils' after a then-popular British firework. Though smaller and less lethal than the Mills bomb, the advantage of the Red Devils was that you could carry more, and follow close on the frighteningly loud explosion to finish off a stunned enemy.

As the force set out by army truck heading for the port, only Sutherland knew of their intended destination. Tucked into his battle tunic was Operation Instruction No. 166, marked 'MOST SECRET. OFFICER ONLY', outlining the plans for the coming raids.

By the time the force set sail by fast Motor Launch – an 86-foot-long vessel reminiscent of the fondly remembered Little Pisser, and designed chiefly for submarine chasing – Sutherland's patrols had been welded into tough fighting units. B patrol, led by Lamonby, included Dick 'Jeff' Holmes plus two others. C Patrol, led by Lassen, consisted of Jack Nicholson, Sydney Greaves and Ray Jones. The third force – A Patrol – was scheduled to follow four days later, aiming to hit Timbaki Airbase at the same time as B and C Patrols struck their targets.

Despite their friendship, there was some good-natured banter between Lassen and Lamonby, as the Motor Launch sped towards the distant target at approaching twenty knots. Only Lassen and Sutherland among the men on that vessel were veterans of raiding operations deep behind enemy lines. The remainder were new to guerrilla warfare, and it was now that the Athlit training was to be put to the test.

As the cloak of night descended over the Mediterranean and the slender craft motored across the dark water, so the tension began to mount inexorably. Crete lay some 600 miles to the west of the raiders' departure point, so they had ample time in which to contemplate the mission now before them. Several miles out from Crete's southern coastline the Motor Launch slowed to a crawl, creeping in as close as possible to their intended landfall at Cape Kokinoxos, a spit of land pushing south into the sea.

At just past midnight the launch cut her engines and dropped anchor. Hearts were pounding among the dozen-odd raiders, as they prepared to launch their inflatable dinghies and paddle to shore. Before Lassen and Lamonby's patrols lay the daunting challenge of traversing the entire breadth of Crete – the largest of the Greek islands – for they were landing on the southern shore, and the target airfields lay on the opposite coast.

No more than thirty miles as the crow flies, the real distance Lassen and Lamonby's patrols would have to trek was many times that, as their route twisted and turned, and climbed and fell across Crete's incredibly rugged interior. A range of high, snow-capped mountains running east to west lay across their path – consisting of the White Mountains rising to some

8,000 feet, the Idi Range rising to a similar height, and the slightly lower 7,000-foot Dikti Mountains.

In among the towering peaks lay countless knife-cut gorges, plunging valleys, dead-end high plateaus and massive, echoing cave systems. On the southern coast, their intended landing point, the climate was more akin to that of North Africa, temperatures climbing to the mid-40s degrees Celsius. As they crossed the island heading north the climate would become progressively more Mediterranean, but even then the midday heat would still reach the debilitating low-30s.

Not only that, but each man would be laden down with some 70–80lbs of personal kit, weaponry, explosives, food and water – a crushing load to carry in such heat and across such terrain. It was all the more fortunate then that Jellicoe's men had had a chance to acclimatize to such scorching temperatures and physical rigours, during the previous months' training at Athlit.

The task before the raiders was made all the more difficult in that each patrol was supposed to hit its target on the same night, to maximize surprise. D-Day for the mission – the hour to launch the attacks – was in just twelve days. That was the time available to the men to navigate their way across the impenetrable spine of the island, to find and recce their targets, and to set their final plan of attack, all the while trying to avoid contact with the German and Italian garrisons, or their roving patrols.

During the war for North Africa Crete had been a major transit point for the German Afrika Corps, and its airbases remained key to air operations across the eastern Mediterranean.

There were reported to be four German or Italian troops on the island for every native Cretan. The island was crawling with the enemy.

It was fortunate, then, that there was some extra help on hand. As the raiders paddled silently towards the rocky shoreline, a British operative was supposedly awaiting them on shore.

When Allied forces had been driven out of Crete in 1941, the British had chosen to leave behind a scattering of men to help organize the Cretan resistance. Those men had learned to speak Greek and had lived the same hard life as the locals. They'd needed to possess nerves of steel to remain hidden in the remote mountains, as German and Italian troops did their best to hunt them down.

Spearheaded by the Greek Sacred Squadron, a unit made up of former Greek soldiers and officers now fighting to free their homeland, the Cretan resistance at first consisted largely of peasants armed with a smattering of antique rifles and shotguns. But in spite of their lack of modern weaponry, the spirit and morale among the Cretan guerrillas was high, and their intelligence on enemy movements across the island was second to none.

Their leader, Monoli Bandouvas, had been among the first to offer the foremost British stay-behind, Major 'Paddy' Leigh Fermor, his full support. Under his role as an honorary Cretan guerrilla leader, Fermor – who after the war became a famous travel writer – was appointed an SOE agent. Disguised as a shepherd named 'Michalis', he had survived in the rugged mountains for approaching two years now. Together with his

Left: Danish Viking. Anders Lassen VC, top right, the fearsome raider-commander, with Stephan Cassuli, lower left, at their secret Turkish 'pirate base'.

Right: Tools of the trade. A raider, with American M1 Carbine, pistol and lethal, 7-inch-bladed, Fairbairn-Sykes fighting knife: 'It never runs out of bullets.'

Who do you think you are kidding, Mr Hitler? A patrol shows off a picture of the Führer; Hitler had ordered that any raider, if captured, face torture and execution.

Above: The *Maid Honour*, a covertly armed Q Ship.

Right: Graham Hayes MC, *Maid Honour* crewman, in typically dashing form.

Right: The crew of *Maid Honour*. Top to bottom; Geoffrey 'Apple' Appleyard MC, Free Frenchman Andrew Desgranges and Gus March-Phillipps DSO.

The crucible. Santa Isabel Harbour, Fernando Po, showing the 7,872-tonne *Duchessa d'Aosta* – the raider's chief target – moored close to shore.

Lord Jellicoe, left, on the bridge of the *Tewfik*, their HQ ship when in Turkish pirate waters, together with a captain of the Greek Sacred Squadron, motto: 'Return victorious or dead'. Note the ever-present massive pot of tea.

A force of the Long Range Desert Group and SAS – those who were urged by Churchill to 'recreate at sea the fame they had won on the sands of the desert'.

Mission accomplished. Reconnaissance photo from the German Federal Archive, showing Kastelli Airbase, Crete, the target of Lassen's devastating June 1943 raid. Damaged aircraft lie scattered about the airfield.

Bad hair day. On a Motor Torpedo Boat after the return from a successful mission, with a good half of the patrol dressed in items of captured German uniform.

Below left: Bad beard day. Mixed Greek partisans, Greek Sacred Squadron fighters, plus Special Forces. On the far right, second row is Jack 'Zucky' Mann, veteran radio operator with Churchill's raiders.

Above right: Dog of war. An SBS comrade with puppy. Andy Lassen's Irish patrol had a motley collection of camp followers – dogs first and foremost. Lassen even took his favourite, a Maltese terrier called Pipo, on raiding missions. He proved as fierce as a lion!

A typical raider ship. SAS/SBS crew prepare to attack a German-held island, sneaking past the enemy by posing as local fishermen.

Above: Lassen's Irish Patrol set sail for the notorious raid on the German force garrisoning Santorini – what became known as 'Andy Lassen's Bloodbath'.

Right: Sergeant Jack Nicholson DCM, MM – a tireless Scott, who became Andy Lassen's right-hand man. He was once cautioned by his commanding officer to: 'Keep an eye on Lassen. Restrain him'. As if that were ever possible!

Right: Prizefighter. Douggie Pomford being treated for a grenade wound. He ran away to the circus with only his dog for company, and went on to win Britain's Golden Gloves middleweight amateur boxing championship: it was a perfect résumé to join the Special Forces raiders.

Left: Hot-tub. Porter 'Joe' Jarrell, the American medic-turned-raider. When asked whether he killed or cured people, he'd answer: 'A bit of both, actually.'

Left: Armed and dangerous. Dick Holmes, right, with weapon at the ready, amongst typical terrain. He'd liken their Mediterranean raids to 'terrorism'.

Major Anders Lassen MC and two bars, VC, discussing the forthcoming Lake Comacchio raid, in which he and his men were tasked to cross impossible terrain, so spearheading the Allied breakthrough in Northern Italy.

Wounded during the fateful Comacchio raid: back row, left to right: Unknown, Hank Hancock, Mick 'Gippo' Conby, Trooper Randal. Front row: Unknown, Corporal Pollock, plus Sergeants Ronald Waite, Sean O'Reilly (Lassen's 'bodyguard') and Patsy Henderson.

very capable second in command, Captain Bill Stanley Moss, Fermor had set up a network of Cretan intelligence agents and guides all across the island.

It was Fermor's agents that Jellicoe's raiders intended to rely upon to help them navigate their way towards their targets, and to avoid contact with the enemy en route. As would become a common refrain with such operations, they would prove largely impossible without the succour and aid of the locals – and winning their hearts and minds would become a number one priority.

In among the calm and the thick, inky darkness, a pair of rubber-hulled boats nosed into the rocky shore. They bumped silently against the beach, Lassen leaping out from the one, Lamonby from the other. A voice called out softly from the shadows. It was Gregorius Hnarakis, one of Leigh Fermor's top men on Crete. Gregorius looked as broad as he was tall, and he was clearly hugely strong. The smile he flashed was almost as wide as the breadth of his shoulders, and the hand he extended to Lassen offered a bone-crunching greeting.

Boats unloaded and hidden, Gregorius led the raiders some two miles inland, their route taking the course of a narrow, boulder-strewn riverbed. It being June it was dry underfoot, but it remained tough going in the clinging darkness. The Greek never once complained. Quite the contrary – Gregorius had become renowned among Fermor and his men for laughing when he was happy, and laughing even more when faced with hardship or danger.

Lassen for one found himself drawn to the man – a citizen of a nation, like his native Denmark, suffering under Nazi occupation.

'Gregorius, we will go into that aerodrome, and I am certain we will come out again,' Lassen assured him, as the two men led the way through the darkened valley.

Gregorius gave a throaty laugh. One the descendant of Danish Vikings, the other of the Ancient Greeks – the two men shared the instinctive, easy bond of natural-born warriors.

They reached their lying-up point – a series of caves to either side of the dry valley – and rendezvoused with Leigh Fermor. This was where Sutherland plus the radio operators would remain hidden for the duration of the mission, together with extra supplies of ammunition and provisions. All being well, the raiding parties would rendezvous with their commander here at mission's end, to be lifted off the beach by similar means as in their arrival.

The following day the trek inland began. At first Lassen was struck by the sweet scent of strawberries and thyme that lingered in the valleys, southern Crete being a fertile region rich in agriculture. But the terrain soon steepened as the route wound inland climbing the Kokinoxos Ridge, tilled fields giving way to rough forest and dry thorn scrub which ripped clothing and tore at exposed skin. In the heat it proved pain-fully slow and brutal going.

At first Lassen and Lamonby's patrols marched together, for the two airbases lay no more than a dozen miles apart just inland from the island's northern coast. The men were kitted out with Italian Army rucksacks – favoured because they were large enough to carry the kit that was required, yet light and durable at the same time. Devoid of the iron frame that most large backpacks then had, a ground sheet was stuffed between the carrier's back and the pack, to cushion the load and prevent chafing.

The first casualty – a victim of the punishing terrain – wasn't long in coming. One of the men on Lamonby's patrol suffered a twisted ankle. There was no option but for his massive pack to be carried in turn by the others. The strapping Dick Holmes – feet clad in huge Canadian parachute boots – was the first to take the burden. Jack Nicholson from Lassen's patrol volunteered next, the lithe Scotsman demonstrating a strength and stamina that belied his wiry frame.

The terrain proved to be crawling with enemy forces. Some four days into the climb the patrols entered a V-shaped gully, the rock walls on either side throwing back the heat like a furnace. Towards the end of that feature lay Apoini village and the parting of the ways – Lamonby's patrol continuing due north towards Heraklion aerodrome. Lassen's patrol would swing north-east, heading across the rugged terrain of the Viannos, in the western foothills of the snow-capped Mount Dikti, each footfall taking them closer to their target – Kastelli Airbase.

Until now both patrols had had radio operators attached to them, but they had driven themselves to exhaustion carrying their 100lb loads of wireless kit and batteries. In fact communications for the patrols had proved nightmarish, as Lassen's last message to Sutherland at his coastal base and to Cairo Raider Force Headquarters, reflects.

B and C sigs together as two sets much too heavy to carry. Sigs are being left behind . . . Impossible come up during day because of enemy. Will come up 2100 hours. Only one call for both sigs due to lack of time. Unable to establish com first time as hiding underground.

The message paints a picture of patrols so harried by the enemy – hiding during daylight hours; secreting themselves underground – that they are hard pushed to find any time to establish radio communications.

'We had to send all messages in Morse; never in voice,' Jack Mann explained. Radio operators like him were specialists attached to whichever patrol needed them most. 'With those messages being doubly encoded, this took real time and effort to get right. All codes can be broken, of course, but the theory was that by the time the Germans had cracked a doubly-encoded cipher message sent in Morse, we would be long gone.'

Lassen's message also reflects how impossible it was to carry heavy radio sets and batteries across such punishing terrain. The patrol's radiomen were to be left at Apoini, where they would act as a relay station to both Sutherland at the coastal base, and Raider Force HQ. If the raids went to plan, a 'SUCCESS' signal was to be sent from there, so triggering the information campaign to be orchestrated from London.

At Apoini Gregorius also had to part company with the raiders, and Lassen's patrol was passed on to another guide, Vasilis Konios, who was more familiar with the terrain that lay ahead. Thanks to his contacts with the nearby villages Vasilis was able to supplement the raiders' fast-dwindling food stocks

– largely oatmeal, raisins and tins of corned beef, augmented by a smattering of scavenged US Army K rations. With Lassen and his men camped out in the high valleys, Vasilis dropped down into the villages, returning with hard-boiled eggs, cucumbers, fresh baked bread and, of course, local Cretan wine.

But he also returned with worrying news. The Germans had patrols out scouting all the Cretan settlements. The enemy was well aware of Leigh Fermor's activities and those of his Cretan agents, and they were searching in the villages for any sign of a British presence. Lassen's patrol would have to exercise extreme caution now. They would have to camp out where the enemy least expected them – sheltering under borrowed blankets on ice-cold, wind-whipped rocky ledges, or in frozen caves dank with fettered shadows.

They knew if they were caught they were prime candidates for Hitler's *Sonderbehandlung*, his Commando Order: to be annihilated to the last man.

Chapter Thirteen

From Vasilis they were passed to another guide, Cheritoc Karfopoulos. Cheritoc Karfopoulos rapidly earned the nicknamed 'Harris' due to the impossible contortions required to speak his Greek name. Harris was young, slim, with wide dark eyes and glittering white teeth, and he was supposed to double as their interpreter for the remainder of their journey.

That evening, Harris took them into one of the many vineyards of the warmer, lower slopes, so the exhausted raiders could indulge in a proper night's rest. Leaving them wrapped in their blankets, Harris headed up the valley to fetch some food from what was his home village. Upon arrival, he stumbled into a German patrol.

Somehow, the enemy soldiers – hailing from the 22 Luftlande Infanterie-Division – had become convinced that the hated 'Tommies' and their 'Banditen' comrades were in the village. Harris was lined up together with his elderly parents, and the rest of the villagers – people who hated the German occupiers with a vengeance. He watched with a growing sense of awe and pride as his mother stared a German soldier in the face, and swore blind that there were no British anywhere around.

But despite such denials, the German soldiers were determined to smoke out Lassen and his men. As they went about their house-to-house search, Harris managed to slip away, taking with him a bundle of typical villagers' clothing. He hurried back to the vineyard, woke Lassen and his men, and they did their best to struggle into the odd assortment of garments. Disguised as local Cretans they moved out, seeking to put as much distance between themselves and the German patrol as possible.

But after a long, hard march Harris could find nowhere obvious for Lassen and his men to hide up. They were forced to seek help from one of his contacts, a Cretan family who were avid supporters of the resistance, and whose two teenage daughters proved to be stunningly beautiful. Lassen and his men were fed a warm and hearty meal, shown to some stone beds with branches forming a makeshift mattress, and invited to get some much-needed sleep.

Shortly afterwards the 22 Luftlande Infanterie-Division patrol arrived in the village. The family woke Lassen and his men and bundled them into a tiny, under-floor cellar-cum-cubbyhole at the back of the house. The four men almost suffocated in there, but the ruse proved successful. As the house was searched from end to end, Lassen, Nicholson, Jones and Greaves remained utterly quiet and unmoving in the claustrophobic darkness, and finally the Germans moved on to the neighbours.

By now the raiders' food supplies were utterly exhausted, as were their cigarettes – essential for calming frayed nerves. Lassen gave Harris some of the Greek money that they'd been issued with prior to setting out, and he set off to replenish their stock of smokes. He returned with a bulging bag and handed them back all of their money. The villagers had provided all the cigarettes the raiders could wish for, and they had refused to accept any payment in return.

But the drama of that long night was far from over. Their search complete, the German patrol made themselves well at home. They turfed some local families out of their homes and took up temporary residence. Lassen knew they had to get out of there. The longer they stayed, the higher the risk of discovery.

The village lay in a narrow, steep-sided ravine, and their onward journey would take them close by the German positions. They waited until well after midnight, before creeping past. Thankfully, the village dogs – often their worst enemy – chose not to bark and to give away their presence. They were able to melt into the enveloping darkness at the far end of the gorge – whereupon another night's march, one most likely devoid of rest, beckoned.

By the time they reached the outskirts of Kastelli Airfield, Lassen's party was on the brink of collapse. It was only the Benzedrine tabs that they kept popping that were keeping their bruised and battered bodies going. The amphetamines would prove indispensible to those charged with such gruelling behind-enemy-lines missions, but in time Lassen for one would become virtually addicted to them.

Guided by a new resistance fighter, Nereanos Georgios, Lassen and his men crawled through a narrow opening into a tiny cave overlooking the airbase. The planned night of the attack was two days hence. In the interim, they would need to keep a close watch and to get a sense of the airfield's defences. The main road running to and from the aerodrome lay below the cave entrance, with German army vehicles buzzing to and fro. They would have to be extremely careful not to be spotted.

Whenever the coast was clear Lassen studied the airbase with his field glasses. It appeared to be about a half a mile wide, and it was set into the side of a steep hill. The raiders could see the targets in the distance: lined up alongside the runway were the feared Stuka dive-bombers and Junkers-88 *Schnellbombers*, the prized German twin-engined fighter-bomber. There were also a few Messerschmitt fighter escorts, plus various older reconnaissance aircraft.

They could clearly make out the fuel and ammunition dumps used to refuel and rearm the warplanes. Those had to be the other key target that they would aim for. At night they could see the searchlights stabbing the darkness all around the airbase perimeter. There didn't seem to be any guard dogs, which was a relief, but they couldn't be sure whether the fence encircling the airbase was electrified, and what kind of sweep and range the searchlights might have.

Without establishing those factors they would be going in blind, and the odds were hugely stacked against them as it was. They were also hearing worrying reports from the locals. Georgios hailed from a nearby hamlet, and the word from the villagers wasn't encouraging. Apparently, the Germans had placed permanent guards on the landing strips, with tents pitched on the grass below each aircraft, so they could maintain a permanent close watch. The locals reckoned it would be impossible for Lassen and his men to hit most, if not all of the warplanes.

'Pay no attention,' Lassen admonished his fighters. 'This I consider to be a stupid exaggeration.'

Lassen was painfully aware that neither Greaves, Jones nor Nicholson had any experience of behind-enemy-lines raiding operations. They were novices at such work, and the last thing he needed right now was the locals undermining the morale of his men. Lassen the experienced raider felt especially driven to lead by example, and to show not the slightest hesitation or doubt.

But it wasn't easy. The garrison at Kastelli Airbase was reportedly 100-strong, even before the aircrew, ground crew and auxiliaries – firefighters, air traffic controllers and the like – were counted. Up against those sorts of numbers, Lassen's four-man raiding force was outnumbered some thirty-to-one and would be heavily outgunned.

Moreover, Lassen knew from pre-mission briefings that the villagers might well be right. *Generalfeldmarschall* Kesselring, the overall German commander in the Mediterranean, was reported to have issued the following orders to his airbases on Crete: '1. Guard of one man per aircraft with relief sleeping near by; 2. Guard to move continuously around aicraft at never more than 2 yards distance; 3. During air raids guard not to take cover but to lie down if bombs actually falling near and even then to keep aircraft under observation.'

Lassen decided they needed to do a close target recce, to get a better sense of which aspects of what the locals were telling them might be accurate. He volunteered to lead it, and the only person it made sense to take with him was Georgios, their Cretan guide.

Leaving the rest of his patrol to get some much-needed sleep, and to start making their Lewes bombs, Lassen and Georgios slipped away for their close encounter with the Kastelli Airbase defenders.

A dozen-odd miles northwest of Lassen's position, Lamonby's unit – B Patrol – was facing its own problems. After a similarly arduous trek they'd made it to the village of Ano Arkhani, just south of Heraklion Airbase, but the area was crawling with the enemy. Hiding out in the rocky high ground, they could see 200 German soldiers drilling in the village square below.

Their guide was a young Cretan called Janni. He'd set off to recce the airfield, only to return with the most dispiriting news: Heraklion Airbase appeared to be devoid of any aircraft. In fact, it seemed as if the Germans must have closed down Heraklion, as they shifted their warplanes to other bases across the island – most notably Kastelli, which was Lassen's target.

But Janni did have one item of potentially cheering news. A couple of miles to the west of where Lamonby's men were laid up there was a massive fuel and ammunition dump, one containing thousands of drums of precious aviation fuel, plus bombs. Deprived of fuel and munitions, no German warplanes could fly: that, Lamonby decided, would have to be their target.

Disguised as local shepherds, Lassen and Georgios made their way through the vineyards that lay to one side of the airbase. Driving their flock of goats before them they managed to approach the fence line. It consisted of an outer barrier of vertical wire supported by posts, plus an inner barrier of coils of Dannert wire. Lassen and Georgios drove 'their' flock right against the outermost wire. It didn't appear to be electrified, and as far as Lassen was concerned that meant that they were on for cutting their way into that airbase.

Lassen also got a close look at the base facilities, mapping out in his mind exactly where the key targets and the defences were situated. Those defences were intimidating enough, not to mention the reinforcements that lay close by. To the north of the airfield, some 3,000 German troops were stationed at the village of Kastelli Pediata. To the south, some 300 mixed German and Italian troops were billeted in Mouktari village.

Georgios, Lassen's Greek guide, was daunted by what lay before them. 'There is little cover and the Germans are everywhere,' he protested. 'Attacking this – I wouldn't wish it on my worst enemy.'

'With so many juicy targets I didn't even notice the Germans,' Lassen replied, his ice-blue eyes levelled at Georgios. 'Time to get busy.'

'But entering that aerodrome – Spiro, it will be like jumping into the fire.'

Lassen flashed a smile. 'Jump quickly, and we won't get burned. Let's get back to the others.'

'Spiro' was the nickname the local Cretan resistance fighters had bestowed on the Dane. Someone among their number had decided that Lassen looked and acted like the dashing medieval knight Ipotis, mentioned in many an ancient English manuscript. Somehow, Ipotis had morphed into Spiro – a common Cretan name, and perhaps the nearest Greek bastardization of Ipotis anyone could think of.

But having observed Spiro-Ipotis at close quarters, Georgios was fearful. He worried that Lassen was so driven by the mission that he was blind to the dangers before him.

Back at their cave base, Lassen sketched out the key features of the target: the ranks of warplanes, the aircraft hangars, the fuel and ammunition dumps, the taxiways, plus the barracks that housed the guard force. Bearing in mind how closely the Stukas and *Schnellbombers* were guarded, Lassen split his force into two. One group – Nicholson leading Greaves – would attack from the eastern side of the airbase, hitting the fuel and ammo dumps, plus any warplanes they could reach. Lassen and Jones, meanwhile, would attack from the west to cause a 'diversion' that would enable the others to go about their work undetected. That way, at least Nicholson and Greaves would get the chance to liberally sow their Lewes bombs.

Moreover, by striking from both the east and west, neither party would have to cross the open expanse of the airstrip, which ran north–south, effectively cutting the airbase in two. Zero Hour for the attack was set for 11.30 p.m. on 4 July – so that coming night.

As for Georgios, after a spirited argument with Lassen it was agreed that he would accompany Nicholson and Greaves as they went in, but he was to wait at the perimeter fence to help guide them out again. After both parties were done the patrol would regroup at a prearranged RV and begin the long trek back to their costal base, where Sutherland should be waiting.

'What's the plan if things go wrong?' Sergeant Nicholson asked, giving voice to the worry that was on everyone's mind. 'What if we're spotted on our approach? Or once we're on the base setting the charges?'

'No one is going to get seen during the approach.' Lassen was silent for a beat. 'Make sure of that. And if you are spotted on the airbase, blow it all to hell and get moving.'

Lassen was getting the gauge of Nicholson now. The quiet Scot had a calm unflappability about him, coupled with a plain way of speaking that reminded him of his *Maid Honour* brothers-in-arms, Appleyard and Hayes, who had proved themselves to be such superlative agent-commandos.

Stealing through the deepest pools of moon-shadow, Georgios led the four raiders along the secret pathways that crisscrossed the vineyards, bringing them as close to the airbase as the cover would allow. A bare few hundred yards separated them from the nearest wire, but it was now that the team had to split up – Lassen and Jones heading northwest, Nicholson, Greaves and Georgios towards the east.

There was a hurried, whispered parting in the darkness – Georgios reaffirming that they would 'fight like the brothers' – and then the final stage of the infiltration got underway. Crawling on their bellies, Lassen led Jones out from the cover of the last of the gnarled and twisted vines. The stretch of open, dusty grass and scrub lying before them appeared horribly exposed, especially with the searchlights sweeping back and forth across its expanse.

Lassen kept watch for a few, tense minutes, then made his move the moment a searchlight flashed past – bent double, scuttling towards the enemy guns and the wire. Dressed only in light order – carrying nothing more than a backpack full of Lewes bombs, plus a pistol, grenades and knife – he and Jones were able to move across the open-ground quickly, but not before the beam of the searchlight swung towards them.

Pinned under the blinding light they dropped down and froze. The two men had to repeat the performance several times before they reached the first barrier – the wire. With the island of Crete alive with resistance fighters, the Germans had reinforced their positions mightily. Kastelli Airbase was no exception, the Dannert wire before them constituting a daunting obstacle to overcome.

Before the war the German industrialist Horst Dannert had invented an oil-tempered form of steel wire. It was so strong that it could be produced in concertinas that were self-supporting. In other words, coils of this high-grade wire – which was extremely difficult to cut – could be strung across the ground without stakes or posts, and with just the odd retaining staple hammered into the earth. It was the forerunner of modern-day razor wire.

Cruelly barbed, this was what Lassen and Jones now faced. As they were engaged in cutting through the Dannert wire a sentry on the opposite side seemed to detect something. He lit a cigarette, and stood there scanning the fencing, his unmoving presence blocking their onward progress. Perhaps he had heard the distinctive sound of blades snipping through strands of wire, as Jones and Lassen worked their way through the fencing.

Time was running on, and their way forward was blocked. Lassen reached for his Fairbairn-Sykes fighting knife, and moving silent as a wraith he stole through the shadows and killed the sentry – the first of the enemy to die that night.

Waving Jones forward, they pushed onto the wide loop of track that ran around the airbase – a taxiway for warplanes waiting to use the runway.

As they skirted around a hangar-like building, they could hear a warm murmur of voices coming from inside. It was a Saturday night, so doubtless the minds of those manning Kastelli Airbase were drifting to thoughts of loved ones back home. Soon now, Lassen and Jones would shake them out of any such cosy reveries.

Several hundred yards to the east Nicholson and Greaves had found the going relatively easy, Georgios leading them to a point where no sentries seemed to block their passage through the Dannert wire. But as they'd snipped the first strands they were forced to freeze, a searchlight sweeping its beam across them. Nicholson was a firm believer in using mind over matter to conquer any fear he might feel. He put such skills to good use now.

'Keep perfectly still,' he hissed at Greaves, 'but don't drop down. If we move an inch, they'll see us.'

Sure enough, it seemed to be movement that drew the operators' eyes – and the intense white light swung past them with barely a pause. By freezing each time the light flashed by, Nicholson and Greaves managed to cut their way through the wire undetected.

With no immediate sentries to deal with they stole onto the eastern edge of the airbase well ahead of Lassen and Jones. They crept across to the ghostly silhouette of the nearest aircraft. It turned out to be a Fi 156 Storch, a skeletal-looking two-seater observation plane that fully deserved its name – *Storch*; Stork – a long-legged, big-winged bird.

The *Storch* had unrivalled short take-off and landing capabilities, but it was hardly the choicest of targets. Yet it would do for a start, Nicholson decided. As far as he could tell it had the added advantage of having no sentries posted anywhere near it.

Crouching in the cover of the *Storch*'s fixed, spindly-looking undercarriage, Nicholson pulled out the first of his charges. Up close the Lewes bombs didn't look like much. A stodgy lump of what resembled bread dough – but was in fact plastic explosive mixed with thermite gunpowder – each was around a pound in weight, oily to the touch, and stuck like a hedgehog with detonator, fuse and timing pencil.

The key to the Lewes bomb's destructive power lay in getting the charge as close to an aircraft's fuel tanks as possible. That way, the flash of the thermite exploding would ignite the aviation fuel, rendering the target into a seething fireball. Their first charge was placed on the *Storch*'s wing-root fuel tanks – where the wings met the fuselage. Presuming the aircraft had been refuelled to capacity, there should be some 40 gallons of aviation fuel ready to be triggered by the explosion.

Having broken the glass phial that triggered the timing pencil, Nicholson and Greaves were ready to move onto the next obvious target, a Ju-88 *Schnellbomber* situated a few dozen yards away. But as they flitted across to it, Nicholson spotted three figures gathered beneath the aircraft's streamlined fuselage. Just as the local villagers had warned, the most prized warplanes lining the Kastelli Airbase runway had groups of guards stationed beside them round the clock.

Beyond that first *Schnellbomber* Nicholson could see another, and for some reason it appeared to be unguarded. Sneaking past the nearest sentries, he and Greaves made their cautious way toward that aircraft. Creeping around the sleek fighter-bomber's nose cone, they reached up with two Lewes bombs, placing one each under the aircraft's wing, where the right and left fuel tanks were situated.

Then, in the far shadows, Nicholson spotted the unmistakable gull-winged silhouette of a Ju 87 Stuka. The distinctive dive-bomber was reviled by Allied troops, and especially those who had been on the receiving end of a Stuka attack. When serving in 7 Commando at the start of the war, Nicholson was one of only sixteen survivors after a bloody confrontation with the enemy, and he knew the Stuka well. Its howling siren struck the fear of God into even the most steely-hearted soldier.

Nicholson wanted that Stuka.

Lying low for a minute or so, he and Greaves studied the dive-bomber carefully – all the while knowing that the timing pencils on the *Schnellbomber* and the *Storch* had been triggered, and the countdown to the explosions was underway. Figuring they could dodge any sentries, Nicholson led Greaves towards the squat silhouette of the Stuka, as a heavy quiet and a tension seemed to creep across the airbase. Reaching up to place the first Lewes bomb, Nicholson heard the sudden dull crack of a low-velocity bullet echoing across the airstrip. It had sounded like a single pistol shot.

It had come from the west, and Nicholson didn't doubt it meant that Lassen was in action.

Chapter Fourteen

Flares burst in the angry night, as Jones shoved the last of his charges onto a target. Burning with a blinding white light like a miniature sun, each flare oscillated gently to and fro as it drifted beneath its parachute towards earth. The western edge of Kastelli Airbase was cast into their harsh white light. Jones felt himself horribly exposed under the blinding glare, which was almost as bright as daylight.

Having felled a German sentry with his pistol Lassen had thrown caution to the wind. He was going at it hammer and tongs with a scavenged German machine gun, as bullets popped and fizzed all around him. The guard force in the barracks was returning fire, and a wailing alarm pierced the staccato crackle of gunfire.

Jones hurried on to a final target – a *Schnellbomber*. It was inconceivable to leave without planting a charge on that. As he dragged out another Lewes bomb, an armoured halftrack slewed onto the runway, disgorging six German foot soldiers. The enemy had him and Lassen penned in on three sides now, and they were moving to block their only exit – the hole cut in the fenceline.

Lewes bomb set, Jones ran to link up with Lassen, as bullets snarled all around him. The Dane unleashed a final, savage burst with the machine gun, then jumped from the enemy bunker and ran. As he did so, he dropped a grenade behind him. It tore apart the gun emplacement, lacerating the position with shrapnel.

Jones and Lassen sprinted for the gap they'd cut in the fence, just as there was a massive *boom* from behind them. One of the warplanes to their rear dissolved in a seething fountain of flame, punching a mushroom cloud of thick oily smoke high above the runway. Two further blasts followed in quick succession, as the first of the Stukas writhed under the impact of Lewes bombs, followed an instant later by the hollow *whump* of their fuel tanks exploding.

Almost at the same time a massive eruption of fire fisted skywards towards the east of the airbase, from the direction of the ammunition dumps and the fuel store. With all the gunfire erupting at Lassen's end of the operation, the Germans had rushed their troops to that side of the airbase, leaving Nicholson and Greaves with a clear run at things.

In fact, Nicholson and Greaves were convinced that Lassen and Jones had either been captured or most likely killed – for how could anyone survive the volume of fire that was raking the western side of the airbase? As the German garrison was drawn to the savage firefight around Lassen's position, Nicholson and Greaves figured that he and Jones were done for.

In truth, the wild Dane and his fellow English raider were running as if they had the Devil and all his demons at their backs. In all the confusion of the surprise attack they managed to lose the enemy and make the fenceline, slipping through the hole cut in the wire. Yet once they were through, a breathless but elated Lassen called a halt. From behind wild cries and curses rang out in German, punctuated by further explosions and sporadic bursts of gunfire.

Figures were darting to and fro like ants, as the Germans hunted for the elusive attackers. Amazingly, they seemed to have no idea where the raiders might be. Above the airbase the sky was lit a fierce, burning orange, and in the glow of the dozen or more fires that were burning to either side of the airstrip Lassen could see further targets . . .

He signalled Jones to lie low and wait. Once all seemed relatively quiet around their position, Lassen indicated that they were going back in. On the one hand, it was borderline insanity to return to the airbase, now the element of surprise was well and truly lost . . . but on the other it was the last thing the enemy would be expecting.

Jones, as fearless as a lion, was swept up in Lassen's wild enthusiasm for the fight, and both men prepared to crawl back through the wire.

As the two raiders – one tall, slim and blond, the other shorter, stockier, with a shock of dusky hair – squirmed back through the hole they'd cut in the Dannert wire, Nicholson was leading Greaves out the other way. In their wake they'd left Lewes bombs on the first Stuka that Nicholson had so wanted to destroy, plus another they'd spotted lying in a blastproof shelter. By then a truck-load of German reinforcements had arrived, dispersing in all directions as they hunted for the saboteurs, and Nicholson and Greaves had come under sustained fire. Nicholson had sensibly decided to withdraw, and as they made their way back to the outer fence they managed to garland the fuel dump with the last of their Lewes bombs. He and Greaves had wriggled through the wire, while behind them the generator room exploded in a mass of plastic explosive and thermite sparks, after which a fuel truck was practically torn in two by a cataclysmic blast.

As its cargo of burning aviation fuel sucked in oxygen and boiled and flared, Nicholson and Greaves escaped into the darkness. The heat of the explosions was strong on their backs, the two men sprinting for the cover of the vineyard and comparative safety. Searchlights swept the terrain to either side of them. Several times they were forced to hit the deck, fearing the bullets they were sure would slam into their backs. But finally they reached the first rank of the ancient grapevines, and slipped into its cover.

In Nicholson's mind there was no point waiting for the others, or even making for the agreed RV. Neither he nor Greaves were in any doubt that Lassen and Jones were finished. With barely a pause to link up with Georgios, who'd waited faithfully for them, they set off on the long trek that lay ahead. Behind them, Kastelli Airfield was racked with further explosions and long bursts of gunfire.

A dozen kilometres to the north-east of Kastelli Airbase, Patrol B was also going into action, albeit against a very different kind of target: the fuel and ammunition dump packed with 200,000 litres of aviation fuel, plus thousands of pounds of bombs. Over the past few hours, Janni, their youthful Cretan guide, had kept a watch on the sentry routine at the dump. During the night hours guards with dogs patrolled both the fuel and ammo stores, so the raiders would have to take extra care.

As Janni had led the four-man force down from their hideout in the hills, Dick Holmes had been struck by how brave and skilful their Cretan guide appeared to be. Demonstrating an admirable fearlessness, Janni had led them across the main road running into nearby Heraklion town, and at just before midnight they were in position to attack. The problem was they could see a German officer with a fierce-looking German Shepherd prowling the grounds ahead of them, and they would need some ruse to get them past the dog undetected.

For twenty minutes they remained secreted in an olive grove, scoping out the plan of attack. Finally they agreed to split up. Janni would lead Holmes to the fuel dump by crawling along a narrow gully, which should keep them out of sight of the officer and his dog. The gully terminated some thirty yards short of the massed ranks of fuel drums, where-upon they'd face a dash across the darkness to get in among them.

Meanwhile, Lamonby and the others would head for the adjacent bomb dump, which had the added barrier of a Dannert wire fence.

At first, all went well. Holmes and Janni reached the end of the gully, whereupon Holmes readied his backpack of Lewes bombs and darted forward alone. There was a high earthen berm encircling the fuel dump, so Holmes had no option but to make for the one narrow opening leading into it. Having stolen through that, ahead of him lay a central passageway leading between the shadowed heaps of drums.

He hurried ahead, knelt at the central point, and to left and right planted the first of his charges, shoving them as far under the metal drums as he could reach. That done, he pushed out to the fuel dump's perimeter and did the same again. Holmes felt surprisingly calm and collected, despite the fact that he knew the German officer with his dog must be prowling about somewhere nearby.

Charges placed, he hurried back to the entrance, stuck his head out to check that the way was clear, and almost ran right into the enemy patrol. There before him not thirty yards away were the sentry and his dog. Holmes ducked back inside and took cover. Aware of the acid eating through the timing pencils that he'd triggered, he knew he had to get out of there before the charges blew.

Just then another sentry with a dog turned up, and the two men began chatting away in German. They were stationed at the entrance and Holmes was effectively trapped. To make matters worse, both of the dogs were whining and growling in a most worrying way, and Holmes felt certain they had sensed him.

After nattering away for what seemed like an age – and now and again ordering their dogs to be quiet – the sentries finally moved on. Holmes seized his chance, crept out of the fuel dump and made it back into the gully without being detected. With Janni at his side he retraced his steps to the RV, only to learn that Lamonby's group had failed to make it into the bomb dump due to the sentries and the wire.

Before leaving, Janni had one last task to execute. Taking the Union Jack 'decoy' flag from one of their backpacks, he dashed down the gully and left it in a place where, come daybreak, the Germans were bound to find it. That way, they would be less likely to take reprisals against the local Cretans.

Or so everyone hoped.

At 0110 hours the first of Holmes's charges went off. The resulting cataclysm was so intense that streams of burning fuel were blasted over the earthen berm and spurted through the bomb dump, setting off the explosives stored there. As a result, it too was blown sky high – the heavens above the fuel and ammo dump turning a terrible, bloody red, and a massive pall of toxic, oily smoke blotting out the stars.

At Kastelli Airbase all was fiery chaos and confusion too. Lassen and Jones were still very much alive, but only just. As their comrades headed for the hills, they had made a mad dash back through the hole in the fence. But even as they'd squirmed through they could see that the way ahead was blocked. A phalanx of German troops was pouring onto the runway to hunt for whoever was blowing their airbase to smithereens.

Lassen made a snap decision. Signalling Jones to wait he ripped off his hat, so exposing his white hair, pulled out his Luger, and stepped into the open.

'Over there! Over there! Intruders!' Lassen yelled in German, shooting into the darkness.

The German soldiers followed his lead, firing into the night, after which Lassen dashed off after the imaginary intruders, drawing the German soldiers with him. Jones took the cue and dropped into the cover of a drainage ditch from where he could see how Lassen was faring, and how he might be able to help.

A fire truck came tearing across the runway. Men wielding hoses began pouring water onto a stricken Ju-88. But just as Lassen and Jones had hoped, the blistering heat from the burning aircraft proved too intense for the German fire crew. In an instant the next sleek fighter-bomber in line burst into flames, the force of the blast throwing the fire engine half across the runway.

As further *Schnellbombers* were caught in the seething fire-storm, Lassen seized his chance and slipped away from the phalanx of German soldiers that he had been 'commanding'. He strode towards the main gate to try to bluff his way through, but the gate guards were immediately suspicious. Guns were raised.

'I'm with you, fools!' Lassen barked. 'Partisans all over the place! We need more men! They're hitting the barracks!'

Several of the guards leapt into action, and Jones watched in disbelief as, for a second time, Lassen led a group of German soldiers into the thick of things. And then came the big one: to the eastern side of the airstrip the ammunition dump went up like a mini-nuke, and in an instant the entire base was lit up by a series of long, searing blasts.

Ammunition cooked off – powerful, juddering explosions ripping the night apart, and rendering the sky above the airbase one huge firework display. In the searing light the guard nearest Lassen must have finally got a proper look at his face and uniform. Lassen noticed the immediate change in his demeanour. As the German barked a yell of alarm, Lassen decided there were too many for him to take on. He made a break for it, dashing into the shadows.

Bullets whined and snarled after him as the Germans gave chase. Lassen found himself running for his life, and he and Jones sprinted back towards the fence and safety. After the months of Athlit training they were fitter than the enemy, but they were also exhausted from the rigours of the long trek into the target. It was the Benzedrine as much as anything that gave them the edge, but neither man was able to outrun a well-aimed German bullet.

Lassen and Jones must have got disoriented in all the confusion, for when they made the wire they couldn't find their entry point. In a mad scramble and with hands cut to pieces, they fought their way across the Dannert fence and dropped onto the far side.

But it was then that a guttural cry split the darkness: '*Halt! Hände hoch!*'

Lassen froze as a torch pinned him in its beam. An anti-aircraft battery had been positioned in a bunker lying outside the base perimeter, to better deter Allied warplanes. The German gunners manning it had spotted Lassen and Jones and had them covered. They ordered Lassen to drop his weapon.

'*Hände hoch! Hände hoch!*'

'*Dummkopfs!*' Lassen roared, his German ringing with officer-like authority. 'Idiots! There are Tommies inside the aerodrome, plus the partisans. Turn your gun and engage them!'

'Sir!'

As the Germans gunners spun around their weapon to open fire on the imaginary enemy, Lassen and Jones managed to slip away into the shadows of the night. It was yet another narrow escape, but the Dane still didn't appear satisfied.

Kastelli Airbase was crawling with enemy, but Lassen figured there was one part of the target area that remained quiet. If they could sneak through the wire once more and sow some final chaos there, their work would be well and truly complete. Buoyed by his commander's apparent fearlessness, Jones figured what the hell – they may as well give it a try.

No sooner had they sneaked through the wire for a third time, than the two raiders were challenged. Striding up to the nearby sentry and calling out an order in German, Lassen raised his Luger and fired. Amid all the ammo cooking off, he hoped no one would notice the lone pistol shot that had felled that sentry. But as he and Jones stole further onto the airbase, a fierce barrage of fire was unleashed in their direction.

Lassen estimated they had at least twenty enemy soldiers converging on their position. He replied in the only way he saw fit, by hurling grenades. As the powerful Mills bombs exploded and fragmented, sending shards of jagged steel tearing through the fiery darkness, Lassen spotted a final target. Without a word to Jones he darted forward, diving into the cover of the vehicle.

Coming to his knees beside the massive caterpillar tractor, he grabbed his backpack, placed his last Lewes bombs against the fuel tank, and broke the timing fuses. That done Lassen went to ground, dropping behind some fuel drums piled at the edge of the runway. By now Kastelli Airbase had been transformed into a sea of fire, and the Dane couldn't help but thrill to the spectacle. Trouble was, he was caught in the midst of the chaos and practically surrounded.

The only side of the airbase that seemed quiet was the far southwestern end, and it was towards there that he moved. He jinked between patches of cover staying out of the light, but as he ran for the safety of the dark exterior he realized that he could no longer see Jones. He reached the fence, but still there was no sign of his fellow raider. In the confusion of the battle Lassen had lost him.

For the fourth time that night the Dane turned away from the beckoning darkness, and stole back into the fiery maw of Kastelli Airbase. He had one aim now: to find Jones and get him out of there. The nightmare scenario was that Jones had been captured, for there was little doubt what would befall him then.

Tiptoeing ahead, Lassen crept to within a few yards of the nearest German sentries. Keeping to the shadows he listened to voices thick with shock, fear and anger, but only for long enough to be certain that no prisoners had been taken.

It looked as if Jones must have escaped. If so, it was high time he made his own getaway.

Slipping through the wire, Lassen headed for the vineyard that he knew lay somewhere close at hand. To his rear the last Lewes bombs went up, punching through the heavy caterpillar tractor's fuel tank. The vehicle lifted with the impact and slammed down onto the scorched and blackened ground in a seething mass of flames.

On either side of the runway lay the skeletal remains of German aircraft, many with wings blown off, their carcasses burning fiercely. The fuel and ammunition dumps had been destroyed, as had several vehicles. Any number of the airbase garrison were dead, and many more were injured. To say that Lassen's mission had crippled the Luftwaffe operation on Kastelli was something of an understatement. But the Dane's euphoria was to be short-lived. Come sunrise, things weren't looking too good.

Lassen had been forced to go to ground in the only patch of cover he could find – laid flat on his stomach in a farmer's cabbage field.

Chapter Fifteen

As Kastelli Airbase burned, and the fuel dump at Heraklion consumed itself in a searing firestorm, so two of the raiding forces – Nicholson's and Lamonby's – had melted away into the night. Convinced that Lassen and Jones were either killed or captured, Nicholson and Greaves headed first for a mountainside rendezvou with a Cretan partisan – one who'd volunteered to play a very special part in the operation.

After a two-hour trek into the highlands, Nicholson and Greaves linked up with the man who'd volunteered to be their runner, and take the 'SUCCESS' message back to the waiting radio operators at Apoini – from where the signal would be sent on to Cairo and London, triggering the wider information operation.

That done, the two raiders disguised themselves as local shepherds; cover for the trek back to the coast. At least dressed thus they could risk making some of the long journey by daylight. Time was of the essence. Word was out that the Germans had set a price on the saboteurs' heads, and that they would take brutal reprisals against any villagers who sheltered them.

Trouble wasn't long in coming. A patrol of German infantry came thundering into the village where Nicholson and Greaves were hiding for the night. The two raiders hurried into the thickly forested hills rising above the village, only to sense other, shadowy figures flitting through the darkness.

The entire population of the village also seemed to be fleeing for the safety of the highlands. Once they were a good distance away from the enemy, Nicholson and Greaves paused to catch their breath. They asked why the villagers had also run for the cover of the forest. The Cretans explained that the Germans would very likely take hostages, and threaten to execute them unless they revealed the whereabouts of the British raiders.

'Then why don't you give us up to the Germans?' Nicholson asked. It was a genuine question. The last thing he wanted was to be the excuse for a massacre.

The villagers had looked at him as if he were insane. Give the British up? It was unthinkable.

In spite of such dangers, at least Nicholson and Greaves were on the move and heading south. Lassen meanwhile had been forced to lie low for hours on end, his body pressed into a ploughed field and covered in dirt, as German patrols charged about. He was still dangerously close to the airfield, he had no water, and all he had to live off was raw cabbage and onion.

The Germans who were hunting Lassen and his fellow raiders could have few doubts now who had attacked their airfields. Already the information war had broken out. On receipt of the 'SUCCESS' signal, a brief communiqué was issued to the British press: 'Small British land forces carried out raids on airfields in Crete last night. The operations were successful, a number of enemy aircraft being destroyed on the ground. All our patrols withdrew successfully.'

To Lassen lying trapped in that cabbage field, his withdrawal doubtless didn't feel that successful, but the British media pounced on the story anyway. 'SMASH AND GRAB LAND RAID ON CRETE AIRFIELD', ran one headline. 'British troops landed on the Axis-held island of Crete last night. They destroyed large quantities of petrol and many enemy planes before successfully withdrawing . . .'

The BBC was also broadcasting its message of hope to the Greek people – one penned by the Political Warfare Executive and specifically designed to counter the German reprisals.

> Special message to the people of Crete. You have heard the communiqué that announces raids in Crete by British forces. You know those forces neither asked for nor received any assistance from local inhabitants. The Germans know this too . . . The Germans know that you have no responsibility for these raids. If they take any action against you they are committing a breach of International Law. They know well that they will be punished for any outrages they commit. The day is coming when they will pay for all their crimes.

The German media countered by downplaying the raids: 'Exploits by British saboteurs are insignificant from a military points of view.' It also claimed that the British raiders enjoyed little if any local Cretan support: 'Collaboration on behalf of the local population was completely lacking . . . If this action signifies the skill of the offensive in the Mediterranean announced by Mr Churchill, the German side wants to . . . withstand attacks on a much larger scale.'

Fortunately for Lassen, local Cretan support would continue to prove spirited and outstanding. Towards the evening of the second day the farmer came to tend his cabbage fields. Lassen decided to take the risk of making contact. The Cretan immediately offered help. Once dusk was upon the fields he returned and led Lassen to the nearest village. There he was reunited with both Jones and Georgios, their guide. Jones had been sheltered by the villagers pretty much from the off. As for Georgios, having pointed Nicholson and Greaves towards safety, he'd doubled back to Kastelli to come to the aid of his brother warriors.

'Any *maya*?' Lassen kept gasping, 'maya' being an Arabic word for water, one that Lassen had picked up in Athlit.

One after the other Georgios fetched him eight bottles of water, before the Dane's raging thirst – resulting from forty-eight hours under a burning Cretan sun, surviving on a diet of cabbage and onion salad – was quenched.

By now, the enemy had begun to wreak their first bloody revenge. The German commander, based in nearby Heraklion town, had taken dozens of villagers hostage. He threatened to shoot them unless the 'foreign saboteurs' – their blond, German-speaking leader first and foremost – were handed over. One by one they began to execute the villagers, but still none of the Cretans would talk.

The executions left Lassen incandescent with rage.

He and Jones were passed from village to village, as they made their way back towards their coastal base, and the promise of extraction and safety – but at every step of the way they were dogged by rumours of continuing German atrocities.

It was 8 July – four days after the raids – when they finally rendezvoused with Lamonby's patrol, plus their radio operators and kit, in the hills above Apoini. The first thing Lassen set about doing was making contact with Cairo headquarters. The message sent, marked 'Most Immediate – Most Secret – Officer Only', reveals much about his tortured state of mind, as the local Cretans suffered at the hands of the enemy.

Sixty-two Greeks shot. Women and children imprisoned. Ten more to be shot daily until our capture. Greeks still helping at risk of lives. Population needs morale boost after misery caused by British troops. Suggest strong air attacks on barracks and daylight strafing if possible.

By anyone's reckoning this was a strident *cri de cœur*. The situation was made all the worse by the fact that the Germans had 'definitely shot Lt Lassen's guide', according to another radio message, this one from Lieutenant Lamonby. All messages sent to Cairo HQ would be picked up, and relayed if necessary, from the main raider base on the Cretan coast. There, Sutherland – the overall mission commander – was growing increasingly worried.

Sutherland had spent the last two weeks making a thorough reconnaissance of the area, and he had men out watching all the obvious routes for the raiders' return. So far, only one had made it back. It was A Patrol. Their target, the aerodrome at Tymbaki, had – like Heraklion – proven devoid of any aircraft, and they had seen zero action.

By 'D plus 5', 9 July, Sutherland was starting to feel a real sense of unease at the continued absence of B and C Patrols. They were overdue, and without radio contact he had no idea of what fate might have befallen them. It wasn't until dawn the following day that he finally got his first positive news. Nicholson and Greaves arrived, fully disguised as Cretan shepherds, and they were able to brief Sutherland on all they had achieved.

A short while later a Cretan SOE agent – one of Patrick Leigh Fermor's men – turned up with more news. As feared, the Germans had executed dozens of villagers in retaliation for the raids. But on a more positive note both Lamonby's and Lassen's patrols were inbound to Sutherland's position. Lassen had managed to gather some twenty Cretan men to add to his number, all of whom had helped aid their escape in one way or another. Those Cretans were intent on getting lifted off the island, so they could join the Allies in their fight against the German invaders.

But with all his patrols having now resurfaced, Sutherland faced a potentially insurmountable problem. Even as his radio operator was making the call to arrange their extraction, his radio died. The batteries had finally given up the ghost. Without being able to send that signal to Raider Force Headquarters, in

Cairo, no pick-up boat would come. Sutherland was acutely aware how vulnerable they were: hundreds of German soldiers were combing the southern coast, seeking to catch the raiders before they could make their getaway.

He decided to attempt a makeshift solution. He took the batteries from two of the patrols and linked them up in series, in the hope of raising enough power to send the vital message. Having cobbled them together in that way, his radio operator was finally able to confirm that contact had been made with Raider Force Headquarters in Cairo.

'Request reembarkation urgently night 11th–12th,' read the message calling in the Motor Launch to pluck them off the coast. 'Sigs as previously arranged. 12 extra to be taken off. Confirm times date. DUMP requests answer urgently.'

'DUMP' was the codename for Sutherland's base. Confirmation was given that the Motor Launch would be there as requested. Now all the raiders could do was wait.

The '12 extra to be taken off' were those of the Cretan partisans that Lassen had drawn with him who wanted to join up with Allied forces. They were a colourful and lively bunch. Armed with ancient, bone-handled daggers and even older-looking guns, their traditional black Cretan hats framed their lined, weatherbeaten features. They were the proud people of a proud nation that had been crushed under the Nazi jackboot, and to a man they thirsted to fight. The main challenge was keeping them quiet and well hidden, as the raiders waited for the pick-up boat to arrive that coming night.

Suddenly, a cry rang out from one of the sentries: 'Jerries!'

Two German soldiers were wandering down the dry river valley in which the raider force was secreted. Moments later they were pounced upon by a dozen commandos bristling with weapons, and they promptly surrendered. But Sutherland knew that where there were two Germans, more were bound to follow. He organized search parties, but it was now that the Cretan fighters decided to take matters into their own hands. As one they rushed up the valley to take the fight to the hated enemy.

Shots rang out. The two German captives had been part of a larger patrol. Those enemy soldiers still at large fought a skilful retreat, falling back among the cover of the rocks and beating off the Cretan attackers. Sutherland was beside himself. This was a near-disaster. The gunshots would be audible for many miles around, and if the Germans escaped they would bring reinforcement in real numbers. The Motor Launch wasn't due for several hours, and in the interim the raiders were pinned with their backs to the sea.

He ordered Lamonby to take four men to stop the Cretans from firing, and then to deal with the Germans. The gunfire died down and the Cretans wandered back to base, but without Lamonby or his men. Finally, as dusk fell the main force of raiders headed for the beach and their rendezvous with the Motor Launch. Inflatables were made ready and loaded with gear. Finally the four raiders returned, but still there was no sign of Lamonby.

Apparently, Lamonby had insisted on going on alone to deal with the Germans. Desperate to bring him in, Sutherland sent

Lassen and Pomford, two of his prize fighters, to investigate. As they headed up the dry river valley, a single shot rang out. It echoed back-and-forth across the enclosed space, ominously. They pressed ahead, calling out to Lamonby: 'Ken! Ken!' Not a word of reply came from the silent hills. Lassen and Pomford continued searching until just before the Motor Launch was due, when they were forced to make a dash for the beachside evacuation point.

By now Paddy Leigh Fermor had arrived, so he could see the raiding force safely off 'his' island. Leigh Fermor offered to continue the search for Lamonby once the raiders were gone. One way or another, they would find the missing man.

And so, as the faint hint of sunrise lightened the eastern sky, Sutherland's raiders sailed away from Crete, their ranks swollen with a dozen Cretan partisans, but sadly minus one of their own – Lieutenant Lamonby. Lassen hoped and prayed that his friend might be injured, or perhaps have twisted an ankle in the rocks. If Leigh Fermor's men found Lamonby, they'd be able to bring him out at a later date.

As the Motor Launch slipped into the darkness, Sutherland was able to breathe a long sigh of relief. His raiders had managed to escape from the encircling enemy, complete with their two German prisoners. They'd left behind them one German airbase and an ammunition and fuel dump in smoking ruins. Even so, the execution of the innocent Cretan villagers weighed heavily upon them all: it would not be forgotten.

Lassen vowed to learn the name of the German commanding officer on Crete who had ordered the executions, and exact revenge.

Much of the German weaponry captured during the raids the men would keep for themselves, for it was far superior to British kit. It also meant they could scavenge ammunition off the enemy when out on operations. In fact, a great deal of their uniform and other kit – not to mention watches, and personal gear – was taken off the enemy dead. They favoured Italian boots and water bottles, but German weaponry and ammo wherever they could find it.

One of the prisoners had been captured with his self-loading rifle – a Walther G43, a real prize for the raiders. It was a cutting-edge piece of German engineering, and it would be handed over to British high command, yielding an intelligence bonanza. The German prisoner who'd yielded up that Walther G43 had been an English student before the war. As a result he spoke excellent English, and turned out to be a friendly-enough kind of a fellow. Before returning to Raiding Force Headquarters, in Cairo, for mission debriefings, Lassen and his men took both their German captives – Ulrich and Heinz – for ice cream sodas in Groppi's, their favourite café and one of Cairo's most famous eateries.

That evening the prisoners were left in the care of Nicholson and Greaves, as Lassen and Sutherland were busy. Nicholson and Greaves didn't exactly fancy a night in, baby-sitting two German captives. So they sneaked back to Groppi's for an evening meal for four. They cautioned Ulrich and Heinz to keep their heads down, for Groppi's was crawling with British and Allied officers. Dinner seeming to have gone down all right, they retired to the cinema to enjoy a movie, before rounding off the night with a few drinks in a local café.

Ulrich and Heinz had several years as prisoners of war ahead of them. They perhaps deserved one last night of comparative liberty, courtesy of the Special Forces raiders. As with many Germans, the average foot soldier was neither markedly better nor worse than his equivalent in the Allied forces. It was the misguided architects of Nazism – the kind of men who believed the execution of fifty Cretan villagers was justified – who were the focus of the raiders' ire.

Perhaps inevitably, Cairo Headquarters found out about the way in which the two German prisoners had been treated. The high-ups were furious, and they attempted to take it out on Sutherland. The lean, ruggedly handsome Special Forces commander gave an easy-going laugh, and pointed out that at least the prisoners had been handed over in a positive and cooperative frame of mind.

Sutherland's report on Operation Albumen – marked 'MOST SECRET – OFFICER ONLY', and written in the immediate aftermath of the mission – emphasizes what an incredible feat the raiders had pulled off: 'This operation I consider to be one of the most physically exacting ever undertaken by Special Services troops in the Middle East, since distances of well over 100 miles of mountain country were covered by night over a period of three weeks in enemy occupied territory . . . The results achieved are a tribute to the leadership, keenness and determination of the patrol commanders and all ranks concerned.'

In his contribution to that report Lassen writes in glowing terms of his wingman, Ray Jones. 'Throughout the operation and especially during the attacks, the coolness under fire, determination and keenness of 1469628 Gnr. Jones was of the highest order . . . by attracting attention to ourselves, we permitted Sgt Nicholson and Cpl Greaves to carry out a successful attack from the Eastern side.'

But for Lassen, the Kastelli raid and those that had gone before – Sark first and foremost – would also weigh heavily upon him. As he explained to a new recruit: 'Never use your knife if you can avoid it. If you have to kill – then shoot. I have at times been forced to use my knife – it's terrible.'

The very night that they had hit Kastelli and Heraklion, Operation Husky and the Allied invasion of Sicily had begun – its success at least partly due to the number of German warplanes destroyed at Kastelli.

In his top secret after-action report, Jellicoe outlined the key role the raids played in safeguarding the Operation Husky convoys from air attack: 'As enemy aircraft known to be in the Athens area could have been transferred to Cretan airfields . . . the patrols, apart from the destruction they wrought, provided a good insurance against such a danger. No air attack was made on the slow HUSKY convoys.'

Italian resistance on Sicily crumbled, and the Allies thrust rapidly northwards onto the Italian mainland. By the start of September the Italians had sued for peace, signing an armistice with the Allies on 3 September 1943.

But the Germans were having none of it. They moved swiftly to reinforce Italian-held territory with their own troops, in effect forcing the Italians to fight on against the Allies, or to turn against their erstwhile German comrades. Either way, Operation Husky had drawn blood: it had pulled huge numbers of German troops away from northern Europe to the defence of Italy. The battle for Europe's 'underbelly' was well and truly joined.

Immediately after the success of Operation Albumen, Sutherland recommended several of his men for decorations. There were Military Medals for Dick Holmes, Jack Nicholson, Ray Jones and Sydney Greaves, plus a bar to his Military Cross for Lassen.

Lassen's citation read: 'Pretending to be a German officer he bluffed his way past three sentries . . . Throughout this attack, and during the very arduous approach march, the keenness, determination and personal disregard of danger of this officer was of the highest order.'

Sutherland would also earn a bar to his own MC for the raid on Crete. But before any of the decorations could be awarded, there was dark and difficult news awaiting those who had done so well during the recent raids.

Upon their return to Athlit, Lassen and Nicholson – the Small Scale Raiding Force veterans – learned that tragedy had struck. At around midnight on 12 July 1943 – just as they had made it safely off Crete – Geoffrey Appleyard had been killed. Banned from combat operations due to illness and exhaustion, Appleyard had still insisted on accompanying his men on a mission over Sicily, though he would not join the parachute drop itself.

The Armstrong Whitworth Albemarle aircraft – a twin-engined British troop transport – had dropped her parachutists at 2330 hours on the 12th, but never made it back to base. There had been intense anti-aircraft fire over the drop zone and the Albermarle had most likely disappeared somewhere over Sicily. Appleyard and all others aboard her were lost in action, presumed dead.

In a chilling coincidence, just a few hours after Appleyard's death Graham Hayes – the other *Maid Honour* founding original – was executed by the Gestapo. He was shot by firing squad in Paris on 13 July, after spending approaching a year in captivity.

By the end of the second week of July 1943, all bar one of the *Maid Honour* founding fathers – March-Phillipps, Appleyard, Hayes: M's pioneering SOE agent-commandos – were dead, killed at the hands of the enemy.

Only Lassen remained.

Worse was to come. It was confirmed that Lamonby – one of Lassen's closest friends in Athlit, and the man they'd been forced to leave behind on Crete – was dead. Wounded by the German enemy that he'd been hunting, Lamonby had died at a local hospital.

In exchange for the dozen or so warplanes destroyed, the fuel dumps blown up, and the death and injury caused among his own forces, the German commander on Crete had already exacted terrible revenge. One British raider – Lamonby – had been killed, and fifty-two Cretan villagers had been executed. As Sutherland wrote in his report on the Crete raids: '. . . as a result of reprisals, a state of terror exists throughout the area.'

'I was appalled . . .' remarked Jellicoe, of those massacres. 'There was a very, very strong mutual bond and this was something that Andy [Lassen] was very responsive to. He understood almost instinctively the people and had a great feeling for them, especially I think "un-grand" people – he was frightfully good with Greek fishermen and Greek peasants, and with their wives and families. It meant a great deal to him, that connection.'

But *Generalleutnant* Friedrich-Wilhelm Müller – the dreaded 'Butcher of Crete' – was far from done yet. On 14 September 1943 he issued his now infamous directive to the men of the 22 Luftlande Infanterie-Division. By anyone's reckoning, Müller's orders were extreme. His men were to lay waste to the entire region of Viannos – long a hotbed of resistance, and the principal area wherein the British raiders had been sheltered – a place of simple mountainside villages, each consisting of clusters of low, white-walled houses lining labyrinthine dirt streets. They were to execute all males over the age of sixteen, plus anyone seized in the countryside *regardless of their gender or age*.

In response to that order, two thousand German soldiers threw a wall of steel around the target area. They spent the first few hours rounding up locals and insisting that their intentions were 'entirely peaceful'. Some of the Cretan males foolishly believed them, and were persuaded to come out from hiding in the forests. Mass executions followed, interspersed with dynamiting properties, torture, looting and burning down buildings.

Some forty-eight hours later 500 or more Cretans from twenty separate hamlets had been executed, and a further 200 had been taken captive. Many of the villages – Kato Symi, Amiras, Pefkos, Agios, Loutraki, Mythoi, Christos – had been burned to the ground. The survivors were forbidden to return to the smoking ruins of their homes, or even bury their dead.

In short, Viannos had been rendered into a ghost land.

Chapter Sixteen

Jellicoe, Sutherland, Nicholson and Lassen all knew that the average German soldier was no more guilty in this war than the average Brit or Dane. They were conscripts, and they too were the victims of the Nazi regime. It was the senior commanders – those who blindly followed Hitler's will; those who ordered the massacre of hundreds of Cretan civilians – who took the lion's share of the blame.

'I am so poor at hating,' Lassen had been heard to say. 'I believe I would even be able to shake hands with the Germans . . . once Denmark is free again.'

After Crete, Churchill issued orders to Jellicoe that his free-lance pirates should do as had been done in coastal Europe: they should set 'the Aegean aflame'. With fierce fighting underway in Italy – and with German forces putting up stiff resistance – Churchill knew there weren't the conventional forces available in the Allied ranks to take the Greek Islands, so Jellicoe's raiders would have to muddle through.

'There is no time for conventional establishments,' Churchill urged, 'but rather for using whatever fighting elements there are . . .'

Jellicoe's raiders were to spread terror in the German ranks across the necklaces of islands strung through the waters of eastern Mediterranean. Those islands provided air and sea bases to support the German stand in Italy, and Churchill wanted those targets hit hard.

Yet at the same time Britain's Prime Minister decreed that aid should go to the native villagers – ground down under the Nazi jackboot; many close to starvation – to help them through the worst. And so was born the concept of 'hearts-and-minds' operations.

With Sutherland and Lassen's help, Jellicoe cajoled and bribed local Lebanese seamen into putting a fleet of ancient caiques – traditional wooden fishing boats somewhat reminiscent of the *Maid Honour* of old – at their disposal, forming a fleet that they christened the Levant Schooner Flotilla. So began a series of combined raiding and hearts-and-minds operations – taking food and supplies to local islanders, while striking hard and fast against the German enemy.

The fame of the fearless blond Viking warrior who led many of those missions, and who drew the locals to him as naturally as a river follows its course, spread like wildfire. So too did the fear he inspired in the hearts of the senior German officers, those who had become Lassen's all-consuming target. One of them would write in a letter to his commander – a letter that was captured by the raiders: 'The British come like cats and disappear like ghosts.'

Jellicoe and his men could have wished for no better endorsement for the war they were waging.

With Italian resistance crumbling, no one knew for sure the status of the Italian garrisons manning many of the Greek Islands. Would they stand and fight, or would they throw their lot in with the British? The Italians feared both the Allied attacks they knew must come, and their erstwhile allies, the Germans. And they feared too the Greeks – those whose menfolk made up the resistance, and who secretly sheltered the British raiders.

The Italian troops had been issued with a briefing document urging them to be on their highest guard regarding the Greek islanders. It summed up their commanders' worries regarding the long-suffering but spirited locals: 'Although apparently passive, the Greek population is very hostile to you. You are surrounded by enemies . . . who are ready to attack you if you take the slightest risk.'

Jellicoe ordered his men to prioritize three targets lying to the far eastern end of the Mediterranean, just off the coast of Turkey: the island of Leros, with its seaplane base and floating submarine dock; Cos, with its three landing strips, plus the southernmost island, Symi. Symi would be the first hit, as it was seen as being the stepping stone to the others.

All three are situated in the Dodecanese island chain, in the Aegean Sea, the stretch of water lying between Greece and Turkey. Turkey had ruled the Dodecanese until 1912, when the Italians seized the archipelago. In the autumn of 1943 the islands remained Italian territory, though populated almost entirely by native Greeks.

At the port of Haifa, just to the north of Athlit, Jellicoe, Sutherland, Lassen and their men readied the Levant Schooner Flotilla. In using the caiques – those often ungainly-looking 10–30-tonne wooden fishing boats, powered mostly by sail – as their raiding craft, they were aiming, to sneak past the enemy, just as they had managed with the *Maid Honour*. They would pose as local Greek or Turkish fishermen, or when the circumstances demanded it they would fly the German or Italian flag.

They developed a system to navigate at night, and a near-perfect system of camouflage. Navigation had to be basic yet foolproof – a method that enabled young officers with little or no seafaring experience to travel long distances to land troops on an exact spot. It had to work with vessels showing no lights sailing in the depths of the night. The method developed, based upon easily identifiable silhouettes, was simplicity itself. Basically, a course was set by compass for a specific point, at which an unmistakable landmark would appear on the port or starboard bow – say a dog-shaped mountain. That sighted, a new course would be set to another landmark, the caique thus zigzagging her way to her intended destination.

From the regular armed forces they managed to beg, borrow and steal some standard camouflage netting. It was re-engineered using a different scrim – the scraps of cloth tied to the netting – to suit the colouring and texture of the island shoreline. The standard scrim reflected too much light; it needed to be a dull, dark grey to blend in with the rocks. Up and down the coast they sailed between Haifa and Athlit, mooring here and there at sunset, sunrise and midday, testing out different combinations of scrim, and the best way to drape the netting so as to break up the boat's outline.

Next they asked a friendly RAF pilot to overfly one of the caiques they'd camouflaged, to search for it with the naked eye and photograph its position. The pilot failed to spot the craft, and on the recce photos it appeared like a continuation of the shoreline. Camouflage and navigation thus perfected, the raiders felt able to sail far into enemy territory posing either as locals or as the enemy, and remain hidden when moored along the shoreline. The further they pressed into hostile seas the safer they hoped to be, for no German or Italian would expect them, or be on the look-out for a British raiding party.

New recruits were drawn to the gathering force. One of the apparently least suitable for the coming raids was Porter 'Joe' Jarrell – 'Joe' for 'GI Joe', Second World War slang for an American soldier. Jarrell was a chronically shortsighted Canadian-American, who'd served with the American Field Service, an ambulance unit that was attached to the British Eighth Army.

A conscientious objector, he had at first refused to take up arms, but he had distinguished himself as a medic on the field of battle. Then an RAF flight had attacked the British lines by accident, resulting in horrific casualties. Jarrell had found himself trying to tend to the dying and dead among the burned and blood-splattered sands, and wondering what on earth he was there for.

He'd volunteered for a combat unit in the US Army, only to be told that with his jam-jar glasses and flat feet he couldn't serve on the front line. Next he'd tried the Greek Army and the French Foreign Legion, but had ended up going to the only unit seemingly willing to have him, and to offer him the chance of battlefield exposure – Jellicoe's raiders.

Jarrell little knew what he'd let himself in for. At some stage this maritime wing of the SAS had been given its own name, the Special Boat Squadron (SBS), though none of the men had paid much attention to the rebranding exercise they'd been subjected to. Porter 'Joe' Jarrell joined up with Jellicoe's raiders as a medic, believing the 'SBS' to be some kind of reincarnation of the Long Range Desert Group.

After studying the quiet young American's file – he was a graduate from the University of Middlebury, Vermont, in the far north-east of the USA – Jellicoe had offered Jarrell an officer's commission. But knowing nothing of the realities of Jellicoe's unit, Jarrell had presumed that he'd spend his life square-bashing and polishing kit if he were to go for an officer's commission, and so he responded to Jellicoe with a polite no.

'Thank you very much, sir, but I'd prefer to remain in the ranks.'

Upon joining the Athlit raiders and getting a taste of the brutal training regime, Jarrell decided that the only way to keep his chunky glasses on was to tape them to the back of his head. He also tried unsuccessfully to wean the Athlit raiders off rugby and convert them to American football.

When serving with the American Field Service Jarrell had been attached to two British armoured car units in the desert, and he'd done a short stint with the French Foreign Legion in the mountains – but he'd never come across anything like the bunch of piratical renegades and desperadoes that he encountered in Athlit.

'They were really tough,' said Jarrell, of his first impressions of Jellicoe's men. 'They had a Cockney barrow boy very proud of splitting a man in half with a burst from a Bren. A Glaswegian told me about getting into an argument in Cairo with an American who he knocked down and kicked in the chin . . .'

Being a 'foreigner' Jarrell naturally fell into the Irish Patrol, although he was noticeably reserved compared to the Irishmen's fierce volubility. There were those among the Brits who didn't thrill to being ordered around by Lassen – a man who couldn't pronounce his Vs and Ws properly – but the Irish Patrol welcomed all-comers. Even so, few could believe that their shortsighted 'Yank' medic was cut out for the kind of work that lay ahead. In fact Porter 'Joe' Jarrell would prove himself a raider par excellence, and he and their heavily-accented leader would become inseparable.

Another 'foreigner' drawn to the Irish Patrol was Dion 'Stud' Stellin. Stellin was in his early twenties and, like Lassen, he was tall, blond and strikingly handsome. He shared with the Dane an easy success with the ladies – hence the 'Stud' nickname. Stellin, a New Zealander, had travelled to Britain in 1938 knowing that war was in the air. He'd volunteered for the Army, joining the Durham Light Infantry, and from there he'd drifted into Special Forces work, soldiering in the Middle East and across the Mediterranean.

Stellin came to Jellicoe's raiders having already fallen for the Greek Islands and their people. He loved the dramatic, timeless scenery, the food, the wine, the music, the dancing and . . . the dusky-eyed women. He railed against the occupiers, whose brutal excesses had caused so much suffering among an ancient people. In that sense he and Lassen were kindred spirits, and Lieutenant Stellin would become one of the Dane's closest comrades.

If nothing else Stellin and Lassen would be united by the fact that in the raids to come, the Germans would put a price on both of their heads.

The raid on Symi would launch the Dodecanese campaign. But this would be no butcher-and-bolt operation. Jellicoe's men were tasked to seize and hold Symi, so it could become a base of operations. From there they'd fan out across the island chain, seizing them one by one, and compelling the Italians either to fight, or join forces with the Allies.

That at least was the theory. It would fall to Lassen and his Irish Patrol to spearhead the action.

Lying on the island's north shore, Symi town straddles a high mountain saddle, with one end terminating in the narrow, deep inlet that forms the harbour, the other dipping into Pedi bay on the far side. The scenery is truly spectacular, with white-walled houses clinging to precipitous mountains that plunge into deep, azure waters. Sheltered by towering cliffs, Symi harbour is rarely troubled by even the slightest disturbance; in September

1943 its waters were little prepared for the cataclysm that was coming.

On 12 September 1943 – two months after the raids on Kastelli Airbase and Heraklion – a pair of caiques packed with forty-odd men pulled out of Haifa harbour, bound for the Dodecanese. Ahead lay a journey across the Eastern Mediterranean of some 500 miles. At the same time Jellicoe himself set sail with a larger force of men and caiques, to push north from Symi and attack Leros and Cos.

No one knew the strength of the garrison on Symi, or its make-up. Was it solely Italians, or Germans as well? Would they capitulate, or would they stand and fight? Either way, crucial to the success of the attack would be maintaining the element of surprise.

In order to reach Symi the flotilla would have to sail past the larger island of Rhodes, at the southern end of the Dodecanese chain, with its garrison of 40,000 German and Italian troops. Rhodes guards the gateway to the Aegean: by the time the raiders reached Symi they'd be at least fifty miles inside enemy territory. The last thing the Symi garrison should be expecting was to get hit by a British raiding force.

Five days after leaving Haifa the two caiques crept into Symi's darkened harbour, the slightest noise from the ships' decks seeming to echo across the mirror-still waters like a gunshot.

In peacetime the welcoming lights from Symi's harbour-front glisten and glow upon the calm. But in September 1943 the town was subject to a strict blackout, and not a glimmer of illumination was to be seen all around. The two caiques drifted to a stop mid-harbour and dropped anchor. Gun batteries had been sited high on the rocky cliffs, and in the faint moonlight the caiques would be sitting targets, should the gunners be alert and poised to open fire.

In overall command of the raiding force was Major Jock Lapraik MC, an officer new to the SBS. What Lapraik needed more than anything now was solid intelligence. Where were the enemy positioned? How were they armed? Was the harbour deep enough for his ships to sail right in and land his fighting force? Two men would have to go ashore to investigate. Anders Lassen and Douggie Pomford volunteered, climbing into a folbot and paddling silently into the night.

They stole under the lee of a cliff and were swallowed by the moon-shadows, pulling strongly towards the quayside. The waters all around were silent, as if the very sea itself were holding its breath. Lassen and Pomford made landfall and followed the shoreline into Symi town. The harbour-front also forms the main street, and on their right were rows of shadowed houses. From one or two came the sound of muffled voices, plus the odd snippet of voices raised in muted song.

They passed a Greek café, its doors thrown open to the street. In hurried whispers Lassen and Pomford conferred with the locals and secured the intelligence that they sought: there were 140 Italian soldiers stationed on Symi, but no Germans. At this time of night the Italians were very likely fast asleep in their billets. Lassen and his men should be able to take them by total surprise.

Word spread along the seafront like wildfire: at last, the long-hoped-for liberators had come! By the time Lassen and

Pomford had reached the harbour, the first of the church bells had already started to ring. One by one the dozen churches dotted around Symi harbour took up the call: at long last the English commandos – *which meant freedom* – were here!

At the quayside Lassen sought reassurances that the water was deep enough to call the caiques alongside. But no one seemed able to give a straight answer. Frustrated, he took matters into his own hands. He jumped off the quayside fully clothed and dived to the bottom. As the 'British commando' sank below sight in the dark water, the locals fell silent. There were a few tense moments before Lassen's blond hair bobbed to the surface, lit a glistening white in the moonlight.

'Pomford, signal to the ships that it's deep enough,' Lassen yelled. 'Call 'em in!'

By the time the two caiques had come alongside and disgorged the forty raiders, word had reached the Italians that 'hundreds' of British commandos had come ashore and taken Symi. Deciding that discretion was the better part of valour, the Italian force commander decided not to put up any resistance. When Lassen found the Italian, he was ordered to join the British in fighting the Germans, or Lassen would hunt down all his men and shoot them dead for cowardice.

Safely ashore, Lapraik split his men into four patrols. Lassen's was sent to the highest point of Symi town, an ancient, partly ruined fort called the Kastro. Built by the Knights of St John – also known as the Knights Hospitaller, a renowned religious and military order from the time of the Crusades – the Kastro's massive stone towers and walkways offered a panoramic view of the town, plus the bays to either side. To Lassen, this was a prime vantage point from which they could dominate the territory, if only they possessed a weapon with sufficient power and range to do so.

The other landmark of vital strategic import was the Monastery of the Archangel Michael, built on the opposite, southern end of the island, overlooking the anchorage of the Panormiti Bay. Like Greek holy men everywhere, the monastery's Abbot Chrysanthos was a diehard patriot and an enthusiastic supporter of the raider's cause. Lassen decided they needed an early-warning system based at the monastery, should the Germans opt to land in the bay below.

Without the Italians realizing, he had a radio set installed in the monastery, and trained the abbot's nephew how to operate it. Abbot Chrysanthos hated the Germans with a vengeance, but he reserved his greatest vitriol for the Italians, who had for decades 'occupied' what were 'naturally' Greek islands. The Italian garrison may have been persuaded by a mixture of promises and threats to stand with the British, but the abbot – as with all the island natives – didn't trust them for one instant. That clandestine radio set was as much to warn of Italian perfidy as it was of German aggression.

Over the coming days the raiders reinforced their positions and sailed out to recce the outlying islands. Lassen took his patrol around three in one day – Piscopi, Calchi and Alimnia. The first two harboured no enemy forces, but the third, Alemnia, possessed a deep harbour used by the Italians as a submarine base. When Lassen's patrol landed they found the place only recently abandoned. There Lassen and Pomford discovered exactly what they were looking for: among the abandoned Italian defences was a 20mm gun.

More specifically, it was a Breda Model 35 cannon, an Italian-made dual-use anti-aircraft and ground-attack weapon. It was a powerful piece, being accurate to a range of 5,000 feet and effective against 30mm thick armour. Mounted on a tripod it could cover a 360-degree traverse – so in all directions – and it had a rate of fire of 240 rounds per minute. The one Lassen and Pomford discovered had a footplate missing, but it came complete with a generous supply of ammunition.

The Breda was taken aboard their caique and transported back to Symi, whereupon it was carted across the main thoroughfare, Syllogos Square, up the winding streets and into the Kastro. Lassen had it placed in a tower offering a panoramic view of the terrain below, including the sea to either side. While the thick stone structure of the tower gave good cover, the tripod lifted the Breda's 10-foot barrel well above the outer wall, giving all-around firepower.

Lastly, he commissioned the town's blacksmith to manufacture a make-do replacement footplate. With the clandestine radio and the repaired Breda cannon in place, Lassen felt ready for whatever the enemy might throw at them. The Italian troops remained decidedly shaky, but the forty-strong raiding force was itching for a fight.

Yet before then Lassen faced his own problems. He'd been sterilizing a latrine using burning petrol, when there was a nasty blowback. Fire scorched both his lower legs badly. He'd also developed a nasty case of dysentery, a painful and debilitating infection of the intestine: with drinking water and food often not sterilized properly and sanitation far from perfect, it hit most of the raiders at one time or another.

Porter 'Joe' Jarrell, the American medic-cum-raider, took a long look at Lassen's badly blistered legs, which were beginning to turn septic. He declared his injuries to be so serious that the Dane should return to Athlit, or better still Cairo, and possibly even England, for treatment. Weakened by dysentery as Lassen was, it would take longer for the burns to heal.

For over two years now Lassen had been at the epicentre of a relentless raiding campaign, and largely without any kind of a break. Jarrell figured the rest and recuperation was long overdue. But the Dane refused to leave. He got Jarrell to bandage up the burns as best he could, so he could soldier on.

Lassen's fierce desire to stay wasn't only due to his determination to remain with his fellow fighters. He was also acutely aware of the needs of the locals. In spite of his weakened state, Lassen had been down to the docks to help unload heavy sacks of flour and beans for the half-starved islanders. The supplies had been placed under Abbot Chrysanthos's control, so he could distribute them to the most needy.

Lassen also had another responsibility here on Symi. On one of his island visits he'd discovered a small Maltese terrier, which he'd named Pipo. Formerly an Italian officer's lapdog, Lassen had adopted Pipo to be his dog of war. He'd cured Pipo of his addiction to Italian pasta, and got him eating proper raider food, like bully beef. Many saw Pipo as a scruffy, dirty, noisy nuisance, one who peed on just about everything in sight. As for Lassen, he coupled his love of hunting with a love for all things wild, and for him and Pipo it had been love at first sight.

But most importantly there were Germans hereabouts to fight: Lassen could sense that they were coming.

Chapter Seventeen

By early October Lapraik's men had been in control of Symi for two weeks. Reinforcements had just arrived unexpectedly, in the form of twenty officers and men from the RAF's 74 Squadron, Fighter Command. They were en route to Cos – one of the islands seized by Jellicoe's armada – intending to crew-up a flight of Spitfires that had been sent to the Cos airstrips. The RAF crewmen pulled into Symi harbour, not knowing that they were shortly to become a key component of the island's defences.

After seizing Cos and Leros, Jellicoe's men had handed the islands over to squads of elite British paratroopers and a number of follow-up Allied infantry units. Jellicoe's caiques had sailed onwards through the Dodecanese chain, seizing Kalymnos, Samos, Chios and Patmos. On the latter island they'd overheard the Italian garrison whispering worriedly about their safe, which was stuffed full of Italian Lire, plus the odd bundle of Reichmarks. It included the payroll for the 1,000-odd Italian troops stationed on the island of Leros – which the raiders had only recently 'liberated' – a considerable amount of money.

Jellicoe's men hesitated only for the barest instant before forcing open the safe and helping themselves to massive bundles of cash. Henceforth Italian Lire became their kitty and their fighting fund for the battles to come. Such were the spoils due to the pirate raiders as they cut a swathe through the Dodecanese.

But as with all things that seemingly came too easy, there would be blowback. Lapraik, Lassen and their fellows would feel it heaviest on Symi. When it came, the German counter-offensive would employ serious firepower and numbers. Sensing what was coming, Lapraik – an unyielding commander possessed of a strong moral and physical courage – issued stark orders to the twenty RAF men now temporarily under his command.

> Owing to our great strategic importance there is no doubt that we shall be attacked . . . Let there be no doubt about it, they will come; therefore we must be prepared. Consequently it is essential that everyone be absolutely on their toes 24 hours a day. When the guard is called out it will be out in seconds, not minutes as was the case last night. When ordered to stand-to you will be downstairs in the bush like bats out of hell . . . Remember – be quick on the job and keep on your toes because if you don't you've bloody well had it, believe me.

At dawn on 7 October three boatloads of German troops put ashore on Pedi Bay, lying to the east of Symi town. Manning the Breda cannon that morning at Anders Lassen's castle lookout was RAF Flight Sergeant Charlie Schofield who, like Porter Jarrell, was terribly short-sighted. Yet even Schofield had spotted the three craft, which were less than a mile away from his vantage point – putting them well within range of his cannon.

Lassen, fresh from sleep, stared down into the bay, and roared, 'Who the hell are they?'

His words were drowned out by Schofield opening fire.

The German force scattered under the 20mm cannon fire, but they were already ashore. Lassen rallied his men to head them off before they could make it into the town, while Schofield sought to keep as many as possible pinned down on the rocky coastline. The fierce percussions of the Breda's fire brought two immediate misfortunes on Schofield: one, it shattered his glasses; two, it attracted a flight of Stukas, which proceeded to dive-bomb his castle-top position.

Schofield had never been in sustained combat, but he stood his ground. As the Stukas howled in, he yelled out words of reassurance to the fellow RAF men manning his position.

'It's impossible for the Germans to hit this spot,' Schofield declared, gleefully. 'Their bombs will fall short 'cause of the angle of approach needed to avoid the hills.'

It proved true. Time and again the Stukas tried to bomb the 20mm gun emplacement, but their bombs slammed into the slopes below and the houses of the town itself, leaving the tower unscathed.

In the winding streets Lassen's Irish Patrol was already in action. O'Reilly noticed the Dane freeze by a wall. He had an uncanny sixth-sense for finding the enemy, almost as if he could smell Germans. Lassen indicated there were soldiers on the far side. On a signal, Lassen and O'Reilly burst into the open and fired over the German's heads, who promptly surrendered. They took two prisoners, but now it would be down to bitter fighting at close quarters.

The streets of Symi town are labyrinthine, and it was a real art to get close enough to the enemy to engage them – an art in which Lassen excelled. Underfoot, the narrow, winding roads are paved with white cobbles, the steps scaling the steeper slopes worn smooth with time. The hobnailed boots of the Germans rang and clattered as they dashed from cover to cover, while the felt soles of Jellicoe's raiders padded silently through the streets, as they stalked the enemy.

A second patrol, led by Englishman Lieutenant Charles Bimrose, pushed into eastern Symi – the direction of the German attack, but it seemed that the enemy had already seized the high ground overlooking the town. A line of ancient windmills marked the ridgeline, terrain that the Italians had been charged to defend. But the Germans had brought with them a unit of Italian fascists, who were exhorting their brothers through loud speakers to turn on the British. Torn, the Italians it seemed had abandoned their positions.

A German machine gun had been established on the ridge, from where it could pour down fire into Symi's rabbit warren of streets. Bimrose's patrol was the first to feel its heat. He and his men played hide-and-seek with the German gunner, as they dashed from cover to cover. Then Bimrose's patrol was hit in an ambush. A stick grenade was tossed over a wall, exploding at the feet of Seaforth Highlander William Morrison. Bimrose's sergeant was hit by a burst of follow-up fire and Bimrose himself took a flesh wound in the arm.

For an instant his advance faltered, before Bimrose himself, enraged by what had befallen his patrol, charged forward and decimated the enemy position. Two Germans were killed and one wounded, after which Bimrose withdrew his men to better cover. But William Morrison died from the wounds he'd suffered in the grenade attack, and Bimrose's sergeant was seriously wounded.

Bimrose briefed Lassen on what he'd discovered about the German strengths and numbers. Lassen's men had studied the layout of Symi town and knew it well. The newly arrived Germans did not. Lassen held his men back so as to draw the Germans in, and then the trap was sprung. Time after time as they tried to storm the ancient fortress of the Kastro the German troops were ambushed, Lassen himself stalking and killing three at very close quarters.

As the morning dragged on the ancient alleyways rang with savage bursts of gunfire, and echoed with grenades exploding, plus the bloodcurdling cries and screams of the dying and wounded. Bullets zigzagged and ricocheted across cobblestones, chasing the German attackers along the twisting streets, and gradually their offensive began to peter out.

As their battered forces regrouped on the town's outskirts, something extra was needed to drive them back to their boats. Lapraik decided to send Lassen and his patrol to put some steel into the Italians' spine. So far, the 140-strong Italian garrison had played little part in the fighting, apart from giving up the high ground. The Germans needed to be driven off that ridge, so who better to do it than those troops who had first abandoned it.

Lassen presented the Italians with a stark choice. 'You may be shot by the enemy, but if you run you *will* be shot by me.'

In spite of the pain from his burned and blistered legs, Lassen had worked himself up into some kind of a trance – one very likely fuelled by Benzedrine, and doubtless fanned by his fervent killer instinct. With the Italians' resolve thus stiffened he drove them up through the burning-hot terrain, which all about them droned with the rhythmic *chirp-chirp-chirp* of cicadas.

As they hit the ridge, the Italians were forced into action against their erstwhile allies. The last of the German positions were cleared and they were driven back to their boats, Lassen and his Irish Patrol chivvying the Italians, guns at the ready. One Italian was injured in the fighting, but none had been killed, and at least the honour of the Italian nation had been somewhat restored.

By three o'clock that afternoon the German commander had withdrawn his men to the spot where they had first landed, and he started to evacuate his wounded. But the battle was far from over. At four o'clock a larger German vessel hove into view – a landing craft packed full of reinforcements, steaming full speed for Pedi Bay. It was crucial that it be prevented from making the shore.

It was now that the scavenged Breda cannon came into play. Lassen dashed up to the gun emplacement, took control of the weapon and opened fire on the landing craft, using the white plumes of spray thrown up by the falling rounds to walk them on to the target. Within moments the 20mm armour-piercing rounds were tearing into the vessel, its overcrowded deck being swept by a whirlwind of shrapnel.

Lassen kept at it until the ship's commander, fearing the gun was going to sink her, made an about turn and set a course back to Rhodes – not a man among his assault force having managed to put ashore.

Seeing the German boats disembarking from the beach, Lapraik ordered his men to give chase. They readied one of the caiques at anchor in Symi harbour and set sail, but it proved too slow to catch the German ships. Yet its very presence forced the retreating armada to alter course, driving the vessels into range of the Bren guns that Lapraik had positioned along the Kastro's thick walls.

The Bren is deadly accurate out to 600 yards, but its maximum range is three times that. The German vessels were well within that distance. Lapraik's machine guns raked the ships' exposed decks, targeting them for the entire length of Pedi Bay, and until they turned south around the headland for Rhodes. The battle for Symi was finally over, but no one among the town's defenders believed for one moment that the wider war for the island was done.

General Ulrich von Kleemann, the overall commander of Axis forces in the region, was furious when he heard about the defeat. He had some 40,000 troops stationed on nearby Rhodes, yet a handful of British raiders and turncoat Italians had defeated him. He ordered the island to be bombed into oblivion.

At 0800 hours the following morning the first flight of Stukas swept in. Coming in at around 5,000 feet, the Ju-87s rolled through 180 degrees above the town and plummeted in a 90-degree dive towards earth. Air-brakes kept the dive speed constant at a maximum 600kph, and the first bomb was released some 400 metres above the target, at which stage the pull-out began – the Stuka leaving a thick black plume of blasted smoke and dust in its wake.

Packed with 650lbs of bombs, the Stuka was designed as a precision ground-attack aircraft. But over Symi that morning the bombing proved largely indiscriminate, and designed to terrorize the island population. Every two hours a new wave of dive-bombers swept in, and it quickly became clear that the entire population of Symi was to be made to pay for the German defeat. As they screamed out of the burning blue, even Lassen – who seemed to feel no fear – found that the Stukas could strike terror into his soul.

Another of Lapraik's men, Lance Corporal Robert McKendrick, was killed, and all across the town there were civilian casualties, as Symi's ancient streets were torn apart. Most of the buildings were built without any cement, and even a near-hit from a Stuka collapsed them into a pile of rubble and dust. Bereft of any air cover, Symi was hugely vulnerable. The Stukas were able to dive so low that the island defenders could see the faces of the pilots through the Plexiglas cockpit, the banshee wail of the aircraft's sirens drilling into their ears.

Just after lunch Lapraik's headquarters took a direct hit. Lapraik escaped unharmed, but two of his men were trapped beneath the heap of rubble. One was Tom Bishop, originally from the Grenadier Guards. The other was Sidney Greaves, who together with Nicholson had done such a sterling job on the eastern side of Kastelli Airbase three months earlier, as Lassen and Jones had hit the western side.

A former miner serving in Lapraik's force led the search party, as they tunnelled in to free the two men. Porter Jarrell, the American medic-cum-raider, was at the forefront of the rescue operation, as was an RAF doctor, Flight Lieutenant Leslie Harris. As the Stukas continued with their terrifying strikes, the rescuers managed to clear an airway to the lower of the two figures, Sidney Greaves. He was trapped by the heavy debris lying on his stomach, and Bishop was above him, his foot pinned under the wreckage.

With Stukas tearing through the skies, the rescue force faced a terrible dilemma. They needed to free Bishop in order to get to Greaves, but if they tried to move the weight off Bishop's foot, the whole lot might collapse and crush Greaves completely. The only option was to amputate Bishop's foot where he lay, drag him free and then attempt to prop up the wreckage and lift Greaves out from below.

To make matters worse, the RAF doctor had suffered a wrist injury in the blast, so he would only be able to guide Jarrell through the operation. He'd lost most of his medical equipment under the debris, and Jarrell only carried the bare basics. Together, they managed to gather a few forceps, some tourniquets, a scalpel and scissors, plus some chloroform to deaden the pain. But the only tool available with which to amputate the leg was a small carpenter's saw.

Despite this, Bishop agreed to the amputation in an effort to save his brother warrior's life. With the RAF doctor and Jarrell hanging half-inverted in the narrow space, and with others holding onto their feet at ground level to keep them from falling, the operation got underway by flickering candlelight.

After the tourniquets had been wound tight to cut off the blood flow, Jarrell began sawing through Bishop's leg, under instructions from the doctor.

The wreckage rang with Bishop's cries of pain. Another flight of Stukas howled and wheeled overhead, like dark birds of prey, but neither Jarrell nor Harris paused in their task. With the foot finally sawn off, they were able to drag Bishop clear, whereupon he was given intravenous blood. But the shock and the bomb blast that he'd suffered, plus the crushing injuries must have proved too much.

Bishop died shortly after they'd pulled him free.

Undeterred, Jarrell crawled back into the dark, dust-choked hole, squeezed through a gap between the debris and managed to reach Greaves. Whispering words of encouragement and comfort to the injured man, Jarrell managed to get an injection of morphine into him, and then a rubber tube was lowered via which he was able to feed some water into Greaves' parched, dust-dry throat.

But in spite of such efforts Sydney Greaves died before he could be pulled free. Porter Jarrell had spent some twenty-seven hours crawling among the shattered debris of the headquarters building, trying to save two men's lives. At any moment a hit from a Stuka could have sent the rest of the building crashing down on top of him. He emerged blood-spattered, caked in dust from head to toe, utterly exhausted and on the point of collapse.

Flight Lieutenant Leslie Harris, the RAF doctor, summed up the terrible situation, and Jarrell's actions and his nature, succinctly. 'It was one of the most horrific operations I've seen. I couldn't perform it myself because I had a wrist injury through falling on the rocks, so I could only guide . . .' Jarrell, he said, was 'a fantastic bloke, with his Red Cross on one shoulder and a machine gun over the other . . . They hadn't a hope in hell, but we thought that we had to try something.'

At dawn on 10 October – three days after the German assault force had been beaten back from the island – the Stukas returned in earnest. Wave after wave pounded the town. That morning, Lapraik received orders to withdraw. At first he resisted, although the suffering of the islanders was causing all the raiders – Lassen more than most – serious anguish.

Lapraik agreed to evacuate his wounded, along with the German and Italian prisoners. On 12 October, after further savage bombing sorties, the orders to withdraw were repeated. Finally, the raiders bowed to the inevitable and pulled out. They could be proud of the fact that no ground force had vanquished them, and that in leaving Symi they were saving the long-suffering islanders from any further death and devastation.

Yet even as they sailed away from Symi Island, Anders Lassen was about to be called back in again.

Chapter Eighteen

A week after their withdrawal, Lassen received a message via the clandestine radio at Abbot Chrysanthos' monastery, warning him that a force of Italian Fascists had been installed on Symi. After their defeat at the hands of the British raiders, the Germans were reluctant to reoccupy the war-torn island. But they were happy to send in the Italians, who'd been offered a stark choice: either they would fight in Hitler's cause, or be sent to the prison camps. The Italians had been ordered to keep a close watch on Symi, and especially on the rebellious islanders.

Following the radio call from Abbot Chrysanthos, Lassen sailed back to Symi with his Irish Patrol, aiming to do what they did best – a snatch and grab raid. Striking by surprise in the darkness, Lassen and his men took eight Italians captive and blew up their radio station – the one through which the Italians were supposed to keep General von Kleemann, the German commander on Rhodes, acquainted with any developments on the island.

The Italians had long suspected Abbot Chrysanthos of being in league with the British. The abbot knew that the Italians had him under surveillance, but still he kept his secret radio functioning, feeding intelligence back to the raider force. Following Lassen's return, the Italians proceeded to take their revenge.

They killed the abbot and his radio operator nephew, silencing the radio once and for all.

When Lassen learned of this he asked permission from Jellicoe to launch a third raid. Permission granted he sailed to Symi, attacked an Italian artillery post at night, killing the officer in charge of it and several of his men. And so the spiral of attack and counter-attack, revenge and counter-revenge spun out of control, as unrest spread across the Aegean as far as the Greek mainland.

In a repeat of the atrocities following the Kastelli and Heraklion raids, civilian resistance was brutally suppressed, German tanks steamrollering houses, their occupants crushed under their tracks. In one town, Kalavrita, on mainland Greece – long a focal point of guerrilla activity – the Germans executed every male above the age of fifteen. They were marched onto a field on the outskirts of the village and machine-gunned. The dead amounted to some 700 – from grandfathers, to fathers and schoolboys.

By now Jellicoe's raiders had been fighting in Greek territory, alongside Greek partisans, and sheltered by Greek civilians, for six months or more. Most, like Lassen and Stud Stellin, had learned to speak more than a smattering of Greek. To many, it was becoming like a second language – mispronounced and bastardized but understood nonetheless. The mutual respect and affection between raiders and islanders kept growing.

Islanders and raiders shared much in common: a burning individualism; a tendency towards anarchic thoughts and actions; a certain raggedness of dress; an abiding disrespect for mindless authority; an innate affinity with the underdog; an in-born toughness and physical endurance; an incurable love of the black market.

Raiders and islanders had grown exceptionally close, Jellicoe's fighting men risking their very survival to help the locals. Radio operator Jack Mann had been sent on a raid on the island of Chios, in the Aegean. He and a fellow raider had managed to trap a German E Boat by posing as Greek locals, and forcing the six-man crew to surrender. But dealing with the plight of the locals had proved harder than fighting the enemy.

Mann had been called to a house crowded with civilians, where a nine-year-old-boy was said to be dying. 'They asked if we had a doctor,' Mann recalled.

'We didn't. But Fred said to me: "Zucky" – that was my nickname in the unit – "why don't you see what you can do for him?" The islanders were literally starving to death before our eyes. I had some Vitamin C tablets, sugar and water, and I mixed up a rehydration solution for the boy. He'd hardly drunk it, when the colour came back to his face and he perked up mightily.

'Then this massive queue formed outside, as everyone kept calling to me in Greek: "Doctor! Doctor! Doctor!" Of course, I had no medicines to speak of and no formal medical training. What could I do? We ended up giving them all the food we had. They were starving. Luckily, another patrol pulled into the island and we managed to get some supplies off them, otherwise we'd have starved ourselves!'

As news of German atrocities reached their ears, Jellicoe's raiders – Lassen, Stud Stellin, Nicholson and O'Reilly first and foremost – thirsted for vengeance. Thankfully, across the Dodecanese island chain they were about to return to what they did best – butcher-and-bolt raids. Holding territory as they had tried to do on Symi and the other islands really didn't play to their strengths.

By means of hit-and-run attacks they could strike terror into the hearts of those they most wanted to terrorize – the German commanders. But first, they would need to regroup, and replace those men lost to death and injury. Then they would need to find a secret pirate base – somewhere in neutral waters – from which to launch the coming attacks.

Lassen's actions on Symi earned him his third Military Cross, with the following citation: 'The heavy repulse of the Germans from Symi on 7 Oct 43 was due in no small measure to his inspiration and leadership on the one hand, and the highest personal example on the other. He himself, crippled with a badly burned leg and internal trouble, stalked and killed at least 3 Germans at close range. At that time the Italians were wavering and I attribute their recovery as due to the personal example and initiative of this Officer.'

It was October, shortly after the withdrawal from Symi, when Sutherland – Jellicoe's second-in-command – learned of the award. Feeling it would be good for morale to give Lassen the decoration pretty much immediately, Sutherland cobbled together a replica of the ribbon that denotes a second bar to the MC, using paper and dye, plus rosettes fashioned from the lid of a Players cigarette tin.

Once the short ceremony to present the honour was complete, the raiders drank everything in sight long into the night.

Jellicoe's raiders had recently been boosted by the welcome arrival of the 'Iros Lochos' – the Greek Sacred Squadron – to fight alongside them in the Dodecanese.

Under the renowned leadership of Colonel Kristodoulus Tzigantes, the Sacred Squadron sported a distinctive badge – a sword surrounded by a laurel wreath, inscribed with the motto 'Return Victorious Or Dead'. In the case of the Sacred Squadron's fighters, those were to prove far from boastful words. Lassen had already bonded with Colonel Tzigantes during operations in and around Symi.

Halfway through a raid by Stukas on Leros, Lassen had amused himself by trimming Pipo's coat, transforming him into the 'Lion of Leros'. Poor Pipo looked more like a poodle at the end, but he did indeed seem to possess the bravery of a lion. He'd bark furiously in the direction of any approaching Stukas, his acute hearing warning the raiders long before any warplanes might be audible to the human ear. As for Colonel Tzigantes, he seemed to greatly enjoy the Lion of Leros episode, and he and Lassen had become fast friends.

As Christmas 1943 came around, the men of the SBS – together with those of the Sacred Squadron – prepared for their deployment . . . to Turkey. Neither the Allies nor the Axis powers particularly wanted to provoke neutral Turkey into joining the war, but Jellicoe's raiders needed a base from which to strike deep into the Dodecanese, and Turkish waters were the obvious location from which to do so.

Training for the coming campaign was interrupted by the all-important Christmas feast. The raiders had just sat down to a fulsome dinner, rustled up by their miracle-worker of a chef, when a brigadier emerged onto a makeshift stage to make an announcement. Apparently, the celebrated performer with the BBC Variety Orchestra, Miss Judy Shirley, was there to sing a few numbers, to 'reward' the raiders for their efforts in the Dodecanese.

Miss Shirley had come at the behest of the Entertainment National Service Association (ENSA), a branch of the services with the job of entertaining the troops while overseas. She was blonde, pretty and no doubt blessed with a fine voice, but few of the assembled throng gave much of a damn. As she stepped onto the stage and fine dinners began to go cold on their plates, someone was heard to yell above her singing: 'Get that cow out of here!'

The brigadier turned puce with embarrassed fury, but at least he had the sense to withdraw with Miss Shirley, and leave the soldiers to eat in peace.

Six hundred miles to the north-west of Athlit, General von Kleemann was doubtless sitting down to his own Christmas feast in his fine castle overlooking Rhodes Harbour. Untroubled by Miss Judy Shirley's dulcet tones, von Kleemann's mind was turning to the defence of his command – the Dodecanese. The British raiders may have been driven out of his islands, but he felt certain they would return. Consequently, he had reinforcements pouring into the region.

A fresh brigade of elite mountain troops had been put at his disposal, in addition to the 999th Infantry Division. A flight of Junkers transport aircraft, some equipped with floats, were ferrying in both men and war materiel, and a newly arrived fleet of barges was shuttling back and forth between the islands. Von Kleemann was an astute commander: he positioned his troops wisely for what he feared was coming.

He retained one division on Rhodes. To the three islands lying south and west he sent 800 men. To those key islands lying to the north – Leros, Cos and Symi – he sent over 6,000 troops. But with the smaller islands that remained he was uncertain what was the best approach. Rather than man each one with a token force, which would be highly vulnerable to British raiders, he decided to rotate a larger force, garrisoning each only for short periods at a time.

From Raider Force Headquarters, in Cairo, von Kleemann's actions were being closely monitored. The German commander now had no fewer than six divisions of fighting men spread across his domain. The strategy developed by Raider Force Headquarters to counter von Kleemann was ingenious: it was to trap – *and terrify* – those troops on their islands, so they could play no further part in the war. It was broken down into three movements.

In the first, British submarines and Beaufighters – a fighter-bomber variant of the Bristol Beaufort – would scour the islands from below and above the waves, seeking to whittle von Kleemann's fleet down to the point at which the German general was no longer able to evacuate those troops he had garrisoning the islands. Jellicoe's raiders would play a key part in this stage of operations – sinking von Kleemann's ships in their harbours, or seizing them on the high seas.

The second movement would be spearheaded by Jellicoe's raiders. They would switch their attacks to isolated, outlying garrisons, forcing the Germans to take to the seas to reinforce those under assault and evacuate their wounded. Once those ships had been lured out of their harbours, British submarines and Beaufighters would strike once again.

The third phase, which lay entirely in the raiders' hands, entailed pure banditry. Jellicoe's men were to launch the *nervenkrieg* – to borrow a German phrase – 'the war of nerves'. In the *nervenkrieg*, every garrison was to suffer the terror of a night raid complete with sabotage and kidnapping. With food and ammunition in short supply, with mail deliveries and leave a thing of the past, and with their horizons reduced to isolated, sun-baked patches of scrub, rock and sea, the German – and Italian – soldiers would always be on edge, fearing the next attack.

This was to be the phase of the collapse of morale, of desertions and of mass surrender.

In order to launch phase one, the raiders needed to get themselves established in Turkish waters. Quietly, some forty-odd potential bases had been recce'd all along Turkey's Aegean coast. The ideal location for the main base quickly became obvious: it was the sixty-mile-long Gulf of Cos, running east of the island of Cos far into Turkey, and surrounded by dramatic mountains and thick forests on all sides.

On 20 January 1944 a very special flotilla set sail from Beirut, the capital of the Lebanon lying to the north of Athlit. It consisted of a fleet of the raiders' caiques, plus a 180-tonne schooner, the *Tewfik* – one that Jellicoe's raiders had somehow managed to procure. In the *Tewfik*'s hold were some 4,700lbs of explosives. Not much of it was going to be wasted in the coming months.

In the lead caique were Anders Lassen, Stud Stellin and the Irish Patrol, and all – even medic-cum-raider Porter Jarrell – were spoiling for a fight. There was also a new recruit among their number – Freddie Crouch. Twenty-six-year-old Crouch was a former policeman who hailed from the East End of London. In the coming weeks Crouch would prove himself to be a born raider: a diamond geezer, as his fellow Cockneys might call him. Crouch would be steady as a rock under fire, and he was destined to become one of Lassen's stalwarts.

The raiders packed onto those ships had an extra reason to be happy, in addition to their sailing to war with a large boat packed full of plastic explosives. They also had their pockets stuffed with gold sovereigns. It wasn't the first time they'd been sent to sea carrying gold, which was useful as a universally accepted form of currency, one that could be used to pay guides or informers and to purchase supplies. But any sovereigns left over rarely made it back into Jellicoe's hands.

More often than not they were 'the first casualties of a successful operation', as Porter Jarrell described it.

Jellicoe had long suspected Lassen of hoarding sovereigns surplus to operational requirements. The men were in the habit of stuffing the small gold coins between the double soles of their boots, to better hide them. Following one raid Jellicoe had even gone as far as searching the Dane's clothing while he was in the shower. The raiding force commander found nothing.

Jarrell was able to explain where the missing coins had got to. 'Andy had taken the gold pieces into the shower!'

The gold was earmarked for the raiders' post-operations party kitty. While they fought hard these men played just as fiercely. Lassen's wartime sweetheart was a dancing girl who performed at the Hotel St Georges, a Beirut cabaret – the diminutive, dusky-skinned and utterly delightful 'Aleca of Alexandria'. Lassen had got into the habit of ending their epic training sessions with an equally epic session in the hotel bar. He'd make his way there in his jeep, driving at typically suicidal speed, before joining the bewitching Aleca over drinks, whereupon the real partying began.

But right now, as the armada set sail for Turkish waters, partying couldn't be further from the soldiers' minds. There was work to be done.

The shores of the Gulf of Cos offered the raiders some 200 miles of dark, pine-forested coastline, overhanging shadowed inlets and narrows screened from passing boats by islands. Such a bay might at first glance appear to be empty, but upon closer inspection it would reveal a squat, ugly schooner riding at anchor, with a host of inflatables and folbots tied up alongside.

A distance away lay a fleet of Motor Launches, plus a flotilla of distinctive caiques. Here and there were other assorted craft, from which some of the raiders were busy fishing for their supper. In the stern of the fat schooner – the *Tewfik* – squatted a distinctive, semi-naked figure, Lassen, a scruffy little dog at his side. The Dane was whittling away at a length of wood, fashioning a bow with which to hunt wild boar in the forest, Pipo glued to his every move.

Down below in the dark interior of the ship sat Sutherland, pipe clamped between teeth, transcribing the raiders' first operational orders. To the front of the ship, Sergeant Jenkins – he who had only recently conjured up that fine Christmas feast – was busy, busy, busy. He was trying to stop one raider from pinching a tin of sausage meat, accusing another of doing the same, while attempting to get his Greek cooks to refrain from preparing octopus for supper – *again*.

'No octopus.' He shook his head vigorously. 'Not octopus. Not again. *Please.*'

On the hatch beside him Donald Grant, a bespectacled American war reporter, reclined in a deckchair. He was busy compiling an article for *Look*, a now defunct American glossy news magazine. For a moment Grant put his writing pad down, picked up a recently acquired Luger pistol, and polished it proudly. Grant had been into action alongside these men on their previous Dodecanese raids, and he was an instant convert to the way these piratical raiders did things. Luger cleaned, Grant turned back to his writing.

Dressed in sand-coloured baggy windproof pants and blouses these taciturn characters unloaded supplies that the Navy had brought them, hoisted the heavy bundles on to their shoulders, gestured for me to follow and set off along the dirt road at a steady pace. As we walked along I realized I was the only one making any noise, so that I finished the two hour journey walking on the soles of my feet in an effort to move as quietly as the rest . . . They were the scruffiest band of soldiers I had ever encountered, carrying an assortment of weapons which they cleaned meticulously.

Grant's welcome into the raiding force had been an unusual one, particularly for a news reporter. Sutherland had asked a group of his officers if they were willing to take a young American newsman with them. 'Well, will he fight?' one demanded. Grant, overhearing the challenge, blurted out, angrily: 'Of course I'll fight!'

The next query had come direct from Lassen. 'Do you know how to carry a pack and a gun?' Grant confirmed that he did. He was quite happy to carry a weapon as well as a pencil into battle. Lassen had handed Grant a German Luger pistol. 'Right, you're in,' he told the reporter.

Lassen liked Americans. He was himself part-American by birth – Lassen's mother was an aristocratic Danish-American – though he never once revealed it to Porter Jarrell, or any other of his fellow raiders. Somehow, Lassen managed to be both an intensely private person, and one who could inspire deep loyalty in others – those who were willing to follow him behind enemy lines on death-defying missions, American newsreporters included.

By the time Raider Force Headquarters in Cairo had realized that the SBS had embedded a journalist within their number, it was too late to do anything about Donald Grant. The high-ups at Raider Force HQ were enraged, but the proverbial chicken had long flown the coop. Grant had already filed the first of his sensational news reports.

These British raiders are some of the finest fighting men in the world today . . . All praise is empty for a soldier who will put on the rags of a peasant and walk through a German garrison, knowing that one false move or word will land him in the torture chambers of the Gestapo. I saw him do this with the calm poise of a man buying a pack of cigarettes in a corner tobacconists . . .

These raiding forces would not be very impressive on a parade down the Mall in London. They pride themselves on their beards while on operations . . . While hiding in the mountains near a German outpost, no-one washes because water is scarce and no-one ever takes his clothes off at night. There is considerable variation in uniform but all are dirty, greasy and torn. About the only common garment to all raiding force men is a strangely hooded jacket, which often makes them appear to be a band of Robin Hood's merry men stepped out of a storybook, complete with knives slung on their belts . . . They took me with them when they ambushed and killed a commander of a certain German garrison . . .

That German officer had been targeted by Lassen, for he commanded a Gestapo unit that terrorized Greek captives using a great black dog that ripped their throats out. Lassen made sure that the dog was hunted down and killed, along with its Gestapo handlers.

Lassen had first been dubbed the 'Robin Hood Commando' back in his Anderson Manor days, when he'd stalked the Dorset fields and hedgerows complete with bow-and-arrow. Now, thanks to Grant's reporting, that epithet had been immortalized in print and for the entire raiding force, the toughest unit of which – the Irish Patrol – the 23-year-old Dane now commanded.

The *Tewfik* bristled with all kinds of weaponry, a good proportion of which was German. To Grant's right and further forward on the schooner's deck, O'Reilly – Lassen's de facto bodyguard – was cleaning a German sniper rifle that had been liberated during the recent battles around Symi. For a moment he contemplated zeroing it onto a target ashore, before reminding himself that loosing off shots against the Turkish shoreline – even practice ones – probably wasn't the wisest of moves, especially since the raiders didn't officially exist in Turkish waters.

Far aft of Grant a figure dressed in a distinctive peaked German forage cap bent over his task, silently working away, his mind totally focused on what he was doing. Despite his German dress, he *was* one of the British raiders – a foremost explosives expert, no less – and he was busy making up the charges for the mission that he'd just been warned by Sutherland was in the offing.

Come dusk the scene livened up noticeably. Those who had been spearing fish or bartering with the local Turkish villagers returned to the mother ship, loudly demanding food. The signallers were badgered for news from headquarters. Was there an update on the plans for the forthcoming raid? Were other targets being lined up for attack?

As the night darkened, Sutherland pulled Lassen to one side. His orders were complete. The first target of the new Dodecanese raiding campaign had been set.

It would be the island of Halki, and Lassen and his Irish Patrol were to lead it.

Chapter Nineteen

It was 31 January 1944 when Motor Launch 1083 whisked the Irish Patrol out of Turkish waters and into those of the enemy. Halki lay some fifty miles to the west of their secret base, and the fast craft made short work of the journey. Braced in the wheelhouse against the biting January wind, Lassen scented the chill air and the fighting that was to come. He was hoping for some German ships to sink in Halki harbour.

Beside him, his dog Pipo – the Lion of Leros – seemed equally ready for battle. Pipo would become a constant feature of Lassen's operations, the four-legged raider being carried on the most arduous treks, and lifted up the worst cliffs and inclines. Pipo had a disgusting habit of peeing on the men's clothing, and even inside their sleeping bags. It didn't exactly win the dog many friends, but Lassen wouldn't hear a word said against him.

Intelligence from Halki suggested that all was not well on the island. The resistance was strong, the anti-German sentiment unyielding, but as a consequence the enemy had cracked down on the locals mercilessly. Malnutrition among the islanders was reportedly reaching crisis proportions, and so – along with all the raiders' weaponry – Lassen had made sure that the Motor Launch was loaded to the gunwales with food supplies. Sacks of flour, bags of macaroni, tins of bully beef and sausage meat and all sorts of other staples were heaped around the boat.

In the face of mass-killing, starvation and economic collapse, the Greek islanders were in greater need than ever. Somehow, Lassen managed to combine extraordinary courage and physical endurance with an innate feel for people's suffering, and an undying empathy for the underdog.

Jellicoe himself would write of Lassen that he had 'a quality which overshadows even his outstanding physical and moral courage . . . that was his sympathy for those who were less fortunate than himself and the love he inspired in them . . . Wherever he went one felt this deep sympathy for the unfortunate, and the affection which these people he had befriended or helped felt for him was quite extraordinary.'

Under cover of darkness the food supplies were ferried in to a remote and uninhabited stretch of Halki's shoreline. But the wind proved strong that night, the rocky shore steep, treacherous and uninviting, and the repeated journeys in a small boat loaded high with stores and provisions were exhausting.

No matter; once the supplies were landed Lassen led a team consisting of Sean O'Reilly – his Irish bodyguard – plus Greek Sacred Squadron officer Lieutenant Katsikis, as they headed for the mayor's house. Unsurprisingly all were asleep at the mayor's residence, the vine-covered outer courtyard locked shut for the night. The three men vaulted over the wall, but the mayor's wife woke up and started screaming, presuming the shadowy figures to be the harbingers of more suffering and trouble.

Lieutenant Katsikis called to her reassuringly in Greek. They were strangers bringing important information, he explained. A voice was heard to utter: 'I am sure that is Lassen and his men.' It was the mayor. Peering out of an upstairs window he'd recognized the blond hair of the Dane whose fame was spreading far and wide across the Dodecanese.

The mayor's wife threw open the door. Lassen explained where the food stores were stashed, and told the mayor to gather his villagers, after which he could distribute the supplies to those most in need. Then he asked about the enemy presence on the island, and their disposition. The mayor told Lassen that there were some half-a-dozen Italians garrisoning Halki, and gave directions to their billet.

'Do you want them taken prisoner, or killed?' Lassen asked.

'Oh, they are not such bad men,' the mayor replied. 'Taken prisoner is probably for the best.'

'All right, let's go and grab the bastards!' Lassen exclaimed.

Lassen led the way through the dark and twisting streets of Halki town, which is hardly larger than the average Greek fishing village. They found the barracks building, stole around to the rear and hammered on the back door. The Italians finally woke up and Lieutenant Katsikis spoke to them, claiming to be a local villager with vital information to give them on partisan activity.

The Italians remained suspicious and refused to open the door. They kept telling Lieutenant Katsikis to come back when it was daylight. Lassen finally lost patience. Cautioning O'Reilly not to open fire, he ordered the big Irishman to kick the door in. No sooner had O'Reilly's boot crashed through the door-frame, than Lassen himself loosed off a volley of bullets above the Italians' heads.

There were six of them, and they immediately surrendered. The raiders searched their premises, seizing six rifles, two Beretta MAB 38 machine guns, plus a wireless receiver. Frustrated at not being able to find any money they could use to fund their campaign, Lassen spotted a safe. He crouched before it, trying to work out how best to get it open. He was in the midst of doing so when an intriguing sound drifted up from the bay below: it was the throaty chug-chug-chug of a motorboat pulling into harbour.

Lassen's eyes gleamed. 'Sounds like a ship. And not a local fishing-boat, either.'

Lassen, O'Reilly and Katsikis grabbed one of the Italians and the four men dashed down to the harbour, only to discover a large German E Boat – a patrol launch – pulling into shore. By its marking they could tell that it hailed from the headquarters garrison on Rhodes, so it was very likely one of General von Kleemann's resupply boats.

Lassen, O'Reilly and Katsikis took cover, hiding around a convenient corner, the Dane shoving the muzzle of his pistol into the nape of their Italian prisoner's neck.

'Call to your German friends,' he told him. 'Invite them ashore for a nice drink.'

The Italian did as ordered, and the yelled reply from the boat indicated that the Germans were partial to coming ashore for a snifter or two of Ouzo.

Lassen eyed O'Reilly and Katsikis excitedly. 'Are you ready?'

Both men nodded, and made ready their weapons. As the boat nestled into the harbourside, Lassen and his men pounced. They dashed around the corner and opened fire. But as O'Reilly tore ahead he stumbled, and his weapon went off, accidentally shooting Lassen in the leg. The stray bullet had caused a nasty flesh wound, and it seemed to drive the Dane into a towering fury.

'You Irish dog! D'you want to kill me?' he kept yelling, all the while pouring fire into the German ship.

Lassen hurled grenades. The blasts tore into the patrol boat, shaking it from stem to stern where it lay in the water. The German crew had been taken utterly by surprise. One moment they were savouring the thought of a few glasses of Ouzo; the next, all hell had broken loose. In the pitch blackness and amid all the horror and confusion they must have presumed their attackers were a legion of the enemy, for those still standing promptly surrendered.

Lassen, O'Reilly and Katsikis boarded the German vessel. In spite of the fusillades of fire with which they'd raked her decks, plus damage from the grenades, she seemed largely seaworthy still. Lassen grabbed the ship's engineer, who'd been wounded by a grazing shot to the back of the head, and he ordered O'Reilly to take the man below decks. They were going to seize the German craft – for then they could use her to properly sneak up on any unsuspecting enemy.

'Get the engines started,' Lassen told O'Reilly, 'and let's get her underway.'

O'Reilly knew no German, so all he could do was point the wounded engineer at the E Boat's engine and make appropriate gestures. The man seemed almost paralysed by terror, and the message just didn't seem to be getting through.

'What are you vaiting for down there?' Lassen roared from above decks. 'Get the bloody engines started!'

O'Reilly decided the engineer needed a dose of the short sharp shock treatment. He levelled his pistol, fired a couple of shots over the man's head, and jabbed a finger at the engine again. Finally the German seemed to get it. Minutes later, the reassuring throb of the powerful ship's engines reverberated through the hull.

Lassen got the Italians and the German crew loaded aboard the ship, the entire lot covered by the raiders' Tommy Guns. A good number of the Germans were wounded, but that didn't stop a fight from breaking out between them and the Italians, once the Germans realized that the offer of drinks had been a false one, used to lure them into the shore.

Leaving the former allies to bicker among themselves, Lassen steered the German patrol boat out of the harbour, to where Motor Launch 1083 was waiting – all the while yelling some choice abuse at O'Reilly for having shot him in the leg. Now was perhaps the most dangerous moment of the mission so far. As the German E Boat approached the British Motor Launch, there was every chance that the British vessel might believe she was being attacked and open fire.

Sure enough, the raiders heard cries of alarm echoing across the night water, plus the sharp clatter of steel-on-steel, as the Motor Launch's guns were made ready.

'*It's Lassen!*' the Dane kept yelling at the British ship. '*It's Lassen!*'

Finally the Motor Launch crew must have heard him, for no one opened fire. All the prisoners were ferried aboard the Motor Launch, whereupon the German patrol boat was slung behind her on a hawser, and they set a course for the Gulf of Cos with their prize in tow.

As they pulled away from Halki, the beach where they had landed the food supplies was alive with villagers. They ceased what they were doing to cheer the raiders' departure, hurling the odd stick of dynamite into the air in an impromptu firework display to salute Lassen and his Irish Patrol.

The German E Boat turned out to be packed full of supplies, including the obligatory live pigs. It was a fine first strike for the raiders' new Dodecanese campaign. Jellicoe's men had been ordered to decimate the enemy's shipping – but it was even better to seize it for their own purposes.

Not only that, but they'd spirited away an entire Italian garrison and a German ship's crew, as if they had been stolen by ghosts in the night. Nothing was guaranteed more to strike fear into the hearts of the enemy.

But one man aboard Motor Launch 1083 was far from happy. Sean O'Reilly sat on the ship's prow, staring into the dark sea, his face a picture of misery. It was no exaggeration to say that the tough and wizened Irish warrior worshipped the young Danish commander, and to have shot him – even by accident – was mortifying.

It was only when Lassen wandered forward, mug grasped in hand, that O'Reilly sensed forgiveness might be in the offing. Lassen handed O'Reilly the tin mug, which contained a healthy measure of the ship's rum.

'Here. Drink this,' Lassen told him. 'It's all right, Sean, it's all right.'

'But, sir . . .' O'Reilly began. 'Oh, sir . . . But I *shot you*.'

'You did,' Lassen agreed. 'And you may be a bloody Irish gunslinger, but you are still my best soldier. I forgive you. I apologize for what I said. But Sean, *do not* shoot me again.'

The two men shared a moment of companionable silence, before Lassen wandered back to the ship's wheelhouse. He needed some advice from the launch's commander – a Lieutenant Adrian Seligman, a regular on such missions – for Lassen's leg wound presented him with a serious dilemma.

'If I report this bullet hole – a mere fleabite by the way – as being caused by enemy action, they will give me a wound stripe or something foul like that,' Lassen told Seligman. In other words, he'd get a minor decoration for something that didn't warrant it. 'But if I say that it was caused by one of my own men, then he may get into trouble . . . and he is one of my best men. What should I do, Adrian?'

The course of action that the two men set upon was not to report the wound at all. That way, Lassen wouldn't be burdened by an honour that he didn't deserve, and O'Reilly wouldn't face punishment.

Back at their Gulf of Cos hideout, the raiders handed over their Italian and German prisoners for interrogation. Jellicoe had shipped in an Intelligence Sergeant to their Turkish base, a South African ironically named Priestley. There was nothing particularly holy about Priestley's methods. He insisted on the truth, and invariably he got it. At the head of all his prisoner interrogation summaries were the words: 'I will say all I can and all that I know.' Woe betide any prisoner who didn't.

After each and every raid, the key commanders were supposed to file an operational report. These were useful documents that other raiders could potentially learn from. But Lassen the man of action detested all such paperwork. His reports – famously – often consisted of no more than five words: 'Landed. Killed Germans. Fucked off.'

Sutherland and Jellicoe found this hugely frustrating, and they were forever pressing Lassen for more details. Invariably, the Dane's response was hauntingly enigmatic.

'It's done. What else is there to say?'

Lassen's reticence doubtless reflected how the relentless violence and the bloodletting was having a cumulative effect. There was a darkness seeping into the Danish Viking's soul. Each raid; each close-quarter battle; each knifing; each grenade hurled into a unsuspecting crowd of soldiers; each time there was enemy blood on his hands – and by now there was a great deal of it – brought Lassen closer to the realization of his true self: that he was a killer almost without rival.

As a consequence of Lassen downplaying his injury – to anyone who asked he explained it away as 'a mere scratch' – the leg-wound wasn't treated properly and it became infected. Eventually, it was clear that Lassen would have to be sent away for proper medical treatment. So it was that the Dane was shipped out of Turkish waters to a military hospital in Alexandria, Egypt's second city, no doubt cursing O'Reilly every step of the way.

Some days later Lassen was rolled out of the operating theatre comatose with anaesthetic, and placed in a ward next to a Lieutenant Cole. A moment later Pipo appeared seemingly from out of nowhere, and leapt onto Lassen's bed. He sat on his master's chest staring at his unseeing face, a picture of doggie misery. So amusing was it that none of the nursing staff could find it in themselves to send the dog 'home' – not that anyone was particularly sure where Pipo's home might be.

However, the matron soon found out and she made it clear the dog had to go. Fortunately, Lieutenant Cole's wife lived not far from the hospital. Although he wasn't himself allowed out, the feisty lieutenant sneaked out the back way with Pipo under his arm, taking the long route home to his house. There he persuaded his wife to keep a close watch on the Lion of Leros, until Lassen was well enough to come fetch him.

Lassen's condition proved so serious that he was in hospital for two months. Even after he had recovered, Pipo's separation from his beloved master wasn't over. Lassen had taught his dog to do a series of silly and amusing tricks, which proved useful when he wanted to inveigle himself into a pretty girl's affections. If he were out of an evening, he'd send Pipo over to a promising table, and once the girls were fully engaged he'd wander over and introduce himself.

Shortly after Lassen was discharged from hospital, the young Lord Jellicoe announced that he was getting married. The bride to be was a beautiful escapee from a Japanese prison camp. She'd ended up in Beirut while trying to make her way back to Britain. There she'd met Jellicoe and in a whirlwind romance the two were married. The wedding celebrations became something of a wild affair, and Lassen ended up losing his false teeth (he'd knocked his two front teeth out a while ago during training).

More worryingly, he also lost his dog. By the time Lassen was scheduled to return to the raider's Turkish pirate base, Pipo still hadn't been found. He offered O'Reilly seven days' leave on one condition: he had to spend it looking for Pipo. Having only recently shot Lassen, O'Reilly – who could take or leave Lassen's dog – felt obliged to accept. Lassen gave him ten pounds to help fund the search, and left him with orders not to return to the Gulf of Cos sans dog.

For the first four days O'Reilly got drunk. On the fifth he sobered up and realized he was over halfway through his leave and no closer to finding Pipo. The Irishman began to comb the Beirut streets, but in a city even then of some quarter-of-a-million inhabitants he had little luck. On the last day he spied a woman with a dog that resembled Pipo. O'Reilly managed to seize it and smuggle it back to his hotel room. It clearly wasn't Pipo, but with a bit of boot polish smeared on here and there, the dog acquired a half-decent resemblance to Lassen's elusive hound.

Figuring it was better to appear with something rather than nothing, O'Reilly duly presented the dog to Lassen. It took him a while to realize the deception.

'Who do you think you are,' Lassen exploded, 'bringing me that dog, when I have given you seven days' leave?'

O'Reilly, caught red-handed in his deception, had added insult to the injury of the recent bullet wound. Lassen was adamant: *Pipo had to be found*. Together with New Zealander

Stud Stellin, the Irishman returned to the streets of Beirut and Pipo was miraculously tracked down. Lassen decided to keep both dogs – part of his growing menagerie of animals – although he was discomfited to see the two fight, and the tough little Pipo come off second-best.

The Lion of Leros had been defeated: Lassen hoped it wasn't a grim portent of things to come.

Chapter Twenty

While Lassen had been away recuperating in hospital, the raids had gathered pace across the Dodecanese. It was a new recruit to Jellicoe's force, Major Ian Patterson, who had led one of the most daring missions. Major Patterson had been second-in-command of the 11th Parachute Battalion, the unit that had relieved the SBS on Cos, once that island had been seized in the previous campaign. Seeing the SBS in action at close quarters Patterson had expressed a desire to join them, and Jellicoe had accepted.

In early March 1944 Patterson got his chance to prove himself in action. Two of General von Kleemann's motor barges packed full of food, wine and reinforcements were reportedly en route for Cos, via the stopover point of Nisyros. Nisyros is a volcanic island almost exactly circular in shape. It was one of those 'minor' islands that General von Kleemann had ordered be garrisoned only temporarily, in rotation.

Patterson and his force of six men managed to get ashore on Nisyros ahead of the Germans. When the enemy vessels pulled into harbour, Patterson was able to study them from the high ground. Each motor barge was armed with a 20mm cannon, plus machine guns, and there were some two-dozen enemy soldiers and sailors aboard. This was no small, lightly armed force.

One of Patterson's men volunteered to dress as a local and go down to the docks to gather intelligence. In this way they learned from the Mother Superior of a local orphanage what the Germans were intending. For whatever reason they were planning to ship all of the Nisyros orphans to Rhodes, and were scheduled to collect them that very day, at three o'clock.

Patterson went to visit the Mother Superior. She was distraught at the thought of losing all her children. But Patterson sensed here the chance to strike, for the enemy would be dividing their not inconsiderable force.

'Would you be prepared to let me use your orphanage in order to capture the Germans?' he asked.

'Anything,' the Mother Superior sobbed. 'Anything, as long as I can keep my children.'

'Then take them up to the high ground, and stay there until the fighting is over.'

Patterson collected up the children's luggage and laid it out in a neat line in front of the orphanage, as if ready for collection. He positioned his men at strategic firing points around the ancient building, and dressed himself up as a 'friendly' Italian priest.

The Germans proved typically punctual. At just before three, a line of men wound their way up the hill. Patterson the bogus priest was there to receive them. He took the Germans down a narrow passage leading into the orphanage's central refectory, whereupon cries of '*Hände hoch!*' rang out.

The Germans managed to open fire, but their aim was poor. Patterson's raiders returned fire with deadly effect, and a brutal battle at close quarters ensued. At one stage Patterson's gun jammed and he was seized by a German. A fellow raider ran forward and blew the enemy's brains out, so rescuing their commander.

Not a single enemy soldier escaped from the orphanage. Two lay dead, seven were injured and the rest were taken prisoner. With no time to delay, Patterson led his men down to the harbour, armed with a Bren gun, grenades and personal weapons. Patterson got the Bren set up on some high ground and zeroed it in on the enemy boats. Below him, two of his men were creeping forward to surprise the German crewmen, who were lounging about sunning themselves on deck – the gunfight at the orphanage being too distant to be audible to them.

But two Germans had been sent to the orphanage to investigate what the delay might be and where the children were. They blundered into the bloody carnage that had been left inside. They came running down the hill, yelling wild warnings at their comrades on the boats. Patterson cut them down with the first burst from his Bren, then turned it on the two ships. Below him, his men ran forward onto the dockside and tossed grenades into the boats.

Some of the Germans managed to get to the vessels' guns, and they began to return fire. Patterson kept cutting them down from his vantage point, and his men tossed their final grenades. All out of Mills bombs, they resorted to hurling their Lewes bombs into the two ships. The plastic explosives ripped into the vessels, the violent blasts bringing an end to the Germans' resistance. A white flag was raised, and those who could came out with their hands in the air.

The entire population of the island seemed to have watched the battle, and they were exultant at the Germans' defeat. The German captain commanding the boats was less enthused. Defeated by a far smaller force, he put it down to 'the black treachery of the Greeks'. He vowed to be back in Nisyros within six months, to take his revenge. In fact, he sailed with the rest of the German prisoners – aboard the two seized ships – for interrogation under the South African Priestley's baleful gaze: *I will say all I can and all that I know* . . . He was never to see Nisyros again, for a POW camp beckoned.

Patterson's adventures weren't yet over. He set sail that evening in the Motor Launch upon which they had arrived on the island. They were well within Turkish waters when the launch's captain spotted two more barges. Presuming them to be friendly the captain pulled alongside. It was only when they tied up to the nearest vessel that they discovered it was crammed full of German soldiers. There was a third barge on the far side, plus a caique armed with a 3-inch gun.

Undeterred, Patterson grabbed his Tommy Gun and leapt aboard, followed by two others. Moving through the dark confines of the ship, they sowed havoc and terror as the Germans tried and failed to identify friend from foe. The German gunboat opened fire on the British Motor Launch, her 3-inch gun killing two of the British sailors. The captain managed to get away, but not before he realized that Patterson and his two comrades weren't aboard.

Patterson, meanwhile, had fought his way to the front of the barge and seized its twin Breda cannon. He put it to devastating effect on the surviving German troops. When the ammunition was exhausted, he yelled orders at his fighting comrades, and all three of them dived into the sea. They struck out for the coast and managed to make the Turkish shoreline. The following day, still decidedly damp, Patterson and his men made it back to the SBS base by local mules.

The pace of raiding grew ever fiercer. Barely had one force returned than another set sail. With Lassen's opportune attack on Halki, and Patterson's lightning raid on Nisyros, General von Kleemann was being given a run for his money. The general ordered news of any raids to be strictly censored, so that the sense of unease and panic didn't spread any further among his troops. But word leaked out anyway, and at his more distant island outposts General von Kleemann's officers slept far less soundly in their beds.

Yet it was now – just as they were riding high – that the raiders' fortunes were about to turn.

By April 1944 Lassen was back in action with his men. But it was another patrol, led by Captain Bill Blyth, that was to come to grief among these islands. Captain Blyth had served as an instructor in the Scots Guards for three years, before being granted his wish and getting a transfer to the SAS Regiment, from where he was posted to Jellicoe's raiders, in the Dodecanese.

Blyth had been given a mission to raid Halki – where Lassen had fired the opening salvoes of the present campaign – as well as the tiny islet of Alimnia. Just three square miles in area, and sheltering no more than sixty inhabitants, to date Alimnia had been an insignificant player in the wider Dodecanese campaign.

But General von Kleemann had been passed a vital piece of intelligence, indicating that a British SBS unit was heading for those islands. Thirsting to strike back at the raiders – *who come like cats and disappear like ghosts* – von Kleemann dispatched four German gunboats escorted by two submarines. The ships were packed with soldiers from the Brandenburger Regiment, the nearest the Germans then had to Special Forces.

The Brandenburger fighters had been drafted in to help General von Kleemann combat the threat of unconventional warfare presented by the British raiders. The German ships landed a contingent of the Brandenburgers on Halki, plus a further force on Alimnia – with orders to lie in wait for the British force.

At well after midnight on 7 April Blyth and four men were put ashore on Alimnia, but then the converted fishing boat in which they had been travelling was spotted by the enemy. Four German gunboats and one E Boat bore down on her. In the firefight that followed her commander, Sub-Lieutenant Allan Tuckey, decided their situation was hopeless and he ordered his men to surrender.

Tuckey and four others were taken prisoner. They were loaded aboard the German E Boat, which set sail for Rhodes. Blyth's patrol had heard all the gunfire, and from the high ground they'd seen the fate that had befallen the boat's crew. Knowing that Alminia would be crawling with the enemy come daybreak, they persuaded a Greek fishing crew to take them off the island that night.

But en route to the Turkish coast the fishing boat was stopped and searched. As luck would have it, it was the E Boat carrying the five men already taken captive that had intercepted the Greek vessel. Blyth and his fellow fighters were discovered and they were taken captive, along with the hapless Greek fishermen.

In just a few hours all ten men who had set out to raid Halki and Alminia had been captured. They were taken for interrogation first to Rhodes, and then on to Athens, before finally in Blyth's case being sent to Stalag 7A, a POW camp in southern Germany.

The questioning of the captives became increasingly intense and brutal. Repeatedly, they were threatened with Hitler's *Sonderbehandlung* – his infamous Commando Order – decreeing that all such captives be handed over to the *Sicherheitsdienst* (SD), the Security Service of the SS, for termination. By early June 1944, after horrific torture, the interrogation of the captives was deemed complete. All but one were released to the SD for 'special treatment' – in other words, likely execution.

Only Captain Blyth would survive, and that only due to the comparative decency of Colonel Otto Burger, the commandant of Stalag 7A. Twice Colonel Burger was ordered to hand Blyth over to the *Sicherheitsdienst*, and twice he refused. Eventually, the SD seemed to have forgotten about Blyth, and he would survive the war.

Among the nine of Blyth's raiders executed was Corporal Ray Jones, the man who had fought shoulder-to-shoulder with Anders Lassen during the Kastelli Airbase raid.

None of the raiders based in the Gulf of Cos could know of the captives' exact fate: that would only become clear many years after the war. But they were under few illusions as to what would happen to any raiders taken prisoner.

Continuous raiding – month after month, year after year – pushed men to the limits, even those as well trained and self-disciplined as Jellicoe's. The narrow escapes and close shaves took a cumulative toll. Many a raider had hidden under a rock, as a German or Italian hunter patrol had paused to have a smoke sitting astride it. In one instance, a Motor Launch packed full of raiders had rounded a headland, only to discover a German destroyer steaming into its path.

The Motor Launch's commander had ordered: 'Open fire – abandon ship!' almost in the same breath.

The raiders had raked the destroyer's bridge with Bren fire, before diving into the sea and swimming to the nearest landfall. Behind them, the Motor Launch had been blasted into match-wood, but at least they'd managed to make good their escape. Yet it had been by the bare skin of their teeth, and as always the thought of capture and the horrors that would follow played heavily on the raiding man's mind.

Acute stress was a natural consequence of such relentless fighting, and over time even the most unlikely candidate might find himself in danger of what the raiders termed 'crapping out' – not being able to take it any more. Invariably, those who 'crapped out' couldn't face going into action ever again. If a man's nerves cracked during a mission, he became a liability to his fellow raiders. It was something they all dreaded.

Some feared that as Lassen drove himself to extremes, he was going to end up being one of those who 'crapped out'. But there was no sign of anything like that happening just yet.

In the face of what had befallen Captain Blyth's patrol, no one in Jellicoe's raiding force was about to lose it. Quite the reverse, in fact. There was, of course, another reaction to such acutely distressing news – one that the forces gathered in the Gulf of Cos were more inclined to. It was to redouble their efforts, and to wreak a campaign of terror throughout General von Kleemann's command, in an effort to make amends for those friends and comrades who had been executed in cold blood.

Fittingly, the charge would be led by Anders Lassen and the men of his Irish Patrol. It would spawn perhaps the Dane's most infamous raid of all – what would become known as 'The Bloodbath of Santorini'.

Santorini forms part of the Cyclades, a chain of islands lying to the west of the Dodecanese, some 150 miles from the raiders' Gulf of Cos base. Santorini is formed of a rugged and bare chunk of volcanic rock some ten miles long by three wide. Sheer, dour cliffs of black basalt rear out of the waves to a height just short of a thousand feet, offering an uncertain welcome to any visitors sailing through her waters.

Human habitation – ancient castles, aged monasteries and narrow, twisting rows of white-walled houses – clusters along the cliff tops, which sweep in a crescent-shaped ridge through waters as deep as the cliffs are tall, being the remains of a half-collapsed volcanic crater. That crater forms an almost circular harbour – one with the added benefit of warm, sulphurous waters to help the local fishermen de-weed their boats.

Santorini is the southernmost of the Cyclades, so it would be the first targeted by the raiders. It would remind Lassen very much of Fernando Po, the island nation off equatorial Africa where he had launched his career as a piratical raider, some three years and what seemed like a lifetime ago. Now Lassen was a triple MC winner, commanding the toughest of the few – the Irish Patrol – and a man very much on a mission of vengeance.

Jellicoe's plan of attack – approved in early April 1944 – suited those ends perfectly. It called for nothing less than the liquidation of the islands' entire garrison in one dark and bloody night.

The fate that had befallen Captain Blyth's patrol had changed things irrevocably for the raiders. No longer would German prisoners be dined at Groppi's, or taken for a few beers and to the movies. The capture and execution of an entire SBS patrol could not go unavenged or unpunished, and from now on Jellicoe's men would be disinclined to take many prisoners.

Just five days after Blyth's patrol had been listed as 'missing' – and few doubted what that meant in reality – Lassen and his men set sail. From the Greek islanders on Halki they had received snippets of news concerning the fate that had befallen Blyth's unit. It was far better to keep busy, than to let minds linger on what kind of treatment those ten captives were being subjected to.

In targeting Santorini, Lassen would be blessed with an unexpected piece of good fortune. One of their German captives – an *Obergefreiter* Adolf Lange – had yielded vital intelligence under Priestley's relentless questioning. Fortunately for Lassen and his Irish Patrol, Lange had been stationed on Santorini throughout the previous year. With the help of a map he was able to detail the number and location of those garrisoning the island – twenty Germans, with some forty Italians in support – including the site of the island's radio station.

The voyage from the Gulf of Cos to Santorini took three days. It was completed wholly at night, with the two schooners lying-up during the day under their specially-made camouflage netting. On board were many of Lassen's old and bold, and all had scores to settle: Sergeant Jack Nicholson, the *Maid Honour* original and Kastelli Airbase raid veteran, who knew by now that fellow Kastelli raider Ray Jones had fallen into enemy hands; the Irishman Sean O'Reilly, who was determined to make amends for shooting Lassen in the leg during the Halki raid, and for putting him out of action for so long.

But there were also several new faces, many of whom were decidedly light on experience. Lassen's second-in-command for the Santorini mission was Lieutenant Stefan Casulli, a man with the fine good looks that went with coming from a family that could trace its ancestors back to the Greek heroes of old. Casulli's parents were well-known, wealthy Greeks, and they had built for themselves a good life in Alexandria, in Egypt, far from the dark troubles that had overtaken their native land. Casulli – with his classical nose, dark smouldering eyes and sensitive mouth – was married with a young family, and he was under no compulsion to go to war.

Yet upon hearing of the actions of the SBS all across the lands of the Greek people, Casulli had volunteered to join the raiders. Lassen and Casulli shared an instinctive bond: both 'foreigners', Casulli's Greece and Lassen's Denmark were reeling under the

Nazi occupation – one that seemed to grow in savagery and excess, as the Axis fortunes worsened. Lassen had met and befriended Casulli's family, growing especially close to his wife and their one young child. He had a high regard for Casulli's abilities as an officer and a spirited leader of men.

Lassen also had a new medic on his patrol as stand-in for the American Porter Jarrell, who wasn't able to make the Santorini raid: Sergeant Kingston, formerly of the Royal Army Medical Corps (RAMC). Another relative newcomer was Sammy Trafford, who hailed from the Royal Marines. After O'Reilly had had the temerity to accidentally shoot him, Lassen had sought out a new 'bodyguard'. Sammy Trafford was it. In truth, the Dane wasn't really in need of a minder: Trafford was more Lassen's driver, the pilot of his boat, and his personal attendant.

Lastly, there was parachutist Jack Harris, another relatively new recruit, one who had never experienced a full-on Lassen raid. Boosted by those newcomers, Lassen's force was some two-dozen strong.

Sergeant Jack Nicholson, Lassen's veteran right-hand man, welcomed the newcomers to the Irish Patrol with distinctly ominous words, although they were doubtless meant to be somewhat reassuring: 'Coming with the killers, are you? Don't worry. You'll be all right.'

In the early hours of 23 April 1944 Lassen's patrol put ashore on the eastern landfall of Santorini, near Point Vourvolous, an isolated promontory. Having dropped the raiders on a darkened stretch of black volcanic sand, the two schooners sailed for the nearby Christiana islets – isolated rocky outcrops some fifteen miles to the south-west of Santorini. Uninhabited, and surrounded by treacherous rocky ledges and shallows, the Christianas should shelter the two schooners from prying eyes, at least until Lassen and his men were done.

Ashore on Santorini, Lassen's patrol shouldered their weapons and their loads. Ahead of them lay a five-mile trek south-west across the island, towards some caves lying near the village of Vourvoulous. The caves were only ever used by goat-herds, and their local Greek guide knew them to be the ideal place for the raiders to hide-up and gather intelligence for the coming raid.

By 0500 hours the men were safely ensconced in those rocky caverns. Lieutenant Casulli, together with their local guide, headed into Vourvoulous village to gather intelligence. Lassen was keen to verify the numbers of the enemy garrison. If *Obergefreiter* Lange's testimony had been correct, there were sixty German and Italian troops billeted in nearby Fira, Santorini's capital. If so, Lassen's patrol was outnumbered more than three-to-one, and especially as he needed to split it into groups, so as to hit a number of targets simultaneously.

Casulli returned with encouraging news. The garrison was said to number no more than thirty-five mixed Germans and Italians. It was still a significant number, but less than the sixty *Obergefreiter* Lange had reported were there. Lassen was inclined to give up-to-date local intelligence more worth than the reports of a German prisoner some months old. There was one other highly intriguing development: the enemy garrison was billeted above the Bank of Athens. If all went well with the attack, the bank might also be there for the taking.

Lassen split his patrol into three elements. A five-man force would hit the radio station, situated on the Imerovigli headland on the northern outskirts of Fira town. A smaller, three-man force would head for the German commanding officer's house in Fira, with orders to kill him or better still, take him captive. The main force, led by Lassen and Casulli, with twelve ranks in support, would hit the main barracks at the Bank of Athens building, in central Fira.

Zero hour for the attacks was 0045 that night, by which time all three raiding parties were to be in position. A good hour prior to midnight the men set out. The caves at Vourvoulos lie no more than two miles north of Fira. Lassen soon found himself approaching its narrow, twisting streets, the white walls and cobbles ahead of him shimmering in the faint silvery moonlight.

He called his men to a halt. From out of his pocket he produced a wad of paper. He unwrapped it, handing around two pills of Benzedrine to each man.

'I vant you all vide avake,' he whispered, as he watched each swallow his allotment.

Lassen was the last to down his, once he was sure everyone had taken theirs.

Apart from the bark of a dog woken here and there at their passing, the raiders flitted through the streets of Fira as silent and unnoticed as wraiths. Lassen, Casulli and their men reached the main thoroughfare – Theotokopoulou Square – apparently undetected. No alarm had been raised. No shot had been fired. So far, so good.

Lassen paused. The town was a maze of narrow streets and even narrower alleyways, and without their local guides they'd have got hopelessly lost. Lassen sensed they were in the very heart of the labyrinth right now, and that getting out was going to prove as much fun as it had been getting in.

Lassen got his men into cover so they could study the target – the Bank of Athens. All seemed quiet, and there were no sentries that he could detect. But they couldn't afford to presume that none had been set. With news of the British raiders spreading far and wide, many of the enemy garrisons were on a permanent state of alert, which was just how Jellicoe wanted them. German and Italian soldiers had taken to sleeping fully clothed, their weapon only an arm's reach away.

The bank was a daunting target. In the faint light it appeared like some ancient, slumbering, thick-skinned monster – a veritable fortress. To make matters worse, the German and Italian soldiers were billeted on the first floor. Lassen and his men would have to break in, sneak through the ground floor and climb the stairs; all without being detected – and all before they could begin their attack.

Lassen decided to hit the bank from two directions – north and south – to increase the chances of at least one force getting in. He sent half of his men, under Lieutenant Casulli, to the south side, giving them time to get into position.

The seconds ticked by: 0045 hours was almost upon them – the time to launch their concerted attacks.

Chapter Twenty-one

Stealing towards the bank, Lassen and Casulli's patrols managed to link up at the foot of the stairwell which led to the billets above. After a hurried confab in bare whispers, Lassen led the twelve men up the dark staircase, treading on the outer edges of the wooden boards, in an effort to stop them creaking.

The atmosphere was heavy with tension, adrenalin pumping through the raiders' fast-beating hearts. None could believe that their presence in the bank hadn't yet been detected. Whatever awaited these men in the darkness above, one thing was certain: the next few minutes would be defined by fear and brute aggression, intermixed with bloody mayhem and murder.

At the top of the staircase rooms branched off from a landing. Lassen positioned one man on either side of each door, leaving two in the centre as a firebase, and putting one as a guard on the exit, to prevent anyone from escaping that way. His force in position, he blew a short blast on his whistle, at which moment several sets of crepe-soled boots went crashing through wooden doors.

The first grenade was hurled into a sleeping room. 'Grenade gone!' yelled O'Reilly.

All along the landing the raiders opened fire, the muzzles of their Tommy Guns and German Schmeissers sparking in the darkness. In seconds the air was thick with cordite smoke and the punching percussion of further grenades exploding, the blasts echoing deafeningly around the close confines of the bank's interior. But then O'Reilly's Schmeisser jammed. The big Irishman started cursing wildly, as he tried to clear it. What a time for his weapon to get a stoppage.

In all the confusion, and with the darkness rent by blinding blasts, agonized screams and savage bursts of gunfire, Lieutenant Casulli and the medical orderly, Sergeant Kingston, kicked through their target door. As they went to rush the room, their entry was met by an immediate blast of fire from inside. One at least of the enemy had woken up to the attack, and was ready and waiting.

Casulli was hit in the chest and blasted backwards, staggering through the darkness, while Sergeant Kingston collapsed onto the floor. Sammy Trafford – Lassen's 'minder' – was the next to be hit, rounds ripping through his upper arm and left leg. He reeled under the blows. Seconds later a fourth raider went down, Guardsman Jack Harris crying out, 'I've been hit! In the leg! I've been hit!'

Harris managed to stagger down the stairs to the bank's outside terrace – but there was no medic available to treat any of the wounded, for Sergeant Kingston himself was down. Kingston had taken a burst to the stomach, and he was in a bad way.

Lassen had tried to dissuade Kingston from coming on the killing part of the raid. 'You cannot be one of the killers *and* our medical orderly,' Lassen had told him. He'd warned Kingston to stay out of the bank, when the fighting proper began. But

Kingston had wanted a slice of the action, and now he was down and very badly wounded.

Jack Nicholson and Lassen opened fire, pouring bullets into the room from where the enemy fire had come. Nicholson raked it with bursts from his favourite weapon – a big, heavy Bren gun – firing from the hip again and again, so as to keep the enemy pinned down. And when cries in German from outside the bank announced that an enemy patrol had arrived to break the siege, it was Nicholson who drove them off with deadly-accurate fire from the Bren.

Lassen grabbed the chance to regroup his surviving forces – he had four men dead or injured, which meant a third of his patrol had been put out of action. They mustered on the bank's terrace, before smashing their way through a pair of French doors – finding themselves in the main dining area, off of which lay three further rooms. They skirted by the large table and the rifle rack, booted open the first two doors and hurled in grenades.

O'Reilly dashed back onto the landing area. He bent over Casulli's prostrate, bloodied form and grabbed the man's grenades. As far as he could tell Casulli was dead, and O'Reilly needed his Mills bombs, for in the dark chaos of this battle the grenade was the only weapon to use. Cowering in their rooms, there was nowhere for the Germans and Italians to hide from a grenade blast. A fragmenting Mills bomb spread instant terror, confusion, injury and death – giving the raiders that crucial edge.

The middle door leading off the dining room seemed to be locked shut. It couldn't even be booted open. Shots were fired at the lock, and the door riddled with bullets, but still it stood firm. It must have been barricaded from the inside. As Nicholson kicked in the bottom panel of the door, O'Reilly readied one of his scavenged grenades. An instant later the Irishman rolled it through the hole in the splintered wood, the raiders jumping aside to avoid the blast.

Inside that room, as with so many of the others, terrified and panicked enemy soldiers had rushed to the windows – both in an effort to escape the blast and to put down fire onto their attackers. Many didn't seem to realize that the raiders were in their very midst. German and Italian soldiers kept lobbing stick grenades into the streets below, and loosing off long bursts of fire. Of course, they were shooting at empty shadows.

One Italian sergeant tried to jump from his window, but it was a forty-foot drop onto the hard cobbles below. The fall half-killed him, after which shots from the wounded raiders gathered on the terrace finished him off. Others tried to rush the exit that led to the stairway, but Lassen's rearguard had it covered. The garrison manning Santorini were trapped, their fate doubly sealed when Lassen learned that his friend Cassuli had been gunned down.

A cold rage rushed through the Dane. He grabbed Nicholson – after Lassen, the longest-serving and most hardened raider of the lot – and urged that they finish the job. Their orders had been to wipe out the Santorini garrison. Nicholson and Lassen went room-by-room now, hurling first a grenade and following on the heels of the blast with bursts of machine-gun fire.

By the time they were done, their orders had been carried out pretty much to the letter. Lassen was certain that every enemy soldier in that billet was either dead or wounded.

Somehow, the injured medic, Sergeant Kingston, had crawled down the bank steps onto the terrace at the front. From there he'd seen five figures jump from a lower window in an effort to escape. He'd managed to hurl a grenade after them, but his throw had proved too weak and they got away.

The fighting over for now, Lassen gathered his surviving men on the terrace. Sentries were set, as they tried to patch-up Kingston's wounds as best they could. Lassen went to double-check that Lieutenant Casulli was truly beyond help. The Greek officer was indeed dead, and Lassen retrieved from his body his dog tags, his gold chain and his diary – to give to a grieving wife and mother of Casulli's young child, whenever he could make it back to Alexandria.

But right now Egypt was a whole world away, and the battle for Santorini was far from over. Voices were heard from down a narrow alleyway close by the bank. There was no doubt they were German. Nicholson, who'd picked up a smattering of the language, tried to lure them out of hiding.

'*Kommen Sie hierher, Kamerad*' – *come here, friend* – he yelled out.

No figures emerged, so he fired a few probing bursts from his Sten, and the voices quickly died away. It was around 0100 by now, just fifteen minutes into the fight, and Lassen and Nicholson knew that there were German and Italian soldiers unaccounted for. Some had got away by jumping from the windows; others had been out on patrol, or would have been billeted in smaller numbers elsewhere in the town.

The element of surprise was completely blown. The advantage would shift to the defenders, especially if Lassen and his men had to fight their way out of the labyrinth that was Fira town, laden down with their wounded and their dead. With Lieutenant Casulli, Lassen made the tough decision to leave his Greek friend where he had fallen. But there was no question of leaving Sergeant Kingston behind: while there was life there was hope.

A door had been wrenched off its hinges to act as a make-shift stretcher for Sergeant Kingston; it had to be abandoned. It was too wide to fit through some of the narrowest alleyways, or up the steepest stairways. Instead, four men had to each grab one of the wounded sergeant's limbs, and with him spread-eagled between them they hurried into the shadows.

Progress proved painfully slow. Sergeant Kingston was fully conscious and in terrible pain, each jolt causing him agony. They'd barely made 150 yards when they reached an open street junction. As Lassen went to cross it there was a challenge yelled in German.

Lassen yelled back a lightning quick response. '*Kommen Sie hierher!*'

'*Nein! Sie kommen hierher!*' the voice retorted, an immediate burst of machine-gun fire punctuating the words.

Lassen responded with a grenade, hurling it into the open space ahead of him. There was the crack of an explosion, a scream from out of the darkness, followed by the sound of boots pounding down the dark street and fading away. The raiders pressed onwards, heading for the Vourvoulos caves, the agreed rendezvous.

When they were still at least half a mile short of the caves it started to get light. Lassen and Nicholson pressed onwards, leaving the rest of the patrol to bring on the injured – Sergeant

Kingston, plus the two walking wounded. Lassen and Nicholson needed to reach the RV and reassure the others. They found the caves crowded. There were eight German prisoners, all of whom had been seized at the radio station on the Imerovigli headland, whereupon the radio station itself had been blown to pieces.

Unfortunately, the team sent to capture or kill the German commander on Santorini, a Lieutenant Hesse, had just missed nabbing him. As they stole up to the front of the house, they'd heard a murmur of worried voices coming from the rear. They'd dashed around, only to discover Lieutenant Hesse making a run for it together with his orderly. The two Germans had made a clean getaway, so Lieutenant Hesse was presumably still at large somewhere on the island.

There was more worrying news from their local Greek guides. That morning, the Germans had been sighted in the nearby Vourvoulos village. From there and from Fira itself they'd already taken hostages. They were threatening to execute them all, unless the locals revealed where the British raiders were hiding. The islanders – resolute and loyal to the last – had no intention of doing any such thing.

Only a small handful of German and Italian soldiers had been seen out that morning. Reports filtering in suggested that well over twenty enemy soldiers had been wounded or killed at the bank – so with the eight Germans taken prisoner they had lost over thirty men. They had precious few able-bodied men with which to carry out their threatened executions, or to mount a hunt for Lassen's patrol.

But that didn't mean things would remain that way for long. It was vital the raiders get away from the island as soon as possible. Lieutenant Hesse, the German commandant on Santorini, was still at large. He was reported to be a very capable infantry officer, and he would doubtless try to signal for reinforcements – that's if there was a radio anywhere on the island that was still operational.

Having radioed the schooners at their Christiana anchorage, and arranged for a pick-up after nightfall, the raiding force set off, retracing their footsteps to the island's eastern shore. Trafford and Harris were walking wounded. They were just about able to make their own way, Trafford laden down with a heavy Bren gun that no one else seemed able to carry.

By the time they reached the coast Trafford was utterly finished. Lassen told him to lighten his load, by disposing of the Bren. There was plenty more weaponry they could scavenge off the enemy. Lassen's priority was to get his men off that island and safely into Turkish waters. Trafford broke down the Bren into its constituent parts and threw them in the sea.

The two men – commander and bodyguard – fell into step, pressing northwards along the coastline under the punishing sun.

Lassen eyed Trafford's leg wound. 'You're no bloody good as a bodyguard now, Sammy. You'll have to bloody go back. Go back to hospital.' Lassen turned to another of the raiders, shaking his head in mock frustration. 'That bloody Sammy got himself shot. You be my bodyguard now!'

The look in the eyes of the soldier said it all. *Be your bodyguard? No bloody fear!*

Sergeant Kingston had been given morphine for his pain, but few believed that he would make it. The only thing the raiders had been able to find to carry him on was a wooden gate borrowed from a local vineyard. Winston was still fully conscious, but even with the morphine the pain was killing him. And as the raiders themselves had learned, in the Jerusalem killing school – *aim for his guts and he's surely dead.*

Santorini island is bare, rocky and windswept. It was obvious that any movement in broad daylight would be seen by all – surviving German and Italian soldiers included. If the enemy force hadn't been so comprehensively devastated – the radio station wrecked and emptied of its personnel; the bank rendered a bloody killing ground – the raiders would have been hunted to their deaths among the open rocks.

As it was, they made the difficult descent to the black beach without being targeted. They found shelter among some caves, which echoed to the rhythmic crash of the surf. Sergeant Kingston was carried to the nearby home of a family who were known to be fervent supporters of the Allied cause. A doctor was called, but he took one look at the wounded British medic-cum-raider and shook his head. Kingston's wounds were haemorrhaging, and without urgent surgery there was little that could be done. The doctor gave him some more morphine, the better to ease his passing.

It was just after midday when the raiders heard the first shots. The gunfire was distant, and it didn't sound as if it was a two-way firefight. They waited for news of what it might mean. Word was brought by the villagers. The Germans had carried through their threat: they had executed their ten hostages, one of whom was the local mayor. They had issued a further ultimatum – to shoot all the inhabitants of Vourvoulos village, if by nightfall the British raiders hadn't given themselves up.

The villagers were adamant: no way were the raiders going to hand themselves in. But Lassen was boiling up with rage. If the surviving Germans and Italians wanted to meet him in open battle, so be it. But kidnapping and gunning down the locals – it was the kind of brute cowardice and spinelessness that the Dane hated.

Grabbing a pencil and paper, Lassen proceeded to scribble a note to Lieutenant Hesse, the German commander on Santorini. Written in German, it reminded Hesse that his name and likeness were known personally to the British raiders. It alerted him to the fact that he was going to be charged for war crimes, for he was the commander who had ordered the execution of the ten islanders.

It finished with a dire warning against any further such actions:

If there are [any further reprisals] we shall return with 1,000 men and kill every German on the island, and not, as at this time, only with 500.

Lassen's note was handed to the German commander by an enterprising and brave Greek. The threats against the villagers, plus the executions, came to a sudden halt.

Sometime around mid-afternoon Nicholson saw Sergeant Kingston finally fall asleep. He had been in enormous pain, and he'd kept telling the others to leave him, and not to stay for his sake. Nicholson fetched Lassen and they examined the wounded man. Having drifted into a deep sleep, Sergeant Kingston had passed away. They wrapped him in blankets and placed a bible in his hand, after which the locals laid flowers upon him, assuring Lassen and Nicholson that they would give him a proper burial.

The islanders took Sergeant Kingston's body to the church, placed him before the altar, and the entire village emptied of its inhabitants as they went to pray for his soul. Meanwhile, Lassen, Nicholson and the raiders headed for their beachside rendezvous with their pick-up vessels. It was the night after the raid and crucial they get off the island. On the nearby, larger island of Melos there was a German garrison of very significant size, and sooner or later they would send a force to investigate the sudden silence that had fallen over Santorini.

But that night a storm blew up and the sea became greybeaten and wild. Lassen, Nicholson and the others took turns signalling across the wind-whipped breakers with their lights, but there were no answering flashes and no schooner emerged from the dark, foaming sea. Come daybreak, the raiders took shelter in the only place they could find nearby – a monastery. The monks fed and sheltered them, as the first signs of the feared enemy activity appeared in the skies above: four Junkers 88 *Schnellbombers* tore overhead at around three hundred feet, accompanied by two seaplanes, plus a Messerschmitt ME109 fighter plane escort.

The search for the raiders was underway.

All that day Lassen and his men hid. The night proved equally stormy, but Lassen knew he had to get his men off Santorini, for any further delay could be fatal. At around nine o'clock that evening a light flashed a distant reply to the raiders' signals, but it seemed to be coming from very far out to sea.

Eventually, a rowing boat was sighted, riding in on the fierce swell. Lassen managed to get four of the German prisoners into the boat, but when it tried to make the return journey out to sea it promptly capsized.

Lassen's men borrowed another boat from the monks, and with that they managed to get out to the nearest ship. It was a Motor Launch, one brought in to use its powerful engines to try to effect the Santorini rescue. Lassen told the ship's skipper that he would have to come in much closer to the shore. He assured the man that he had studied the depth of water, and it was quite safe to do so. In fact, Lassen had done no such thing – but it convinced the captain to bring his Motor Launch to within spitting distance of the beach.

It was close to four o'clock in the morning by the time all were brought off the island. The Motor Launch and the two schooners would just have time to make the Christiana islets before daybreak. They got there, dropped anchor, camouflaged the boats with nets, and fifteen minutes later a flight of five *Schnellbombers* came tearing overhead searching for the British vessels.

Flights of *Schnellbombers* continued to fly search transects over the Christianas for much of the day, but the boats must have remained undetected, for no bullets or bombs fell.

Three days later, having dodged further search flights, the flotilla of ships made it back to the comparative safety of Turkish waters. They anchored at their hidden base in the Gulf of Cos, handed over the prisoners to Priestley, whereupon the surviving men from the Irish Patrol hit the bottle. They needed to drink long and hard after Santorini – which by now had earned the nickname among the men of 'Andy Lassen's Bloodbath'.

As for Andy Lassen, while he seemed happy to speak of the Germans they had killed, he made little if any mention of Casulli and Kingston's deaths. *It is done. What else is there to say?* Yet everyone knew how much their loss had hit him, especially that of his fine Greek friend Stefan Casulli. For two days the flags on the raiding ships flew at half-mast, in remembrance of Sergeant Kingston and Lieutenant Casulli. And Anders Lassen drank two days of sorrow, like a father who had lost a son.

A few weeks later Lassen made it to Alexandria, where he knew that a young wife had refused to accept the death of her husband. Casulli's widow had said she would only believe it if she heard it direct from Lassen himself. Steeling himself for what was coming, he duly went round to visit her.

'Is it true that Stefan is dead?' she asked of him.

Lassen looked her directly in the face. 'Yes, it is true,' he told her, gently.

Again she asked, and again he told her it was true – Stefan, a much-loved husband and father, was gone.

A short while later a set of German orders were captured during a raid. In spite of the recent losses suffered by Lassen's patrol and others, what they revealed was gratifying in the extreme. It proved absolutely the devastating impact the raids were having on General von Kleemann's island garrisons. Typed across the security instructions in bold and capitals was the following phrase: 'WIR BEFINDEN UNS IN FEINDES LAND.'

The German translates roughly as the following: 'WE ARE LIVING IN AN ENEMY COUNTRY'.

Chapter Twenty-two

In spite of the wild successes of the raiding years, Lassen had lost a good many of his dearest friends – two more now in the Santorini Bloodbath. A dozen of his closest comrades had been killed, and it may have seemed like the Danish Viking's luck was turning.

Perhaps as a foil to his loss Lassen decreed that his dog Pipo should be awarded his SAS wings. Pipo duly had his parade, one of the few that Lassen actually bothered to scrub up for.

Lassen never had been one to abide by Army formalities. Throughout his time soldiering – at Fernando Po, on cross-Channel raids, and throughout the eastern Mediterranean – he and his men had little cause to rub shoulders with the wider British Army, or to conform to their rules. In any case, Jellicoe's – Churchill's – piratical raiders were delivering the goods. The relentless raids across these islands were working, and Jellicoe was winning the war against General von Kleemann's forces.

The Aegean campaign culminated in an iconic victory at the raiders' old stalking ground – the island of Symi. Fittingly, it was Major Jock Lapraik MC, who had led the previous Symi operation – during which Lassen had dived in to test the depth of the harbour – who commanded the force that would target Symi for a second time.

This time, as at Santorini, there would be no quarter given. The Symi raid would deliver a crushing blow to General von Kleemann's forces: for the loss of two Greek officers who drowned while coming ashore, Lapraik's men killed 21 enemy troops and took 151 captive. The raid's success, coupled with the wholesale defeat of the Symi garrison, delivered a devastating blow to the enemy's morale.

Almost of equal importance, some nineteen German caiques were sunk at anchor in Symi harbour, and the Germans' gun emplacements and radio stations were blown to smithereens. Tonnes of enemy supplies were thrown into the sea, and by the time the Germans managed to mount a counter-offensive from Rhodes, their troops stormed ashore to find nothing but the remains of the raiders' breakfasts, plus the bodies of twenty-one of their dead. Everyone else – the entire garrison, officers and ranks alike – had been spirited away.

They come like cats and leave like ghosts.

As a result of raids like those on Santorini and Symi, General von Kleemann was forced to boost the strength of all his island garrisons, thereby tying down more men, war materiel and supplies. Such sudden, violent and deadly night attacks shook his men's morale to the core. The German officers knew that right across the region they were struggling to defend their own billets and installations, never mind trying to keep any kind of grip on the restive Greek islanders.

In short, Jellicoe's men had achieved what had been asked of them: the three-stage plan to imprison von Kleemann's legions in their island bases was bearing fruit. By the time the Allies advanced to take the entirety of Greece, there would be no escape for many of von Kleemann's garrisons – including tens of thousands of German soldiers based upon Rhodes and a string of other islands. Overrun, outflanked, demoralized and trapped, they would be taken prisoner en masse, playing no further part in the war.

It was time for Jellicoe's force to move on. Their pirate base in Turkish waters had played its part in the battle for the Aegean. Churchill had urged Jellicoe to 'play for high stakes', tasking his raiders to 'set the Aegean aflame'. Men like Lassen, Lapraik, Nicholson, Stud Stellin, Porter Jarrell and O'Reilly – not to mention those like Casulli, who had given their lives in the cause – had done just that and more.

But despite the sacrifices made and the successes earned, there were those in the British establishment who decried the activities of the raiders. Foremost among them was the British parliamentarian Simon Wingfield-Digby. Ironically, Wingfield-Digby was the Conservative Member of Parliament for West Dorset, the area where the *Maid Honour* Force and the Small Scale Raiding Force had undergone so much of its early training.

Wingfield-Digby apparently thought that war in the mid-twentieth century could still be a gentlemanly affair. He sought to upbraid Churchill in the House of Commons over the Aegean campaign. 'Is it true, Mr Prime Minister,' he demanded, 'that there is a body of men out in the Aegean Islands, fighting under the Union Flag, that are nothing short of being a band of murderous, renegade cutthroats?'

No doubt Lassen, O'Reilly, Nicholson, Stud Stellin and all – even the American medic-cum-gunman, Porter Jarrell – would have found that description somewhat apposite: they *were* a band of murderous, renegade cutthroats, and damn good at it they were too.

Churchill – rarely a man lost for words – had an entirely suitable riposte for the Honourable Member for West Dorset: 'If you do not take your seat and keep quiet, I will send you out to join them.'

Had Wingfield-Digby accepted Churchill's generous offer – and there is little evidence that he did – he would have joined Jellicoe's men as they embarked upon a wholly new campaign, one marking perhaps the most audacious episode yet of all their raiding activities. The SBS – a few hundred lightly armed men in an assortment of converted fishing boats and small patrol craft; both British vessels and those seized from the enemy – were about to more or less single-handedly liberate the entirety of mainland Greece.

Few countries in Europe have ever been won with such a light force overcoming such mighty odds.

The SBS handed over the Aegean campaign to the Greek Sacred Squadron and Jellicoe's raiders withdrew from the Gulf of Cos. Turkish waters were to see them no more.

Under Jellicoe, who'd just been promoted to Brigadier, the SBS and a handful of associated units – chiefly some RAF Regiment men – were regrouped to form a unit codenamed, with wonderful irony, Bucketforce. Jellicoe's appointment as Brigadier was a deliberate stratagem, and all part of the bluff. It helped give the false impression that he commanded a full brigade of men, instead of a beg, borrow and steal force of a few hundred raiders.

Churchill wanted Jellicoe to liberate Greece, to help relieve the pressure on Allied forces slogging it out with the German enemy as they tried to push into northern Italy. As with the previous island campaigns, the more enemy forces Jellicoe's raiders could tie down, capture or trap, the better. Initially conceived as a minor attack on an aerodrome, Bucketforce's assault morphed into what was to become the liberation of almost the entirety of the country.

On 24 September 1944 Bucketforce parachuted onto the south-west corner of mainland Greece, seizing the airfield at Araxos to form a bridgehead.

Having seized Araxos, Jellicoe's force began pushing west towards the Greek capital, Athens. Wherever German and Italian garrisons were encountered who didn't seem inclined to surrender, the raiders used bluff, theatre and subterfuge – interspersed with some very aggressive raiding – to force a way through. With his men outnumbered many times over, Jellicoe and his key commanders demanded the Germans surrender, 'or face annihilation'. The bluff kept working, as his raiders swept the demoralized Axis troops aside.

Lassen, meanwhile, was given the role of leading a seaborne force island-hopping towards the Greek capital . . . and so the race to liberate Athens was on. Across a dozen or more islands – Spetsia, Hydra, Paros, Aegina and many more – Lassen never knew what to expect. On some, the German and Italian garrisons had already withdrawn, their will to resist utterly exhausted. On others, the German garrisons were drowning their sorrows in strong local liquor, and in their cups they were more than ready to fight.

It was mid-October when Lassen and his fleet of ships began their approach to Athens, via the port at Piraeus. Jellicoe's force was also making its final push on the city, and it looked as if they would arrive more or less simultaneously, from land and sea. By now Lassen's seaborne raiders had gathered 100-odd vessels. A fleet of Greek warships had been added to the SBS's usual motley collection of caiques, schooners and Motor Launches.

The voyage north to Athens proved an unforgettable experience, one rich in emotion. The Greek coast was still dark – a faint band of golden light in the east presaging dawn. Many of the ships were crewed by Greeks, men who hadn't seen their homeland since the Germans had driven them out, four long, war-torn years before. The route ahead passed through a series of minefields, and at the head of the convoy sailed the mine-sweepers, clearing the path.

As the sun rose it touched the sea, lighting up the columns of water thrown up by the exploding mines with a burnished gold. Three vessels, including one minesweeper, were lost to the mines, but the convoy proved unstoppable. As the ships approached Piraeus harbour the Greek population lined the shore, shooting off rockets and coloured flares in celebration. There were German forces still in the city, but no one doubted for one moment that the liberation of Athens was at hand.

A thick, white mist blanketed the dawn harbour. Out of its swirling mass rose the columns of the Acropolis, washed pink in the early morning light. Those Greeks aboard the ships stood in silent wonder, many with tears rolling down their cheeks. Lassen and his fellow raiders were likewise choked with emotion. They had lived, fought, suffered and bled alongside the Greeks for so long now – and finally, victory seemed to be at hand.

There were no words for such a moment. If only Lieutenant Stefan Casulli had lived to see this day, instead of being shot to death during the Santorini raid just a few months earlier. Such were the vagaries of war.

The Greek vessels were under the command of Andre Londos, a dark and bearded Lieutenant-Commander who'd long-served with the SBS's fleet of raiding ships. Now, he was effectively commanding the Greek Navy in exile, as it returned to liberate the Greek nation. As the church bells rang, and the crowds cheered wildly, he searched the shore with his eyes.

'Where are my children?' he asked, again and again.

Suddenly, he spotted them, running along the quayside to keep pace with his ship. It was just one of countless joyous reunions that early morning on the Piraeus quay, as mothers found sons, and wives found husbands they had long feared dead.

As the ships docked, the quayside rang with the cries of: 'Angli! Angli! Angli!'

While Lassen wasn't strictly speaking British, he had fought for four years in Britain's cause. He was happy enough to be carried through the streets, to be showered with carnations and roses and to be plied with fine wine. Fittingly, Lassen linked up with Jellicoe at the Grande Bretagne – arguably Athens's largest and finest hotel – and the liberation of the great city was complete.

Athens was a hungry city, but far from being a ruin – and she and her people certainly knew how to celebrate. Party followed feast followed dance, and for sure Jellicoe's men needed such distractions. For years now they had lived a hard, tough life, with few if any comforts and beset by danger on all sides. So many nights had been spent on hard mountainsides, in freezing caves, on snow-covered ridges, or in the midst of an enemy-occupied village; it had become a luxury just to sleep on the hard wooden deck of a schooner or a caique. So often, death was only ever a heartbeat away.

For officers like Anders Lassen there had been the added burdens – the weight of command; the responsibility he felt for those under his authority. Few officers have ever nurtured such a dissolute and maverick group of fighting men, earning their love, loyalty and respect in return. Lassen had shaped and honed his Irish Patrol with great care, and for a few short weeks in ancient Athens the raiders were able to shrug off their burdens, and to celebrate life and the liberation of that magical city.

They joined the Athenians in partying as if there were no tomorrow – which for some there doubtless wouldn't be. Anders Lassen, the sole surviving *Maid Honour* original, had been in the raiding business for longer perhaps than anyone. No one partied harder than the Danish Viking. He seemed driven to extract the absolute maximum from life in the time that was available to him.

Lassen managed to get his hands on a jeep, so he was able to roar around the city streets from assignation to assignation. One night while he was carousing the jeep was stolen. No matter. In a city awash with pleasure, partying and unrest in equal measure, Lassen stole a jeep from some American forces recently arrived in town. Once the licence plates were switched, as far as the raiders were concerned the jeep had become SBS property.

Lassen was loath to lose a second jeep, so he took to parking it in the only secure place he could think of: he drove it up the steps of the hotel, into the capacious lift, and had it transported up to the floor his room was on. All was fine until one night the lift got stuck. Lassen sent for some of his Irish Patrol, and together – via a combination of brute force, beer and ignorance – they managed to free the lift and get the jeep parked properly once again.

A few days later Lassen swapped rooms with one of his fellow officers, a young SBS captain only recently married. That man only had eyes for his wife back home, and he seemed admirably blind to the charms of the local ladies. That night he was asleep in his room – formerly Lassen's – when the door burst open and a furious gunman rushed in. He made for the bed, loosed off several shots and stormed out again.

Luckily, the SBS captain had only been hit in the leg. It turned out that the gunman was a Greek officer just recently returned to Athens. Upon his homecoming, he'd discovered that a dashing blond Scandinavian SBS officer had been paying his wife very close attentions, and the only thing to do in the circumstances was to shoot him.

Lassen loved everything Athenian, just as he had thrilled to the Greek islanders. But even here, even now, there was an undercurrent of tension and unrest deep within. Lassen seemed driven to get back to what he did best: waging war. Tiring of the Athens party scene, he hungered for action. Still he was driven to pursue and attack. And Jellicoe was about to give him the mission of a lifetime – one that would enable him to harass and confound the enemy as never before.

Athens lies towards the southern tip of the Greek mainland. At the opposite end of the landmass lies Salonika (Thessaloniki), Greece's second city, on the far eastern coast. With its superlative port facilities, Salonika was a vital trading and commercial hub. It was known to be heavily garrisoned by the enemy. The mission given to Lassen by Jellicoe – codenamed with suitable irreverence Scrumforce – was to clear Greece's eastern coastline of the enemy from one end to the other, an expanse of territory leading up to Salonika.

Athens was one of the first European capital cities to be liberated by the Allies, and it was much in the news. War correspondents had descended on the city en masse. As a result, Donald Grant of *Look* magazine no longer had the scoop on Jellicoe's raiders. After years of semi-secrecy – there had long been whispers in newsrooms of 'the long-haired boys', the 'secret raiders of the Aegean', and to 'rings of steel' being thrown around this or that island – the full glare of publicity was turned upon the unit.

For Lassen, arguably the most famous – or infamous – raider of all, it was time to be moving on. A reporter like Grant – one who carried a gun and shared with them the rigours and dangers of a mission – was Lassen's kind of man. He didn't care a great deal for the regular, mainstream press pack. And anyway, Lassen had his new mission: Scrumforce was calling.

Scrumforce was part of a larger operation, codenamed – with Jellicoe's characteristic dry humour – Pomforce. Pomforce consisted of an army cobbled together from whatever was available, and spearheaded by the raiders. Bolted onto the SBS were the 4th Independent Parachute Battalion, an RAF Regiment unit, plus a battery of 75mm field guns. In all it amounted to some 950 men, under the overall command of Jellicoe.

Its mission – 'a mad expedition' according to many – was to harass and hound the retreating enemy and to chase them out of Greece. Small, fast-moving raider forces were to attack the Germans' rear, and block the roads leading northwards – cutting off the enemy's retreat, and forcing those troops so trapped to capitulate, with Lassen doing similar along the coast.

Lassen – who had just been promoted to Major – departed Athens on 22 October, with forty raiders under his command. In Motor Launches they sped northwards, island-hopping once again as they searched for any enemy who wished to capitulate, or those who might choose to stand and fight. Frustratingly for Lassen, there were few of the latter: the greatest danger they seemed to face was stumbling onto enemy minefields – for in their retreat, the Germans had sown the ground liberally with mines.

On one island Lassen and Stud Stellin went ashore, only for one of them to trip over a wire laid at ground level. They knew instantly that this was a minefield. Frozen in their tracks, they glanced all around, noticing the silvery threads of wires strung across the earth in all directions. They proceeded to tie a piece of string to one of the wires, and with eyes peeled they gingerly backed away, moving as if treading on razor blades.

They took cover behind a stone wall and gave a quick tug on the string. The next instant there was a massive explosion and blasted stones and earth rained down upon them. Lassen and Stellin locked eyes. If that first tripwire had triggered the mine as intended, the consequences would have been dire indeed. It was sheer luck that the trigger mechanism had malfunctioned. Typically, Lassen and Stellin had a good laugh about it. They could laugh, of course, having escaped without getting their legs blown off.

They come like cats. Indeed they had, but Lassen was fast using up all of a cat's nine lives.

Chapter Twenty-three

Other than minefields, the retreating German forces had left behind scorched earth and burned houses, and a traumatized local population. Everywhere were villages plagued by hunger. Lassen called a halt outside of one. Tired, hungry and cold, he and his patrol brewed up some tea. Children were drawn to the fire. One of Lassen's men sliced open a big tin of biscuits with his fighting knife. The children formed a circle, hungry eyes staring silently at the tin.

'Give them the biscuits,' Lassen ordered.

The tin was handed over, without properly thinking through the consequences. As famished kids thrust their hands in to get some, several ended up cutting themselves on the sharp, jagged edges. Lassen was furious, but his anger soon turned to concern. He got the children to form a line, and with iodine and dressings he began to treat each one. Having suffered so many traumas at the hands of foreigners, it was testament to Lassen's innate affection for these people that none of the kids flinched before him, or ran. They could read the heartfelt kindness in his eyes.

It was as Lassen led his Irish Patrol island-hopping along the Greek coast that an extraordinary confrontation arose, one that perfectly defines the Danish commander's unique relationship to his men. Lassen's patrol had formed a scouting party for a unit of British troops who were landing on a small and largely uninhabited island. Few if any enemy were expected, but still it had to be cleared.

The SBS raiders came ashore first, and they soon established that there were no enemy forces present on the island. Nevertheless, the captain of the main force came charging off his landing craft, plunging into chest-high water, pistol in one hand and cane in the other, and urging his men to follow his lead. Two of Lassen's veteran raiders, Dick Holmes and Roger Wright, watched him storm ashore, struggling to contain their laughter.

'Best get out of those wet clothes,' Wright shouted over. 'You'll get your death of cold.'

The officer tried his best to ignore the remark, ordering his men to dig in on the beach. But soaked to the skin, and most likely incensed at Wright's words he finally came marching over. Wright and Holmes were sheltering behind a dry stone wall having a ciggie and getting a brew on, while they prepared to cook up some breakfast.

'Why aren't you men digging in?' the officer demanded.

'We don't do that sort of thing,' Holmes replied, 'especially when there are no enemy in the vicinity.'

'Anyway, we've got nothing to dig with,' Wright added.

The officer fetched an entrenching tool – a small, foldable spade – from one of his men. He handed it to Holmes. 'You have now.'

Holmes took it, dug out a shovelful of earth, handed the tool to Wright and smiled. 'Your turn.'

Wright took a swift dig, threw the dirt over his shoulder, then handed the shovel back to the officer. 'Why are we digging in? There are no fucking Germans anywhere on the island.'

The officer stared at the two men dumbfounded, as they went about preparing their morning feed. He seemed utterly lost for words. He stormed over to his commanding officer, and started gesticulating angrily in the raiders' direction. The senior officer, a major, came marching over, Wright and Holmes coming to an easy kind of attention.

'Don't you men salute officers?' the major barked.

'Not often, sir,' Holmes replied.

'Never on active service, sir,' added Wright.

The commanding officer was steaming. 'And why is that?'

'Might provide enemy snipers with a target,' Wright ventured.

'You said there are no enemy on the island,' the major snapped.

Wright shrugged. 'We've been wrong before.'

The major looked the men over from head to toe, an expression almost of revulsion spreading across his features. Holmes was dressed in his massive calf-length Canadian paratroop boots, topped off by shorts and a windproof, hooded smock stained with the detritus from several raids – including food, gun oil, sweat, mud and the odd spot of blood (not his own). A webbing belt at his waist supported a water bottle, a Fairbairn-Sykes fighting knife, a holster carrying a Colt .45 pistol, plus a homemade canvas pouch holding three spare Tommy Gun magazines.

Wright was equally snappily dressed.

'Who – are – you?' the major demanded.

'Sergeant Holmes.'

'Sergeant Wright.'

'Do you always dress like this?' he snapped.

'Only on active service, sir,' Wright replied.

'Well, why aren't you men digging in?' the major blustered.

Holmes shook his head. 'We don't do that sort of thing.'

'I'm ordering you to,' the major thundered.

Holmes looked at Wright, and Wright looked at Holmes.

'Well, we're not doing it,' they replied.

That was it, the major snapped. 'Mr Watson, put these men under close arrest!'

Two riflemen hurried over. 'Disarm them!' the major barked.

'No, I don't think so,' Holmes remarked, with quiet menace.

The major stood facing the two SBS men, steam practically coming out of his ears. 'But you are in the Army!' he cried.

Holmes smiled. 'Well, only sort of, you know, in a way . . .'

'More of it, than in it,' Wright added, cryptically. 'Look, sir, to settle all of this, our major's just along the beach. Send someone along for Lassen and he'll sort things out.'

Seeing as though he was at something of an impasse, the major agreed. A runner was sent for Lassen.

Minutes later he appeared. He strode across the beach dressed in similar fashion to his men, only with the ribbon of his MC sewn over his left breast, with the two silvery shapes cut from the lid of a Players cigarette tin to denote the bars.

'What the hell's going on?' Lassen asked, as an opener.

The major was staring at Lassen all agog at his 'unconventional' appearance. 'Are these two of your men?' he demanded.

Lassen nodded. 'Yes.'

'Well, they refused to obey a direct order.'

'What was the order?' Lassen asked.

'I told them to dig in.'

Lassen snorted, derisively. 'Oh, we don't do that sort of shit. We've got better things to do with our time.'

The major opened his mouth and closed it again, like a fish drowning. 'But look how they're dressed!' he blurted out.

Lassen took a long, hard look up and down the man. 'You don't need to get dressed up to kill Germans,' he grated. He pointed in Holmes's direction. 'That's Sergeant Holmes. He won the MM for singlehandedly destroying a fuel dump in Crete in 1943 . . . as well as many other successful raids. The other man is Sergeant Wright, also an MM. Both of these men have been in the army since the outbreak of the war and they have probably killed more Germans than you have ever seen.'

The major couldn't think of anything to say.

'Now, if you've finished with my men I'll take them with me. We've got better things to do than dig fucking holes.' With that he turned on his heels and strode away.

Holmes and Wright picked up their folbot and followed after, plodding along the sand of the seashore.

Holmes glanced ahead at the distinctive figure of Lassen, then back at Wright. 'You know, sometimes I love that man.'

Landing on islands that the enemy had already evacuated didn't exactly satisfy Lassen's all-consuming desire for battle; to fight, or to die in the cause. Accordingly, he decided to seize the initiative and advance on Salonika itself. Strictly speaking, his orders only allowed for him to recce the region, but he gambled upon Jellicoe backing him if he were successful in taking the city. However, he faced one seemingly insurmountable problem. He'd just received orders to leave half of his men behind on the island of Skiathos, to consolidate the territory he and his men had seized.

Moving on Salonika involved a push into totally uncharted territory. No Allied forces had operated that far north, yet not a man on Lassen's patrol wanted to be left behind. While Lassen sometimes bent and twisted the rules, and often exceeded his orders, he never directly disobeyed them. He had far too much respect for Jellicoe to do that. But if Salonika – still garrisoned by hundreds of German troops – was to be taken, he would need every fighting man that he could muster.

During the months and years spent operating in the Mediterranean, Lassen's patrol in particular had gathered a coterie of camp followers – people who had attached themselves to the Irish Patrol, almost as Pipo had attached himself to Lassen. Indeed, Lassen had gathered several more strays by now, his second favourite after Pipo being Dog Tom, one whose evil smell seemed to pre-announce his arrival. His assorted human camp followers consisted of volunteer barbers, cooks, mechanics and the like – and when Lassen considered his orders to 'divide his force', it was the camp followers that he chose to leave behind (temporarily).

By such a subtle reinterpretation of his orders Lassen managed to muster some forty men-at-arms. He decided to sail north in two caiques – as opposed to the Motor Launches – for the caiques could easily pass as the local fishing vessels they once were. They would be pushing one hundred miles beyond any other Allied

323

forces, and the last thing the Germans would be expecting was Lassen's raiders to appear in their midst at Salonika.

One of the two caiques was captained by Lieutenant Alec McLeod, a very capable operator from the Royal Marine Commandos. McLeod would need all his seaborne experience for the coming mission, for the route ahead lay across some of the most heavily mined stretches of water in the entire Mediterranean. The other caique was commanded by a Lieutenant Martin Solomon, a man who would play a key role in the coming action, which at times would do justice to a Hollywood movie script.

Over the preceding weeks Solomon had become an apparently unlikely companion to the Danish Viking. He was short, chubby and forever cheerful, in contrast to Lassen's tall, lean, icy wolfishness. There was nothing about Solomon's appearance or pre-war background that suggested a particular toughness: after studies at Cambridge University, he had been a manager for some up-and-coming actors before the war.

But looks can be deceptive. Solomon had won the Distinguished Service Cross in 1940 at Dunkirk, and a bar to the DSC when commanding a Motor Torpedo Boat off North Africa in 1942. Since then he'd distinguished himself during several seaborne raids across the Greek Islands, and Lassen knew well Solomon had the heart of a steely-eyed warrior.

It was dusk when Lassen's patrol set sail, with his purloined American jeep lashed down on one of the caiques and camouflaged under a tarpaulin. Pulling around the northern tip of Skiathos, the caiques were able to hug the coast, for the water remained deep right up to the shore. They sailed past the wooded spit lying on the island's northern tip, the waters ahead appearing millpond-calm and mesmerizing in the evening light.

All of a sudden a sound pierced the stillness, as unexpected as it was moving. The lilting tones of bagpipes rang out from the wooded shoreline, echoing across the sea, the water lit almost blood red with the sun's dying light. One of those Lassen had been forced to leave behind was piping a plaintive farewell.

Disguised as local fishermen, Lassen's force pushed through sixty miles of seas menaced by minefields. Staring through his field glasses Lassen was able to study the German positions along the shore – for the approach to Salonika was heavily fortified. Lassen could see German troops evacuating their gun emplacements, in preparation for what had to be a full-scale withdrawal. His greatest fear was what havoc the retreating enemy might wreak on Salonika and its people; his challenge how he might insert his force into the heart of that city, to try to stop them.

Four days after setting sail, the two caiques pulled into the tiny harbour of Potidaea, lying some thirty miles to the south-east of Salonika in the Gulf of Thermaikos – the long finger of sea that stretches north to Salonika itself. Lassen's caiques pushed up the Roman-era Potidaea Canal, a short stretch of man-made waterway linking the Gulf to the Bay of Toroneos on the far side, where they were able to moor up and hide well out of sight of any prying eyes.

Once his ships were safely hidden, Lassen found he had other priorities on his mind. It was dawn, and he fancied making a deep-penetration recce up country.

With some difficulty his men managed to manhandle the jeep ashore, whereupon Lassen set off at his customary murderous pace. He had with him Sammy Trafford, his 'minder' – now fully recovered from his Santorini Bloodbath injury – Martin Solomon, his somewhat portly, but nonetheless fearless comrade, plus a Greek fighter called Jason Mavrikis, who had long been part of their company.

Lieutenant Mavrikis hailed from the Greek Sacred Squadron, but in early 1944 he'd been attached to Lassen more or less permanently as his translator. The Greek officer had bonded with the Danish Viking, especially over their shared sense of humour.

'Lassen had the real type of humour, not just jokes,' Mavrikis explained. 'Real humour – meaning he could see things from the other side; understand and laugh about what he was doing. He could laugh about himself, which is the hardest thing a person can do.

'He was collecting somehow, respect; a bit of fear of what he would do next, and definitely we would follow him blindfolded wherever he wanted to go. Whatever he wanted to do we were with him – no question about that . . . knowing that he was the best leader of all.'

Lassen, Solomon and Mavrikis headed north on the coastal road that links Potidaea to Salonika, passing through territory still entirely controlled by the enemy. Greek villagers they encountered along the route mistook the blond-haired soldier at the jeep's wheel for a German, and everywhere they fled before him. It was hardly surprising: the rest of Allied forces were one hundred miles or more to the south, and none were expected here any time soon. More to the point, German atrocities in this region had been no less extreme than elsewhere, and in some villages there were rumours of children being deliberately burned to death.

Just after nightfall Lassen and his men stopped in some thick forest to answer the call of nature. As the rumble of the jeep's engine died away, they caught the sounds of voices in the trees. Whoever it was, they were speaking German. Lassen's eyes lit up. Here was the very thing he sought: the chance to seize some captives for interrogation.

Lassen and his men stole through the darkened woodland. They discovered three German soldiers in a clearing, gathered around an armoured car. They were chatting away unconcernedly. Unsurprisingly, they had not the slightest idea that British raiders might be in the area, and they must have presumed the jeep was one of their own. When Lassen and his men burst forth from the shadows, Tommy Guns, Schmeissers and a Bren levelled at the Germans, all three surrendered immediately to the cries of '*Hände hoch!*'

The prisoners were crammed aboard the already overloaded jeep, and Lassen put his foot to the floor for the journey back to Potidaea. Upon reaching the harbour, the German prisoners were worried to see a number of heavily-armed Greeks among the raiders' party. The Germans knew full well how much the Greeks detested them. They gave up their watches, gold rings and cigarette lighters to the Greek fighters without so much as a murmur of complaint.

From the captives Lassen learned what he needed to know. For more than a week now the German forces in Salonika had been blowing apart the city's harbour. The port area had been comprehensively destroyed. Two massive ships had been sunk in the harbour entrance; the main seawall had fifteen massive holes blasted in it; forty smaller vessels had been scuttled along the quayside; all the wharfs, derricks and associated harbourside facilities had been burned down and demolished.

Earlier that day Lassen had been in radio contact with Raider Force HQ. He'd been told that a force of 9,000 British and Allied troops was mustering, preparing to set sail for Salonika to seize it from the enemy. The trouble was, with the port lying in ruins, there would be nowhere for that force to land. Moreover, by the time they reached Salonika there would be precious little of any value or wartime significance worth saving.

In light of what he now knew Lassen sent a cable back to HQ: 'If you do not get here fast we intend to take Salonika ourselves.'

By 'ourselves' he meant Scrumforce – some forty assorted Special Forces raiders.

With that idea now firmly implanted in his mind, Lassen briefed Mavrikis on what he intended, for the Greek would have a vital role to play. The following morning they set off up-country, to launch stage one of the grand deception to assist with taking the city. It was four o'clock by the time they had located the headquarters of the resistance, who here consisted of the communist ELAS (the Greek People's Liberation Army), a group closely allied to the Russians.

In recent weeks ELAS had proven themselves woefully unenthusiastic about fighting the Germans. They seemed happy to let them withdraw from Greece largely unmolested – as if fighting the Nazis was someone else's war now. Their attitude infuriated Lassen, and he proceeded to give their leader, one Colonel Papathanasion, a stiff tongue-lashing. Lassen challenged the Colonel and his men to prove their honour and to fight. Shamed by his words and stung into action, the ELAS were whipped into a force willing to do battle once more.

But Lassen wasn't done yet. It was now time for what he'd called Operation Undercut, the first part of his great deception. He asked the ELAS commanders to point out to him exactly where the German minefields were situated. Poring over a map, he feigned a keen interest in an area far to their east – the seaport of Kavala, towards the Bulgarian border. During a break in the conversation, a couple of ELAS fighters drew Jason Mavrikis to one side. They asked him why Lassen was so interested in minefields and the defences up around that one particular area – Kavala?

It was now that Mavrikis played his part to perfection. 'A very large Allied convoy with an armada of warships and at least three Army divisions has just set sail,' he confided to his fellow Greeks. 'They have heavy armour and artillery in support, and they are awaiting our signal to start the invasion of northern Greece – either here at Salonika or at Kavala. We're here to complete a recce and to call them in.'

Mavrikis claimed that the British III Corps – a Corps that existed pretty much in name only; one used extensively for deception purposes during the war – was positioned to sweep in and seize the entirety of northern Greece. He sketched out on a scrap of paper the order of battle of the Corps, which consisted of the fearsome 34th and 57th Infantry Divisions, plus the elite 5th Airborne Division (none of which in truth existed).

Mavrikis had let this 'slip' in the knowledge that the ELAS would feed the information back to their Russian allies, and knowing that word would almost certainly reach the Germans stationed in and around Salonika. By sleight of hand, Lassen's force of forty with two converted fishing-boats had just grown to one of 30,000 men, backed by warships, artillery and armour. Hopefully by the time news of it reached German ears, it would have been boosted to 100,000-strong.

The following morning Lassen moved his force up to the outskirts of the city, using the caiques. There was the odd exchange of gunfire, but for now his men were ordered to avoid any major confrontations or pitched battles. Having established a temporary base in a deserted schoolhouse on the outskirts of the city, Lassen decided a closer recce of Salonika was required – to better plan their means and route of entry.

During the advance on Athens, Lassen had procured for himself a battered grey suit and hat, of the kind worn by the locals. The hat was a vital part of his disguise, for he'd used it to cover up his hair on the previous occasions when he'd had to pose as a Greek villager. Now, on the outskirts of Salonika, he donned suit and hat again, this time accepting a novel modification to the disguise – a brace of chickens offered him by Mavrikis. They were tied at the feet, so he could carry them slung over his arm.

With Mavrikis swinging a basket of eggs and Lassen his chickens, the two men strode into town, acting as if they were locals off to the marketplace. Lassen didn't for one moment underestimate the dangers of heading into Greece's second city in this way. But he needed hard, actionable intelligence with which to plan the next, most audacious stage of the Salonika deception – and that made the risks worth the taking.

'He gave a fine example to people,' was how Jack Mann described Lassen's apparently fearless behaviour. 'No one could stop him. Once he was going he was going, and once they saw what he did his men followed him anywhere. He was in the front and he never gave an order which he wouldn't do himself. That was Andy.'

So it was that Lassen and Mavrikis wandered into the centre of Salonika, along narrow, twisting passageways thronged with street traders hawking every kind of ware imaginable. Complete with their chickens and eggs they blended in perfectly. While the two men strolled back and forth Mavrikis asked the questions of the locals, providing whispered translations of the few snippets that Lassen failed to catch.

From this Lassen learned that the Germans had withdrawn to the west of the city, in preparation for pulling out completely. They were intending to take the road north-east to Bulgaria, but their number had been considerably weakened already, especially by desertions. A good number of the German commander's men had baulked at the long retreat north towards Germany. There were many unfortunate Poles, Serbs, Russians and other non-Germans press-ganged into Hitler's military. Any number had seen the writing on the wall and slipped away.

Even some of the diehard German Nazis were sensing the way the wind was blowing. The locals were able to relate to Lassen-the-chicken-seller a revealing story. A team of German demolition experts had been sent to blow up Salonika's main power station. But they'd offered the city's inhabitants an alternative: if they could pay them off in gold, they'd make sure the explosive charges did no damage. A loud bang might be heard, but that was easy enough to manufacture. For the equivalent of £100 in gold, they'd keep the power on in Salonika.

Lassen sensed a rare *legitimate* use here for some of their gold sovereigns. If the price could be bargained down to something more reasonable – say £25 – then he'd pay it. As Lassen and Mavrikis turned eastwards to return to their base, a series of loud blasts rocked the city. A pall of black smoke rose high above the area of the airport. It was a powerful reminder – if one were needed – of the urgency of taking the city before all was laid waste.

The intelligence that Lassen had gained via his walkabout proved crucial: the eastern part of the city was devoid of enemy; the battalion garrisoning Salonika had been seriously weakened by desertions; morale – even among the most ardent Nazis – was low. In the SBS major's view, if the right elements could be pulled together, Salonika was there for the taking.

All that day Lassen got his lone jeep blasting back and forth across the high ground, from where it was bound to be seen by the enemy. From various vantage points they loosed off shots against known enemy positions, even using a pair of PIAT antitank bazookas to mimic artillery pieces. The PIATs were fired by launching their grenade rounds in a high arc over the city, as opposed to how they were intended to be used – in a flat trajectory against tanks, bunkers or armour.

The impression given by Lassen's jeep-borne raiders was of a major force gathering on the eastern high-ground overlooking the city. Next, Lassen sent an ultimatum to the German commander in Salonika. It warned him that a Brigade of elite British troops had the city largely surrounded, being an advance force for the 30,000 men and war machines of the British III Corps, now sailing north into the Gulf of Thermaikos. He demanded the Germans surrender.

A message was returned care of the Swiss Red Cross worker who was stationed in Salonika, and acting as Lassen's go-between. The German commander asked for forty-eight hours to vacate the city. If the British held off from attacking him for two days, then he would withdraw his forces without a fight. Lassen sensed a bluff here, in response to his own breath-taking gamble. The German commander was trying to play for time, most likely in an effort to establish if the British really did have him surrounded.

Lassen was having none of it. If he granted the German commander the time he'd asked for, he had little doubt that what remained of Salonika would be blasted into further ruin. The Dane rejected the German commander's terms outright.

Lassen issued a counter-ultimatum: *surrender, or prepare to be annihilated.*

Chapter Twenty-four

Martin Solomon set out that evening in Lassen's jeep, to see if they could secure the first victory of the coming battle – the surrender of a German garrison manning a gun emplacement that blocked their advance. Under cover of darkness Solomon and his men ambushed and destroyed a German truck carrying supplies to that position, after which Solomon penned a note in German demanding that the battery commander surrender, as his position was 'completely surrounded'.

While one of the Greeks scurried off to deliver the note, Solomon and his small force found themselves with unexpected company. Two German soldiers had been drinking Ouzo at a local café, and had presumed that Solomon and his men – with their Schmeissers and German forage caps – were fellow brothers of the Thousand Year Reich. Solomon promptly took the two Germans prisoner.

But that was to be the last of their good fortune that night. Throaty growls echoed out of the darkness, and suddenly Solomon and his raiders found themselves face-to-face with a pair of German tanks, plus six self-propelled guns and several truck-loads of grey-uniformed infantry. These enemy troops and their war machines certainly looked businesslike enough! Driving the two prisoners before them at gunpoint, Solomon and his men hurried off in the other direction and made good their escape in the darkness.

But an awful realization now hit Solomon. In his haste to get away he had left behind Anders Lassen's beloved jeep. He and his men sat in the woods all night long, shivering in the cold and trying to keep their prisoners quiet. Just prior to dawn they were able to sneak back to where they'd left the jeep, and repossess it. They loaded the prisoners aboard, fired up the engine and tore back towards their base.

Once there, Solomon briefed Lassen about the strength of German armour and troops that he had encountered, plus the prisoners he'd seized for interrogation. To round things off, he confessed somewhat sheepishly to having almost lost Lassen's jeep.

'Well done, Martin, very well done!' Lassen replied. Then his eyes flashed dangerously. 'But had you not brought back the jeep I would have slit your throat.'

For the liberation of Salonika Lassen needed transport to get his men into the city. The only thing he could lay his hands on were four of the city's fire engines. Never averse to a bit of theatre, Lassen ordered his men to mount up their dusty red steeds. With his jeep taking the lead and with the Lion of Leros – Pipo – beside him, Lassen led Scrumforce towards the German-held city.

But even a parade of fire engines bristling with weaponry wasn't enough for the Dane. Lassen knew he had to give the impression that a major force was liberating Salonika for his bluff to stand any chance of working. It was a Sunday, the weather was warm and balmy for the time of year, and Lassen's sense of occasion demanded more.

'We need a scout!' he declared. 'A rider in the vanguard!'

A horse was commandeered. Sammy Trafford – Lassen's 'minder' – confessed to having a degree of riding experience from before the war, gained while working on a farm. He mounted the horse bareback and rode ahead of the column, his trusty Bren gun in one hand and an improvised bridle in the other, looking like a Hollywood Injun chief leading his braves into battle.

The parade took on a carnival atmosphere as the procession made its way along the city's main thoroughfare, the Via Egnatia, fire engines ringing their bells for victory. It appeared as if the long-awaited liberation was at hand, and the tanned and war-bitten warriors were showered with gratitude: flowers rained down, bouquets of fragrant herbs were pressed into their hands, and pretty girls climbed onto the running-boards and the fire-ladders to join them. Scores of ELAS partisans had come to join the liberation parade, bandoliers of ammo slung around their chests in distinctly war-like fashion.

Elderly Greek women pressed gifts of eggs, goat's cheese and honey upon the raiders. Bottles of Ouzo were passed around, as the men toasted Salonika's freedom, and grabbed the chance of a quick snog with a local lady delirious with liberation. Oiled by the Ouzo, the raiders started singing a popular comic song of the war, Bing Crosby's 1943 hit 'Pistol Packing Momma'. Somehow, it captured absolutely the spirit and the essence of the moment.

At the main square the ELAS political leadership had gathered for a spot of speechifying and parades. This was a golden opportunity for the communists to claim some of the glory for driving the hated Nazis out of the nation's second city. But even as they prepared to speak, a series of deep, powerful explosions rolled across the city from the dockside. The demolition was continuing, the Germans intent on leaving little in Salonika that wasn't a blasted ruin.

Sniffing danger; the enemy; *war* . . . Lassen completely ignored the assembled speechmakers. He waved his column of fighters forward. As they passed out of the square and headed into the narrow maze of streets that led towards the docks, so the atmosphere began noticeably to darken. The girls, the cheering crowds, the gift-laden grandmas – all gradually melted away as the column pushed westwards. Sammy Trafford abandoned his horse, and climbed aboard the lead vehicle.

Lassen ordered his men to thunder about in their fire engines, honking their horns and sirens and blowing up any opportune targets they could find – using grenades, Molotov cocktails or simply torching them with cans of petrol. The appearance he wanted to give was that a large British force was moving through the city and that serious battle had been joined. Columns of thick black smoke rose above the skyline, adding to that impression.

From his position atop his fire engine, Sammy Trafford swept the terrain to their front with his Bren gun. To either side there were piles of shattered masonry, fields of broken glass and heaps of blasted machinery.

Among Jellicoe's officers, Lassen was known as the one blessed with the most incredible luck. In spite of the near-insanity of many of his missions, rarely had Lassen lost men under his command. He was also blessed with an instinct that seemed to enable him to sense the presence of the enemy in that crucial split-second before the enemy detected him.

That extraordinary sixth-sense came to the fore now.

All of a sudden he yelled: '*Stop!*'

He signalled his colourful column to a halt. To either side of the road there were death's heads crudely daubed in black paint on rough boards, marking the borders of minefields. Rolls of barbed Dannert wire had been slung around strategically-important installations, one of which – a fuel dump – was sign-posted in the distinctive German gothic script used by the *Wehrmacht*, the German military: '*Treibstofflager*'.

That fuel dump was no more than fifty yards away, and Lassen sensed that here they would find their first enemy. The force of forty-odd raiders dismounted from their engines, their bright red flanks glinting somewhat inappropriately in the warm sunshine, and they crept through the narrow confines of the streets. Lassen was at the fore, Sammy Trafford with his Bren on one shoulder, and the solid form of Martin Solomon on the other.

Lassen led his men to within such close range of the German enemy that they could overhear their conversations. A unit of sappers – demolitions experts – were busy laying their charges at the fuel dump. To the outer edges of the *Treibstofflager* were a few dozen German guards, keeping watch as the sappers went about their work.

Some of the raiders, eager for battle and fuelled up with the Ouzo, wanted to charge the enemy in a frontal assault. The irrepressible O'Reilly was in the vanguard, but Lassen argued against it. Such an attack over open ground would be almost suicidal. Instead, he split his force into two, one part of which would hit the fuel dump from the rear. He got his men into good cover, from where the ambush could be sprung. He wanted every weapon to be brought to bear in a scything attack. They needed to win a decisive victory in keeping with the bluff – that a thousand crack British troops were in the process of taking the city.

On Lassen's call his force opened up with forty submachineguns, plus their Brens, and the handful of weapons that the few ELAS troops who had stuck with them managed to bring to bear. For a few moments the sappers tried to return fire, but they were cut down in their droves. Again and again their positions were raked with murderous volleys of fire, the Bren gunners each burning through a dozen magazines of rounds.

Finally, with the raiders running painfully low on ammunition, the surviving sappers and their guard force turned and ran. The Germans had a column of trucks lined up at the fuel dump's exit gate. They swarmed aboard like ants. But as they tried to pull away the raiders turned their guns on the vehicles. Bullets tore through glass, shattering it into storms of blinding splinters. Grenades punched through thin steel, finding the soft human targets clambering about inside.

By the time the battle was over, estimates of the enemy losses were as many as sixty dead and wounded. Lassen's force had suffered just the one casualty – a raider shot in the shoulder.

With the battle of the *Treibstofflager* done and dusted, the German commander in Salonika seemed to lose all further appetite for the fight. Though his force outnumbered Lassen's many times over, it seemed he had bought the bluff. The following morning a long column of German military vehicles began to pull out of the city, as he evacuated it to the last man.

A pall of smoke lay over the last of the German positions, his departing troops torching whatever they couldn't take with them. But much of the city had been saved. By now the red, white and blue of Union Jacks had largely replaced the ELAS banners that had festooned the city streets: it was clear to the city's inhabitants who the real liberators were.

On seeing the flags, Lassen turned to Solomon, who sat beside him in the jeep. 'England's prestige has been saved,' he quipped. 'Now we can have a bit of a fling!'

One of the greatest bluffs of the war – forty butcher-and-bolt raiders posing as a battalion of elite British soldiers – had paid off. But before the partying proper could get underway, Lassen had to send a cable to Jellicoe.

'I have the honour to report that I am in Salonika,' he wrote.

'Give your estimated time of arrival Athens,' Jellicoe cabled back, curtly.

Jellicoe knew that in taking Salonika Lassen had overstepped his orders, hence the message recalling him to base. But at the same time Jellicoe was well aware of the kind of men that he had under his command, officers included. His attitude to such maverick risk-taking was summed up in the phrase: *all's well that ends well.*

In any case, curt message or no, Lassen wasn't about to return to Athens any time soon. For a good week the Danish SBS major became the de facto ruler of Greece's second city, a conurbation of some 150,000 inhabitants. Lassen upheld laws, passed verdicts on disputes, and generally tried to keep a lid on things. Salonika was a seething mass of chaos and exuberance, on a par with post-liberation Athens just a few weeks earlier. There were scores of enemy deserters in the city – Italians, Bulgarians and even a few Germans – which made Lassen's job all the more tricky.

But there was one group of people who were noticeable only by their absence. Salonika had been purged entirely of its Jews. Since Biblical times it had had a large Jewish population, but by the autumn of 1944 every single Jew was gone. They had allegedly been shipped to Krakow, in Poland, but a captured German soldier confirmed that there were no Jews in Krakow any more. Indeed, he'd been told that the Krakow Jews had been deported to Salonika.

Lassen, Solomon and others felt deeply the suffering of the Greek nation, whether Jew or Gentile. Lassen railed at how sinister and evil was this liquidation of an entire Greek people. Yet despite such unspeakable atrocities there was work to be done. He sat side by side with Solomon in Salonika's Hotel Mediterranean, trying to keep a lid on this wild city, particularly the ELAS fighters, who were seeking to settle old scores and take revenge for long-held grievances.

'Andy and I prevent riots and murder, we pass laws, we pardon and we pass sentences,' Solomon wrote, in a rare letter home. 'If we had not come and acted as we did, much blood would have been spilt . . . Andy and I have experienced together the greatest joys and sorrows – in adversity, as on Leros and in victory as here in Salonika. For some reason or other he feels the same for me as I feel for him. He once said to me, almost with tears in his eyes: "Martin, you are a great soldier." That is the best praise I have ever received.'

There were some in Salonika who had profited from the German occupation. There are always quislings, collaborators and profiteers, even among a noble people like the Greeks. Any number came to Lassen, seeking to convert their ill-gotten gains – chiefly looted art, jewellery and gold – into ready cash. In the name of punishing them Lassen took it all, telling whoever came that he would expedite their request, where-upon he promptly distributed the loot around his men. Few of the chancers felt able to complain when nothing materialized in return.

And of course, along with all the hard work came hard play. Naturally, the war-bitten but handsome and supremely confi-dent major proved the uncontested favourite with the ladies in Salonika. One night as his men caroused in the hotel grounds, Lassen emerged naked apart from his boots, shouting: 'Chaps, can't you let your CO screw in peace?'

It wasn't until nine days after Salonika's liberation that the main British force – the 9,000 promised Allied troops – made it to the city. Had Lassen and his men waited for them to get there, Salonika and its people would have been in a far worse state. A British intelligence assessment of the action subsequently concluded:

But for Lassen and his band, Salonika would not have been evacuated as soon as 30 October 1944. The town would have suffered greater destruction. His solitary jeep and few troops were seen everywhere; behind the enemy's lines, with ELAS in the mountains. Their numbers and strength were magnified into many hundreds of men with automatic weapons. Prisoners taken confirm this, their estimate never being less than one thousand men.

Jason Mavrikis, Lassen's translator and Greek Sacred Squadron veteran, put it more succinctly: 'The whole of Salonika was in the streets, and Anders Lassen was something to the local people, because the day before he had negotiated with the Germans and he really managed to save large and important installations, especially the harbour.'

But Lassen, the hero of Salonika, soon tired of acting as city governor. With Athens and Salonika having fallen, all of Greece would soon be in Allied hands.

In recent weeks Lassen had found himself increasingly drawn to the 'big war' – that which would inevitably throw him into close contact with the regular military. 'We must go to the big war,' he kept telling his comrades in the SBS, plus anyone in higher command who might listen. Quite what his force of maverick pirate-raiders might be called upon to do in the 'big war' remained unclear – but Lassen was determined that he and his men would play their part.

The nearest 'big war' was Italy, but in the fierce winter of 1944/45 Allied forces were bogged down in the snows and mud. Northern Italy had become a long and brutal war of attrition, in which neither side was gaining much ground. It was not a war in which Lassen could see an obvious niche for his kind of small-scale raiding operations, but with the coming spring offensive all of that was about change.

Lassen's almost unrivalled reputation for delivering unlimited violence in the night and the darkness, ensured that his desire to go to the 'big war' would not fall upon deaf ears.

Porter Jarrell, the American medic-cum-raider, had been at Lassen's side all through Athens and Salonika and for everything in-between. Like so many of Lassen's raiders, Jarrell saw himself as being especially close to the man who commanded the Irish Patrol; this enigmatic leader had the ability to draw fellow warriors close, while revealing little of his private self.

In spite of Lassen's closed, intensely self-contained nature, Jarrell could tell how murderously hard the Dane was driving himself. As November 1944 in Salonika turned into January 1945 somewhere on the road to Italy, Jarrell feared where his commander's restlessness and battle-hunger was leading him. Lassen had survived four years of constant raiding – action that had killed off every one of his original comrades, and more. Yet it was as if he felt the guilt of the survivor, and was driven by a terrible death wish.

'It was as if a fever was burning inside him,' Jarrell remarked. 'He defied death and exposed himself to the greatest dangers. He was like a restless dynamo, charged with energy . . . When he was on leave it was as if he knew he had courted disaster too often and had to fill those short hours with the life that was running away from him.'

'He didn't seem to know the word fear,' Jack Mann remarked. 'He was a go-getter. He would organize the raids, prepare for it, and he was the real killer . . . You knew he never knew how long he had. He never thought about dying, but he thought – "Well, you know, I may as well have some fun when I'm not fighting . . ." '

Jarrell feared for Lassen's very survival. 'Life had become a race against death. He had already become a legend – but a legend about a human being – full of contrasts in his many-sided character. A legend which bore the unmistakable stamp of his personality.'

That unique and compelling personality – one intensely proud of his soldiers and hugely protective of them; one largely dismissive of rigid military hierarchies – would be to the fore as Lassen led his men into combat in Northern Italy.

Chapter Twenty-five

Lassen turned up in Italy complete with a Volkswagen *Kubelwagen* – the open-topped jeep-like vehicle used extensively by the German military – that he had purloined from the enemy. He also had with him the veterans of his Irish Patrol, plus Pipo – the mischievous Lion of Leros. Unfortunately, the evil-smelling Dog Tom had somehow been left behind.

Yet now that his wish had been granted and he'd got to join the 'big war', Lassen would find himself increasingly fettered by its rules and confounded by its regulations. At first he tore around northern Italy in that *Kubelwagen* looking for some suitable work for his men, but only for so long. One day the British Military Police stopped him and confiscated the vehicle. They didn't seem to understand the concept of such things being seized as the 'booty' of war.

Lassen's repeatedly cabled headquarters to get Dog Tom sent on to him in Italy. 'Kindly send Dog Tom, two jeeps and a barber,' read the first. No response was forthcoming. A second was sent. 'Where is Dog Tom – stop. Lassen beginning to show symptoms of anxiety neurosis – stop.' That too went unanswered.

No Dog Tom was ever forthcoming, and in truth a newly arrived NCO had taken advantage of the Danish major and his dog being separated, and Dog Tom had been shot. Rules and regulations seemed to define and shape everything in the new world order that was Italy with the regular Army.

'The practise of wearing unit headgear at other than the regulation angle will cease forthwith . . .'

'Articles of Enemy personal apparel, toilet items, cameras etc. will in future be described in the correct terminology. They will *not* be referred to as "liberated".'

All this was anathema to Lassen and his Irish Patrol, and at times they must have wondered what on earth they were doing in such a theatre of war.

'The rest of the British Army hated us,' remarked Dick Holmes. 'They disliked us intensely. I mean, no doubt about it we were arrogant bastards. We walked around with scarves on, carried guns, most of us had shoulder holsters and one thing or another that we'd picked up along the way, guns concealed in our pockets somewhere – little Berettas and stuff.'

Little of this kind of behaviour seemed acceptable now that Lassen and his Irish Patrol had joined the 'big war'. The Viking raider's frame of mind wasn't improved much by the attitude of some of the regular Army officers he encountered. They seemed to view his Special Duty raiders as truly a villainous bunch – a band of ragged, renegade, warn-torn desperadoes.

'Your men are a disgrace,' one officer declared to Lassen. 'They are not even shaved! You are not even shaved! What will the enemy think if they see you dead looking like this?'

Lassen's hand went to the hilt of his Fairbairn-Sykes fighting knife: 'Speak of my men like that again, and I'll slit your throat.'

Gradually, bit-by-bit, Lassen's way of waging war was being eroded by an Army High Command who resented the Special

Duty volunteers and their unique *esprit de corps*. As the war shifted in focus away from small-scale operations behind enemy lines to large-scale set-piece battles, the regular Army High Command was gaining the upper hand.

Lassen found himself having to issue orders that ran against everything the Special Forces raiders had long stood for. This one was typical: 'The flogging of kit for personal gain is prohibited.' But he had asked to be a part of the 'big war' and now he was here. He'd made his bed: he was going to have to lie in it.

Lassen had made it to the 'big war' chiefly due to a request by Brigadier Reginald Tod, of the 2nd Special Service Brigade (a unit consisting largely of Royal Marine Commandos). The brigadier, who knew Lassen well, had seen an opening for him and his men in a forthcoming crucial operation – the attempt to break through the German lines and kick-start the stalled Allied offensive.

The conquest of Italy had been spearheaded by the British Eighth Army, working in conjunction with American forces. The Eighth Army had pushed as far north as the Bologna plain, capturing such towns and cities as Forli, Faenza and Ravenna, but their offensive had stalled in bitter fighting, exacerbated by the freezing winter mud and snows. To the west of their positions, the American advance had likewise come to a halt in the rugged foothills of the Apennine Mountains.

Allied forces had thus been halted some 200 miles south of the Austrian border, and just 250 miles short of German territory itself – taking them tantalizingly close to the heartland of Hitler's Reich. Operation Husky – the liberation of

Europe via Sicily and her soft underbelly – was coming up trumps, but only if the logjam on the Bologna plain could be broken, and Hitler was doing everything in his power to ensure that it wouldn't be.

Hitler had ordered the German army to stand firm on their present lines, and not to retreat to stronger positions along the northern Italian Alps. They had twenty-seven divisions manning their front, with good supplies of ammunition. Their morale remained high, and Hitler had demanded that every last inch of Italian soil be rigorously defended. Yet Churchill was convinced that a breakthrough here would spell disaster for the Germans, opening the way for the advance on the Fatherland itself.

The River Po lay between the German forces and the refuge of the Alps. Churchill believed that defeat south of there would deliver a knockout blow – and the Allied commanders, Field Marshal Alexander and American General Mark Clark set their minds to engineering such a defeat.

'If we could break through the Adriatic flank and reach the Po quickly all the German armies would be cut off and forced to surrender,' Churchill argued. It was to this that Alexander and Clark bent their efforts when the stage was set for the final battle.

At the eastern end of the Bologna plain lies the Lower Romagna, a flat, marshy coastal region beginning around Argenta and terminating on Italy's eastern coast in the Adriatic Sea. Dykes, canals and numerous rivers crisscross this region, and in the warmer months its waterways are the breeding ground for clouds of ferocious mosquitoes.

The Eighth Army's front line terminated at its eastern end at Lake Comacchio – in truth a 'lake' in name only. Comacchio was but the most evil-smelling, treacherous, mud-choked patch of shallow, bog-water, among many such swamplands in the Lower Romagna. And perhaps because it ran counter to any easy logic – and thus would be the route of attack least expected by the enemy – it was at Comacchio that Allied forces had decided to attempt their spring breakthrough.

Brigadier Tod, commanding No. 9 Commando and assorted other supporting units, held the front line at Comacchio. Lake Comacchio is some twenty miles by fifteen, and across its length and breadth the average depth of water is no more than two feet; everywhere the lake was plagued by muddy shallows and treacherous sandflats. To the lake's eastern flank lay a narrow spit of scrub-covered sand, which was all that separated the lake from the sea. To the west, the lake petered out into a skein of waterways, quagmires and bogs.

If he could abide the stench and avoid the quicksand, a child could paddle for miles from the fringes of the lake, without the water ever reaching above his knees. Over the millennia the local inhabitants had tried to carve the odd channel through the lake, to try to ease passage from one side to the other, but with little intention of lingering on its stagnant waters. The only vaguely edible things to be caught in Comacchio were thin, tasteless eels, and otherwise it was a rank-smelling, mosquito-plagued death-trap.

But Brigadier Tod saw something else in Comacchio's stagnant expanse. The sand spit separating the lake from the sea was heavily mined and rigged with formidable fortifications.

But if a force could somehow cross the lake undetected and hit the enemy by surprise from the rear, the spit would be there for the taking. If the northern shore of the lake could be held to form a bridgehead, the German positions set to both the west and east of the lake would have been comprehensively outflanked.

Brigadier Tod believed his Commandos were capable of crossing the lake, taking the spit from the rear, and establishing a bridgehead on the northern shore. Thus Lake Comacchio was regarded as being the unlikely – but vital – point of break-through to kick-start the Eighth Army's spring offensive.

What Brigadier Tod needed prior to that was a comprehensive intelligence picture drawn up of the lake, its defences and the usable routes of ingress. He also needed a force to guide his commandos onto target come the night of the attack, one capable of mounting some form of diversionary action.

There was only one unit he could think of with the experience, the skills, the bravery and the sheer gall to undertake such a mission – one that would entail working under the very noses of the enemy in impossible terrain and with absolutely zero cover. This was a job for Anders Lassen and his Irish Patrol.

The mission to take Comacchio was codenamed Operation Roast. The challenges in Operation Roast – both for Lassen's men and those of 9 Commando – were legion. On the night of the assault 1,000 heavily armed men would need to cross many miles of lake undetected. Only the southern fringes of the water lay in Allied hands. The western, northern and eastern shorelines were held by the enemy. Few if any of the channels across the lake had been charted, even in the memory of the locals.

In the centre of the lake lay a handful of 'islands' – uncertain mounds of earth rising barely above the waters, and thickly wooded. One or two ancient buildings lay on the islands, but these had long fallen into disrepair and ruin. The islands were believed to be held by the enemy, but no one on the Allied side knew for certain.

Across such terrain watched by the enemy from all sides Brigadier Tod's Commandos would have to go, with neither sight nor sound of their progress being detected. Lake Comacchio would offer zero cover. If unusual movement or abnormal sounds were detected from the water, the enemy scouts would fire flares, illuminating the desolate expanse of stagnant lake for miles around.

If the men of 9 Commando, or Lassen's Irish Patrol, were so caught, they would be annihilated.

Clearly, if any engine noise were detected on the lake it would attract a barrage of murderous fire from the enemy. Thus, Lassen and his men – plus the Commando force to follow – would have to cross such terrain in Goatley boats, canoes and on floats, using only silent, human means of propulsion – the paddle. When empty, a Goatley has a draft of about one inch. When loaded with ten heavily armed commandos its draft is approaching two feet – the average depth of Comacchio.

It was absolutely vital to the mission's success that Lassen and his men explore and map Comacchio's deep channels – those that might exist – and somehow mark such passages across the deathly shallows.

At the end of March 1945 Lassen's force moved up to the nearby city of Ravenna, bringing with them their folbots, Goatleys and 'Jellicoe' Inflatable Intruders – their rubber assault craft. Lassen immediately made himself busy, zipping about in a jeep to get a sense of the terrain they would be operating over. Briefing followed briefing, as senior officers queued up to give their input into this vital first stage of the planned Allied break-through.

Lassen was used to operating more or less in isolation from senior officers, and unburdened by the chain of command. At Ravenna, things were very different. Where Operation Roast was concerned, everyone and their dog seemed to want to put their proverbial oar in, and it wasn't much to the Dane's liking.

At one briefing, and in the midst of a long speech by a colonel, Lassen rose abruptly to his feet. 'I go now,' he announced.

With that he turned and left the room. Lassen's legendary reputation, not to mention the sheer force of his persona, meant that no one thought to try to stop him.

In the last days of March the Danish major broke away from this suffocating environment, and got down to business. He busied himself on the lake with his men. The days were spent sleeping and updating the intelligence files, the nights out on the water. On one occasion Lassen pushed as far north as Comacchio town itself. There, as in Venice, many of the 'streets' consisted of waterways, and it was possible to paddle right into the centre of the town.

As a result of such night-time sorties, the large map in Brigadier Tod's headquarters became full of coloured pins, each noting a particular feature of the lake, a navigable channel or an enemy position. The full picture on Lake Comacchio was slowly being pieced together, but there were few among Lassen's men who liked what they saw. The lake was nigh on impossible to operate on covertly, and even the veterans of the Irish Patrol felt a growing sense of unease.

If he could help it, Lassen never went on a mission without the unshakeable O'Reilly. He believed it a bad omen if he were forced to sally forth without the Guardsman at his side. But out on Comacchio's haunted waters even O'Reilly felt a cold, clawing sense of dread. Fred Crouch was another old hand who was daunted by the mission that lay before them. He confided to one of his fellows that he'd had a vision of his own death out on the cursed lake, his body sinking into the dark and fetid waters.

Even their veteran commander's actions were starting to be a source of worry to the men. Lassen had always been a risk-taker, but here at Comacchio he seemed to be actively courting danger. During his night visit to Comacchio town he had only narrowly escaped capture.

On another foray he'd paddled his canoe close enough to the enemy sentry positions to eavesdrop on their conversations. He hadn't done so with any intelligence-gathering aim in mind. He'd done so almost to bait the enemy. He'd proceeded to smoke a cigarette as the German voices had drifted across to him, and when one of his fellow raiders had asked what on earth he thought he was doing, Lassen had practically bitten the man's head off.

The wholly unnecessary risks that he was taking horrified many in his patrol. Porter Jarrell, Jack Nicholson, Sean O'Reilly,

Martin Solomon, Dick Holmes, Stud Stellin, Sammy Trafford – none of Lassen's hardcore of operators had ever seen him like this before.

It was almost as if he was actively seeking for that dreadful death wish to be fulfilled.

At dusk of 3 April 1945 Lassen's force moved out to 'occupy' the lake. They climbed into their Army trucks for the drive to the shore, where their boats were pulled up in the cover of some bushes. They loaded the canoes with everything they needed for the coming days – weapons, ammunition, radios and batteries, water and food.

That done, the men brewed tea on the lakeside and waited until it was completely dark. There were thirty two-man canoes lined up ready to take to Comacchio's unwelcoming waters. It was one of the largest missions that Lassen had ever commanded, and it was by far the most daunting.

Finally, the major gave the orders for the men to follow his lead. Amid the sucking slurp of gumboots struggling through the mud, the canoes were carried down to the water. One by one the craft were hauled out into the muddy quagmire, until each was swallowed in the darkness. There followed a long push through the shallows, until there was enough depth to let each pair of men climb into their canoe.

Their intended destination tonight was the island of Casone Agosta, some six miles out on the lake. The crossing took most of the night. Repeatedly, the raiders had to climb out of their heavily laden craft and manhandle them over slick, stinking mud-banks. Stud Stellin managed to overturn his craft completely, getting soaked in the process and losing much of his kit and part of the radio set.

When the raiders finally reached Casone Agosta it proved to be totally devoid of any cover. The only option was to pull the craft ashore and camouflage them with cut bracken. That done, the exhausted men had to dig crude foxholes and sheet them over with camouflage netting. By sunrise, the sixty men and their canoes on Casone Agosta had apparently disappeared.

All that day Lassen, O'Reilly, Stud Stellin and the others lay still and silent in their holes. Swarms of mosquitoes feasted on their blood, but few could afford to swipe them away. The nearest German position was four hundreds yards away. Before the heat of the day rose to unbearable levels the men tried to snatch a few hours' sleep.

Around mid-morning Stud Stellin awoke to find a large-framed figure sitting bolt upright, still wrapped in his camo-netting.

'Get down!' Stellin hissed. 'Get down, or I'll bloody shoot.'

It was only then that he realized the sitting figure looked very much like Major Lassen.

A few minutes later Lassen crawled over to Stud's foxhole. 'Good morning, Captain Stellin,' he smiled. 'Will you give me the pleasure in having breakfast with me? Unfortunately, I can only offer you minced bacon.'

In spite of himself Stellin had to smile. 'Was that you sitting up like a big idiot just now?'

Lassen laughed that it was, and Stellin couldn't help but join in the dark humour. No matter what way they looked at it, the situation they found themselves in was so horribly exposed and indefensible, it was absolutely absurd.

All that day the men remained trapped in their shallow holes, eating, sleeping and defecating where they lay. Only come nightfall were they able to crawl out and stretch and ease cramped limbs. Then the canoes were uncovered, eased into the water, and the second stage of their infiltration began. Their objective now was the largest island, Casone Caldiro, lying towards the northern end of the lake.

It was well after midnight when the canoeists reached their next landfall, a small island lying between the two. Lassen went first, checking for any enemy. The island was found to be unoccupied, and he left Stud Stellin there, complete with a small force tasked to hold the main force's rear. Lassen also left Stellin with some sappers, whose job it was to check for mines, leaving white tape marking the cleared areas, so the commandos could follow on in some degree of safety.

Lassen led the main force onwards into the night. Unbeknown to them, a boat carrying four Germans was also out on the water. It happened to be making for the island where Stud Stellin was even now digging in with his patrol. The German boat landed there completely unawares, and Stellin took four prisoners. This was great for intelligence-gathering purposes, but not so good for remaining undetected. When German patrols went missing, others tended to come looking.

The main island, Casone Caldiro, also proved to be devoid of the enemy. Having checked over a ruined building and assured himself that the entire expanse of land was clear, Lassen ordered his men to dig some proper shelter. If the Germans realized they were here, they'd doubtless shell the island, and there was very little if any natural cover.

The other main problem – apart from remaining undetected – was water. There was a well located within the ruins, but it proved to have only a few inches of dirty, stagnant liquid in the bottom. Still, Lassen and his men knew they would die unless they had water: they forced themselves to drink the murky dregs. And then they steeled themselves for whatever the next few hours might bring.

Three further boatloads of Germans were out on the lake. They rowed past the little island where Stud Stellin and his patrol were dug-in. Stellin could tell they were making for Casone Caldiro, the main island. He let them draw well ahead of his position, before he ordered his men to open fire. It might blow their cover, but he felt he had to warn Lassen that a force of enemy was inbound, and this was the only way he could think of doing so.

Rounds tore across the lake, shattering the tense stillness. Tracer fire lit up the water around the three target boats, as if a swarm of giant, supercharged fireflies were zipping across the lake. In the glare, Lassen and his men spotted the enemy, and Lassen ordered his force to open fire. The Germans were caught in the crossfire from both islands, with absolutely nowhere to take cover or hide.

This was what the men of the SBS had themselves dreaded: getting seen and targeted out on Comacchio's open water. Those Germans who tried to bail out got sucked into the mud, and stuck fast. They were gunned down wherever they became immobilized. Those who tried to stick with their flimsy craft were torn to pieces by the raiders' fire. Just five Germans made it to Lassen's position alive, and they only managed to do so by hoisting the white flag of surrender.

Those five turned out to be Brandenburgers – the same elite troops that Lassen and his men had run into during their Aegean campaign, when the Brandenburgers had been drafted in to help General von Kleemann defend his islands. Under questioning, they yielded vital intelligence, but almost of more importance were the supplies of fresh water that they carried. The Germans knew there was none to be had on the islands, and they'd come well prepared. They'd also brought a quantity of Italian wine with them, which proved more than welcome.

At first light the following morning a boat became visible drifting through the thin grey blanket of mist lying across the dead lake. It was a ghostly apparition. That vessel was barely still afloat and it contained the bloodied corpse of a dead Brandenburger. The bullet-riddled wreck was fetched by canoe, and the German prisoners were made to bury their dead comrade on the shore. They were throwing in the last few shovelfuls of mud, when the first German shells rained down on the island.

Lassen was gathered around a map with his raiders, in the middle of a planning session. On hearing the howl of incoming artillery rounds, men dived into nearby foxholes or crawled beneath the old table that the ruins contained. Three shells hit the building, before Lassen ordered the German prisoners to dig some deep trenches along the island's shoreline. Once they were done, Lassen ordered his men to take shelter in those, but wherever they went the German shells seemed to follow.

The enemy had to have spotters with eyes on the island. As the German gunners zeroed in on the newly-dug trenches, Lassen's men dashed towards a second, smaller ruin on the far side of the island. But they hadn't been there long when the barrage crept over to that building, and the men had to find some new cover.

The horrific game of hide-and-seek with the German gunners carried on all morning. One of Lassen's men was badly wounded, his heel being blasted off and his leg riddled with shrapnel. Another was blown off his feet and thrown in through the doorway of the ruined building. By now, Lassen and his men could only move about by crawling on their bellies, the fire was so accurate and so lethal.

Mindful of the coming mission, Lassen got his men to paint up some warning signs for the commandos, who would be joining them on Casone Caldiro after nightfall. They read: 'You can be seen from Comacchio – enemy observation posts nearby.'

Under cover of darkness the first commando forces started to advance across the lake. They were shipped in using Storm Motor Boats – a plywood-hulled assault craft powered by a 55-horse power outboard engine. The Germans knew the lake was alive with their enemy now, and without using such craft it would be a near impossibility to get the commandos into position in time for the attack.

With the commandos now holding the islands, Lassen would have liked a further 24 to 48 hours to push out night patrols and to recce the terrain leading up to Comacchio town itself. But he'd been sent unequivocal orders, stressing how crucial it was that the mission proceed with all due haste.

The attack must repeat must take place tonight as planned whether reconnaissance has taken place or not – stop. Every reasonable risk must repeat must be taken – stop. These military operations are vital to the completion of present plans – stop. Acknowledge receipt . . .

Those orders were unequivocal: come what may Operation Roast was going ahead that night.

Just before setting forth in their canoes, Lassen shared a quiet moment with his close friend, Stud Stellin. Stellin was struck most powerfully by one thing: for the first time ever Lassen chose to speak about what would happen if one of them were killed. It was eerie and unsettling. Stellin, like nearly all the men, had come to view their iconic leader as indestructible; bulletproof; immortal even.

Yet he was left with the strong impression that Lassen had had a premonition that he was going to be killed.

Chapter Twenty-six

It was just after midnight on 8 April 1945, and time for the first parting of ways. While the main commando assault force would head north-east for the spit, Lassen's men would continue paddling due north, towards Comacchio town. Their mission was to cause as much chaos, destruction and mayhem as they possibly could on the lake's northern shore, as a cover for the big push against the spit.

The commandos' tough Storm Motor Boats were a good deal faster than the paddle-powered canoes. They motored ahead, quickly overhauling the thirty SBS boats. The commandos waved a farewell to the distinctive figure of Lassen in the lead canoe, and he was seen to wave a cheery-seeming *au revoir*. On the surface there wasn't the slightest sign of the turmoil that the SBS major was feeling inside.

As a major, there was no need for Lassen to go on this mission. He could have chosen to remain in the rear, in overall command. But he sensed the extreme danger that his men were sailing into, and it wasn't in his nature to let them face it without him. He also believed it was his duty as a commander to be at the head of his patrol, leading by example.

Gradually, the raiders' last landfall, Casone Caldiro, faded into the night behind them. The faint rustle of the breeze ruffled the still waters, reed beds whispering in the impenetrable darkness. It provided just enough sound to mask the dip and drip of the paddles as they flicked through the turbid waters.

One of the greatest risks now was bioluminescence – the natural light that tiny, single-cell aquatic creatures give off whenever they sense movement or danger. With sixty sets of paddles churning the waters of Lake Comacchio, and thirty prows cutting through its surface, the men would have to row as softly as they could, or they risked prompting the distinctive glowing blue-green light that might be visible to the enemy.

Slowly, silently, with barely a flicker of fluorescence, the raiders edged towards Comacchio's northern shoreline.

Lassen had divided his force into two, with a smaller, separate patrol being commanded by Stud Stellin. Each unit was to hit a different stretch of shoreline on the fringes of Comacchio town, so as to give the impression that a larger force was in action.

Lassen planned to land his force some 3,000 yards from the town itself, and advance up the road leading into it. The route lay across a raised embankment fringed by deep water on both sides, so there would be precious little cover to mask their advance. Without the benefit of any recces, Lassen had little idea what defences the German might have sited along the road, so they would be fighting all but blind.

As the canoes crept closer to the shore, the tension rippled back and forth across his patrol. The lead canoe nudged into the soft mud at the lakeside, and Lassen leapt out to drag it further ashore. To left and right shadowy figures were doing likewise. Boats hastily made fast, each man grabbed his weapon. Lassen mustered them in the cover of a ditch.

So far so good: at least they'd made landfall without being detected. Lassen started the advance, creeping through the stillness with Fred Green, a passable Italian-speaker at his side. Fred was to yell out the cover story if they were challenged. They'd made about 500 yards when a cry rang out through the darkness.

'*Chi va la?*' – Who goes there?

'*Pescatori sulla nostra strada di casa!*' Green yelled back.

This was the agreed response – fishermen on our way home. It was the best they could think of, but with Comacchio boasting only barely edible eels for the catching, it was a decidedly thin cover story. Green had to repeat it several times before whoever was manning the forward guard post seemed to understand. There were some yells in German back down the road towards the town, after which the voice cried out in Italian again.

'*Veni qui!*' – Come here.

Green had no option but to step forward onto the road. The instant he did so a long tongue of flame stabbed out of the night, as a machine-gun nest positioned behind the guard post opened fire. Green and Lassen dived for the only possible cover – the slope leading into the water to the nearest side of the road.

What sounded like a fearsome *Maschinengewehr* 42 'Spandau' poured down a torrent of bullets, which ricocheted horribly off the road. The MG42 could fire twice the rate of rounds of any equivalent Allied machine gun. So rapid was the rate of fire the human ear couldn't distinguish between each bullet, the distinctive continuous *brrrrr* of the weapon lending it the nickname 'Hitler's buzz saw'.

To Lassen and Green's rear agonized cries rent the darkness, revealing that some at least of the 'buzz saw's' rounds had found their target. Unbeknown to them, veteran raider Fred Crouch had just been killed. His dark premonitions of his own death had proved well-founded.

Lassen knew it was time for decisive action or they were finished – pinned down and unable either to advance or retreat. It was so dark that a man lying prone on the ground could barely be seen. He crawled forward, reached for a pair of grenades, and threw first one and then another at the bunker in which the Spandau was positioned. The moment the second grenade exploded he rushed forward and sprayed the position with fire, killing the machine-gunners at close quarters.

Four enemy lay dead at his feet, but the volume of fire just kept growing. Further up the road were two more MG42 bunkers, with a third set to one side. Each was placed slightly higher than the one in front, so they could put down fire in unison. The road was being raked by storms of lead, 7.62mm rounds snapping and buzzing all around like demented hornets. The only way to avoid getting hit was to keep down by the water, but that didn't offer much of a route to advance.

With the bunkers firing in unison, it meant that six Spandaus were in action against Lassen's patrol. It was murder out in the open. But that didn't stop the Danish Viking. Lassen rose again. Sprinting ahead, somehow he reached the next bunker without getting hit. Again, he hurled grenades in through the gun-slit. There was a punching blast, fire and smoke billowing out of the narrow opening, followed by the strangled screams of the dying and wounded inside.

Two more fearsome Spandau machine guns had just been put out of action, and for a brief moment the guns on that road leading into Comacchio town fell silent.

Lassen's voice rose above the quiet, yelling to his men. 'Forward! Forward, you bastards!'

Shadowy figures rushed up to join him. Two men were dragged out of that last bunker injured but alive. Both were Russians who'd been press-ganged into the German army. They were sent back to the boats as prisoners, under guard. But as Lassen led his men forward, so the darkness to their front erupted into blinding points of burning light.

Flares burst in the sky, their intense illumination throwing the road into harsh light and shadow. The moment the raiders were pinned under their glare, the firing recommenced from up ahead, another of Lassen's fellows being blown off his feet in a hail of bullets. Wounded men fell to the roadside, from where those who were able continued to fire into the machine-gun nests that had them so horribly pinned down.

Out on the lake, Stud Stellin could see just how serious Lassen's position had become. But with more flares being fired every minute, there was no way he could risk bringing his canoes in to their intended landing point. They'd be doing so under the full glare of the flares, and he and his men would get blown out of the water.

Stellin tried to get his patrol into land by ascending a high dyke that formed one side of the shore-side road, but almost immediately they came under blistering fire from the hyper-alert German sentries. As probing bursts reached out to menace the forward-most canoes, Stellin made the toughest decision that he had ever been forced to take. He ordered his patrol to turn around and head back the way they had come, making for Casone Caldiro once more.

Ashore, three of Lassen's force lay dead, and many more were injured. But at this stage even sounding the retreat would prove disastrous. There was no way to fall back in safety, when facing the withering fire of a pair of MG42s Spandaus. Lassen crawled back to his nearest men and grabbed some spare grenades. He reorganized those still able to fight. He got them into the only cover there was, half-submerged in the water, and he briefed them to put down a barrage of fire once he gave the word.

That done, he turned back to the battle. He had with him two volunteers – Sean O'Reilly and a Sergeant-Major Stephenson – and together they aimed to take out the last Spandau positions. The three men belly-crawled ahead under a murderous hail of bullets, a slight rise in the road giving them only limited cover from the fire.

They continued to worm their way forwards, and when they were within range for his exceptional throwing arm, Lassen let fly with grenades – O'Reilly and Stephenson passing over theirs, so the Dane could hurl those as well.

The last explosion echoed across the flaming waters, and a lonely cry floated out from the darkness: '*Kamerad! Kamerad!*' – friend. Moments later a torn fragment of ghostly cloth was hung out of the bunker's opening – the white flag of surrender.

Lassen told Stephenson and O'Reilly to stay where they were. He rose to a crouch and scuttled forward, moving cautiously as he approached his third enemy machine-gun post of the night. He stopped a few yards short of the white flag, and in German he ordered whoever was alive in there to come out. The only answer that came was a savage burst of machine-gun fire. Even as he fell, Lassen threw his last grenade, lobbing it in through the gun-slit opening.

The explosion ripped apart the bunker, and the two Spandaus sited inside it finally fell silent. From his position a few dozen yards back, Stephenson had heard that staccato burst of rounds, followed by the answering grenade blast. As the echoes died away, a long, ringing silence fell across that bloodied road, one that seemed to go on and on for ever. And then he heard it – a distinctive cry for help.

'SBS! SBS! Major Lassen wounded!'

Stephenson dashed forward. He found the Dane lying on his back, wounded. He knelt, and lifted Lassen half-up, getting him braced against his knee.

'Who is it?' Lassen asked, dazedly.

'Stephenson. Steve. It's me.'

'I'm wounded, Steve. I'm going to die. Try and get the others out.'

'No, no – we'll be all right,' Stephenson tried to counter. 'Key thing is, can you walk?'

There was no answer. Stephenson tried to lift Lassen onto his shoulders, but he was a dead weight, and Stephenson found his foot snagged in some loose wire. He cursed. He needed help.

'Sean!' he cried. 'Sean! Andy's injured!'

It was then that he realised that O'Reilly too was hurt. The indestructible Irishman – without whom Lassen was barely willing to go into battle – had been shot through the shoulder by that last Spandau burst. Bone and muscle had been torn to pieces, and O'Reilly was losing a great deal of blood. Stephenson tried calling for help a few more times, but to his rear all was darkness and confusion.

Stephenson knew Lassen couldn't walk, and he alone couldn't manage to carry him. He felt around in his side pouch, grabbed a morphine tablet, and fed it into Lassen's mouth.

'What is it?' Lassen asked. His voice was weakening.

'It's morphia. Don't worry, Andy. You're going to be okay. We'll get you back to the boats.'

Lassen shook his head. 'It's no use, Steve. I'm dying. Don't go any further. Leave me and try to get away with the others.'

Pretty much the moment he'd uttered those last few words, Anders Lassen lost consciousness. Stephenson felt a presence behind him. Some of the others had made it forward. He tried to get them to help him lift their commander, but one of them restrained him.

He put a hand on Stephenson's shoulder. 'Steve, the major's dead. He's dead. He's gone.'

Stephenson and the others carried Lassen's bloodied form some way down the causeway, until they again came under devastating bursts of fire. They decided they had no option but to abandon him. Lassen had ordered Stephenson to get out and save whoever he could, and in order to do so they had to leave his body behind.

It was shortly after three o'clock that morning – 9 April 1945 – when the first of Lassen's patrol made it back to Casone Caldiro. Four of those who had set out were dead: Corporal Ted Roberts, Fusilier Wally Hughes, Fred Crouch and Major Anders Lassen. Many more were missing. Of the wounded, Sean O'Reilly was in the worst shape. He'd stuck with his commander to the last, and it had very nearly cost him his life.

Many of the old dependables – Porter Jarrell, Dick Holmes, Jack Nicholson, Sammy Trafford – had survived, but few would ever fully recover from losing Lassen. They were in shock. No one was able to sleep. They sat around talking about the incredible courage of their commander, who had fought on even after he was mortally wounded.

None of them could believe that he was truly gone. When Stud Stellin learned what had happened he refused to countenance that it could be true. The fact that he had failed to get his force ashore made Stellin even more inconsolable.

Anders Lassen died a few months short of his twenty-fifth birthday, less than a month before the end of the war in Europe. Operation Roast was the last mission to be undertaken by the SBS in the Second World War. Once across Comacchio and through the Argenta Gap the British Eighth Army thundered north, reaching Venice by late April. General Clark's Fifth Army made similar spectacular progress in the west.

On 28 April a high-ranking German officer arrived at Field Marshal Alexander's headquarters, to discuss terms for surrender. On 8 May 1945 the war in Europe was declared over. For his part in Operation Roast, Lassen's final action, he was posthumously awarded the Victoria Cross. He is the only member of Britain's SAS ever to have won that award.

The VC citation states:

In Italy, on the night of 8th–9th April, 1945, Major Lassen was ordered to take out a patrol . . . to raid the north shore of Lake Comacchio.

His tasks were to cause as many casualties and as much confusion as possible, to give the impression of a major landing, and to capture prisoners. No previous reconnaissance was possible, and the party found itself on a narrow road flanked on both sides by water.

Preceded by two scouts, Major Lassen led his men along the road towards the town. They were challenged after approximately 500 yards from a position on the side of the road. An attempt to allay suspicion by answering that they were fishermen returning home failed, for when moving forward again to overpower the sentry, machine-gun fire started from the position, and also from two blockhouses to the rear.

Major Lassen himself then attacked with grenades, and annihilated the first position, containing four Germans and two machine-guns. Ignoring the hail of bullets sweeping the road from three enemy positions, an additional one having come into action from 300 yards down the road, he raced forward to engage the second position under covering fire from the remainder of the force. Throwing in more grenades he silenced this position which was then overrun by his patrol. Two enemies were killed, two captured and two more machine guns silenced.

By this time the force had suffered casualties and its firepower was very considerably reduced. Still under a heavy cone of fire Major Lassen rallied and reorganized his force and brought his fire to bear on the third position. Moving forward himself he flung in more grenades which produced a cry of 'Kamerad'. He then went forward to within three or four yards of the position to order the enemy outside, and to take their surrender.

Whilst shouting to them to come out he was hit by a burst of Spandau fire from the left of the position and he fell mortally wounded, but even while falling he flung a grenade, wounding some of the occupants and enabling his patrol to dash in and capture this final position.

Major Lassen refused to be evacuated as he said it would impede the withdrawal and endanger further lives, and as ammunition was nearly exhausted the force had to withdraw.

By his magnificent leadership and complete disregard for his personal safety, Major Lassen had, in the face of overwhelming superiority, achieved his objects. Three positions were wiped out, accounting for six machine guns, killing eight and wounding others of the enemy and two prisoners were taken. The high sense of devotion to duty and the esteem in which he was held by the men he led, added to his own magnificent courage, enabled Major Lassen to carry out all the tasks he had been given with complete success.

Anders Lassen VC, MC and two bars – the last of the *Maid Honour* originals – had died as he had lived, in heroic defence of his fellow raiders and taking the fight to the enemy.

Fittingly, his body was retrieved by Don Francesco Mariani, the priest of Comacchio town, and buried close by where he had fought his final battle, alongside those brother warriors who had fallen with him.

Epilogue

The loss of their commanding officer devastated the survivors of Comacchio. All had seen Lassen as fearless and indestructible and as leading a charmed life. Impossible as it might seem he was now dead. He was buried initially in Comacchio, the town whose liberation had been his objective in the action that was to be his last. His remains were later transferred to the British military cemetery at Argenta. They were laid to rest along with some 600 of those from the many nations who fought and died at Argenta and Comacchio so Europe might be freed from Nazi tyranny. A verse in Danish at the foot of his gravestone translates as:

> Fight for all you hold dear.
> Die as if it counts.
> Life is not so hard
> Nor is death.

The mission to take Comacchio had formed part of an elaborate feint, one designed to convince the enemy that the main push by Allied forces in northern Italy would be along the coast. In truth, the real thrust had concentrated some miles to the west of there, in the Argenta Gap, a strip of land lying between Comacchio's western shore and the Lombardy marshes. At Argenta, the Allies had secured their much-needed breakthrough, and barely four weeks later the war in Europe was over. Arguably, the sacrifice at Comacchio had not been in vain.

The posthumous Victoria Cross was presented to Lassen's parents by King George VI at Buckingham Palace, in December 1945. A second VC was awarded for actions during Operation Roast. Royal Marine Commando Tom Hunter VC was killed while charging down and destroying at least three enemy machine-gun positions. Few British military operations have ever been honoured so highly.

At the SAS lines in Hereford, there are two statues of the unit's founding heroes: one is of David Stirling, the other of Anders Lassen, the two men who pioneered what was to become modern Special Forces soldiering. While Lassen served in Jellicoe's SBS, during the war years it was a part of the SAS Regiment, so the SAS have rightly claimed Lassen as one of their own. Equally, the SBS – now a long-established separate entity from the SAS – also claim the Danish Viking raider as one of their chief forebears.

Many have described Lassen as a real James Bond character: a hard-drinking, hard-hitting womanizer, for whom there were no holds barred when fighting the enemy. Indeed, Ian Fleming's Bond is believed to be based in part upon Lassen, with a good dose of Gus March-Phillipps, Geoffrey Appleyard and Graham Hayes thrown in. But the efforts of Lassen and his men had far wider ramifications over and above their obvious heroics. For example, David Sutherland, Lassen's commanding officer during the Comacchio mission, wrote of him: 'Anders caused more damage and discomfort to the enemy during five years of war than any other man of his rank and age.'

A number of other senior Allied commanders wrote about how the small band of men that Lassen helped lead had achieved the extraordinary, in helping to turn the tide of the war – in the Aegean raids, in Santorini, in Salonika, and even in Comacchio. For example, Field Marshal Alexander wrote to Sutherland shortly after Comacchio, saying: 'The reputation you have made for yourselves in your successful operations in the Mediterranean, then the Aegean Islands and the Adriatic coast will never be surpassed.' High praise indeed.

In the aftermath of war a nation hungry for peace saw no role for irregular, piratical raiders: perhaps rightly, the focus of the world turned to building the peace. The SAS were criticized on the following points: 'not adaptable to all countries'; 'expense per man is greater than any other formation and is not worthwhile'; 'any normal battalion could do the same job'.

The SAS was disbanded immediately after the Second World War, or so the official history goes, the military High Command and their political taskmasters wasting little time in getting rid of the mavericks that had made up their number. Yet less than a decade later the British military was forced to drastically revise its position, and the Special Forces units were reformed – largely in response to the 'Malaya Emergency', in which the need for irregular forces became clear. Fortunately, the SF ethos had been kept alive in various guises, and survivors from the original units resurfaced so the elite SAS could be reformed.

In truth, immediately after the war the then ex-Prime Minister, Winston Churchill, became the chairman of a secret association that kept the SAS/SBS alive until it could be formally and officially refounded in 1953. During that underground period, the SAS/SBS/SOE formed a deniable unit based in France but run from London, tasked with hunting down Nazi war criminals, and in particular those responsible for executing former members of British Special Forces on Hitler's orders. The Nazis they tracked down were not to be brought to justice. They were to be given the same rights as our own had been, and wiped out.

This reflected Churchill's passion for, and his unshakeable loyalty to, the Special Forces that he founded, a commitment that remained undimmed until the end of his days. No doubt Gus March-Phillipps, Geoffrey Appleyard, Graham Hayes and Anders Lassen would have approved wholeheartedly of keeping a secret SAS active, and of its post-war missions, had they lived to see the war's end.

Bibliography and Sources

Books and Academic Papers

Amphibious and Special Operations in the Aegean Sea 1943–1945. Panagiotis Gartzonikas, December 2003, Naval Postgraduate School, Monterey, California.

Anders Lassen Krig – 9 April 1940–9 April 1945. Thomas Harder, Informations Forlag, 2010 (provisional translation by Thomas Harder, 2013, as *Anders Lassen's War*).

A History of the SAS Regiment. John Strawson, Secker & Warburg, 1984.

'Andy' – a Portrait of the Dane, Anders Lassen. Mogens Kofod-Hansen, Frihedsmuseets Venners Forlag – Friends of the Freedom Museum, 1991.

Commandos and Rangers of World War II. James Ladd, McDonald & Jane's Limited, 1978.

Dust Upon the Sea. W. E. Benyon-Tinker, Hodder & Stoughton, 1947.

Ian Fleming's Commandos: The Story of 30 Assault Unit in WWII. Nicholas Rankin, Faber & Faber, 2011.

Ian Fleming and SOE's Operation Postmaster – the Untold Top Secret Story. Brian Lett, Pen & Sword, 2012.

Operation Albumen. Anne E. Jensen and Ole Christensen, Imprint Grafisk, 2010.

The Filibusters: the Story of the Special Boat Service. John Lodwick, Methuen, 1947.

The Invisible Raiders. James D. Ladd, Arms and Armour Press, 1983.

The Regiment – The Real Story of the SAS. Michael Asher, Viking, 2007.

The SBS in World War II – An Illustrated History. Gavin Mortimer, Osprey Publishing, 2013.

The Second World War, Vol. VI: Triumph and Tragedy. Winston S. Churchill, Cassell, 1954.

Unearthing Churchill's Secret Army: The Official List of SOE Casualties and Their Stories. John Gehan and Martin Mace, Pen & Sword, 2012.

Wine Dark, Blood Red Sea: Naval Warfare in the Aegean, 1941–1946. Charles W. Jr. Koburger, Praeger Publishers, 2000.

Appendix One
Gus March-Phillipps – Decorations

Citation for Gus March-Phillipps Bar to his D.S.O.

MOST SECRET

Special Service Brigade
Unit: Small Scale Raiding Force
Army No. and Rank: 99184 – Major
Name: MARCH-PHILLIPPS, Gustavus Henry, D.S.O., M.B.E.
Honour or Reward: Bar to D.S.O., Posthumous Mention in Dispatches
NOTE: These raids for operational reasons have not been announced to the press and the above citation is on no account to be published

Major March-Phillipps was responsible for the original conception of the S.S.R.F. and was its first Commander. He formed and trained the force, and due to his energy and personality the force was ready for its first operation within six weeks of the directive authorizing the formation of the force being signed. The first operation (the first attempt at 'DRYAD') was unsuccessful owing to fog.

In a period of less than three weeks Major March-Phillipps planned and executed three successful small scale raids, all of which he commanded himself, both from the Naval and Military side. In the first of these, Operation 'BARRICADE', a coast defence installation on the East side of the Cherbourgh peninsula was attacked, and a number of casualties caused to the enemy with bombs and small arms fire. The second operation, 'DRYAD', resulted in the capture of the CASQUETS lighthouse from which seven German Naval prisoners were taken together with valuable code books and other papers. The third operation was a reconnaissance in a particularly difficult part of the Channel Islands, and was in every way completely successful. The S.S.R.F. suffered no casualties in any of the operations.

On three other occasions a force commanded by Major March-Phillipps put to sea in M.T.B. 344, but owing to weather conditions having changed on arrival the other side of the Channel the operations had to be abandoned.

He has been at all times an inspiring leader to his force, with a complete disregard for personal danger or hardship, and has in every way shown himself to be a most vigorous and determined Commander.

Major March-Phillipps is reported missing after operation 'AQUATINT' and is believed to have been killed. In the event of his survival and return to allied occupied territory, he is strongly recommended for a bar to his D.S.O. If he is subsequently reported as killed, it is recommended that his name should be mentioned posthumously in dispatches.

Louis Mountbatten
Chief of Combined Operations
12th November 1942

Appendix Two
Geoffrey Appleyard – Decorations

Citation for Geoffrey Appleyard's D.S.O.

MOST SECRET

Special Service Brigade
Unit: Small Scale Raiding Force
Army No. and Rank: 86639 – Captain A/Major
Name: APPLEYARD, John Geoffrey
Honour or Reward: D.S.O.
NOTE: These raids for operational reasons have not been announced to the press and the above citation is on no account to be published

Major Appleyard has taken part in five raids carried out by the S.S.R.F. between the 5th August and the 15th October. During all these Operations he has acted as Navigator on Raiding Craft M.T.B. 344 and as Second in Command on the other four. The success of these Operations has been largely dependent on his courage, determination and great skill in navigation. On all occasions M.T.B. has proceeded unescorted and has often passed through enemy minefields.

On an operation at CAP BARFLEUR which took place on the night of the 14th/15th August, he went ashore with the landing party which escaped undetected after killing and wounding several Germans. On an operation against the CASQUETS which took place on the night of the 2nd/3rd September, he went ashore with the landing party which returned with seven prisoners. This operation was carried out with a wind force 3 rising to force 5 and the landing and re-embarkation took place from a Goatley boat on a very rocky island. It was largely due to his skill that this very difficult Operation was successfully accomplished. During a raid at ST. HONORINE on the night of 12th/13th September he remained in the landing craft due to injuries received on the previous operation. The landing party got into difficulties and he kept the M.T.B. close inshore under heavy enemy fire until eventually forced to turn seawards by direct fire over open sights. He then evaded enemy patrol boats and as quickly as possible returned and scoured the coast on the chance of picking up any of the landing party. During this time he was again under fire and only one engine of the M.T.B. was working. Only when all chances of picking up the raiding party had disappeared did he turn back and successfully navigate the M.T.B. with one engine out of action, through enemy minefields to the home port. He commanded the raid against SARK on the night of 3rd/4th October and led the landing party which spent 3 to 4 hours ashore, capturing one prisoner and killing three enemy, without any casualties to his own force.

Louis Mountbatten
Chief of Combined Operations
12th November 1942

Appendix Three
Anders Lassen – Decorations

Major Anders Frederik Emil Victor Schau Lassen was awarded, both before and after his death, the following honours and decorations:

King Christian X Memorial Medal
The Victoria Cross
The Military Cross and two bars
The Greek War Cross
The 1939–45 Star
The Africa Star
The Italy Star
The Defence Medal
The War Medal

Citation of Anders Lassen's Military Cross

Second-Lieutenant Anders Frederick Emil Victor Schau
LASSEN

(234907) General List

Second-Lieutenant Lassen has at all times shown himself to be a very gallant and determined officer, who will carry out his job with complete disregard for his own personal safety. As well as, by his fine example, being an inspirational leader of his men, he is a brilliant seaman possessed of sound judgment and quick decisions. He was coxswain of the landing craft on an operation and effected a landing and subsequent re-embarkation on a dangerous and rocky island with considerable skill and without mishap. He took part in a further operation on which he showed dash and reliability. He recently took part in another highly successful operation in which he was the leader of the boarding party. Regardless of the action going on around him, Second-Lieutenant Lassen did his job quickly and coolly and showed great resource and integrity. Second-Lieutenant Lassen also took part in another operation, as bowman on landing, and then made a preliminary reconnaissance for a reported machine-gun post.

Citation of Anders Lassen's Second Military Cross

Unit: Special Boat Squadron, Raiding Forces, Middle East
Regtl No. 234907
Rank and Name: WS Lieut Anders Frederick Emil Victor Schau
LASSEN, MC (Danish Subject)
Recommended By: (Sgd) Captain D. G. C. Sutherland, MC,
Commanding Special Boat Squadron, Raiding Forces, Middle
East; (Sgd) Ronald M. Scobie, Lt.-Gen. GCS 21Jul. 43; (Sgd)
H. M. Wilson, General, Commander-in-Chief, Middle East
Forces

HONOUR OR AWARD: Immediate Bar to MC
ACTION FOR WHICH COMMENDED

The officer was in command of the patrol which attacked
Kastelli Pediada aerodrome on the night of 4th July. Together
with 1469628 Gnr. Jones, J. (RA), he entered the airfield from
the West, passing through formidable perimeter defences. By
pretending to be a German officer on rounds he bluffed his
way past three sentries stationed 15 yards apart guarding
Stukas. He was, however, compelled to shoot the fourth with
his automatic, and in so doing raised the alarm. Caught by
flares and ground searchlights he was subjected to very heavy

machine-gun and rifle fire from close range and forced to withdraw. Half an hour later this officer and other rank again entered the airfield, in spite of the fact that all guards had been trebelled and the area was being patrolled and swept by searchlights. Great difficulty was experienced in penetrating towards the target, in the process of which a second enemy sentry had to be shot. The enemy then rushed reinforcements from the eastern side of the aerodrome and, forming a semi-circle, drove the two attackers into the middle of an anti-aircraft battery, where they were fired on heavily from three sides. This danger was ignored and bombs were placed on a caterpillar tractor which was destroyed. The increasing number of enemy in that area finally forced the party to withdraw. It was entirely due to this officer's diversion that planes and petrol were successfully destroyed on the eastern side of the airfield since he drew off all the guards from that area. Throughout this attack, and during the very arduous approach march, the keenness, determination and personal disregard of danger of this officer was of the highest order.

Citation of Anders Lassen's Third Military Cross

Unit: General List while with the Special Boat Sqn, 1 SAS Regt.
Regtl. No: NYA
Rank and Name: WS Lieut LASSEN, Anders Frederick Emil Victor Schau
Recomended BY: (Sgd) D. J. T. Turnbull, Colonel, Commanding Raiding Forces; (Sgd) D. F. Anderson, Lt.Gen., Commanding 3 Corps; (Sgd) H. M. Wilson, General, Commander-in-Chief, Middle East Forces. 19.11.43
Honour or Award: Second Bar to MC
Action for which Commended:

This officer, most of the time a sick man, displayed outstanding leadership and gallantry throughout the operations by X Det in Dodecanese, 13 Sep. 43 to 18 Oct. 43. The heavy repulse of the Germans from Symi on 7 Oct 43 was due in no small measure to his inspiration and leadership on the one hand, and the highest personal example on the other. He himself, crippled with a badly burned leg and internal trouble, stalked and killed at least 3 Germans at close range. At that time the Italians were wavering and I attribute their recovery as due to the personal example and initiative of this Officer. He continued to harass and destroy German patrols throughout the morning. In the afternoon he himself led the Italian counter attack which finally drove the Germans back to their caiques, with the loss of 16 killed, 35 wounded and 7 prisoners, as against a loss on our side of one killed and one wounded.

Citation of Anders Lassen's Victoria Cross

The King has been graciously pleased to approve the posthumous award of a Victoria Cross to:

Major (temporary) Anders Frederick Emil Victor Schau LASSEN, MC (234907) General List.

In Italy, on the night of 8th–9th April, 1945, Major Lassen was ordered to take out a patrol of one officer and seventeen other ranks to raid the north shore of Lake Comacchio.

His tasks were to cause as many casualties and as much confusion as possible, to give the impression of a major landing, and to capture prisoners. No previous reconnaissance was possible, and the party found itself on a narrow road flanked on both sides by water.

Preceded by two scouts, Major Lassen led his men along the road towards the town. They were challenged after approximately 500 yards from a position on the side of the road. An attempt to allay suspicion by answering that they were fishermen returning home failed, for when moving forward again to overpower the sentry, machine-gun fire started from the position, and also from two blockhouses to the rear.

Major Lassen himself then attacked with grenades, and annihilated the first position, containing four Germans and two machine guns. Ignoring the hail of bullets sweeping the road from three enemy positions, an additional one having come into action from 300 yards down the road, he raced forward to engage the second position under covering fire from the remainder of the force. Throwing in more grenades he silenced this position which was then overrun by his patrol. Two enemies were killed, two captured and two more machine guns silenced.

By this time the force had suffered casualties and its fire-power was very considerably reduced. Still under a heavy cone of fire Major Lassen rallied and reorganized his force and brought his fire to bear on the third position. Moving forward himself he flung in more grenades which produced a cry of "Kamerad". He then went forward to within three or four yards of the position to order the enemy outside, and to take their surrender.

While shouting to them to come out he was hit by a burst of Spandau fire from the left of the position and he fell mortally wounded, but even while falling he flung a grenade, wounding some of the occupants and enabling his patrol to dash in and capture this final position.

Major Lassen refused to be evacuated as he said it would impede the withdrawal and endanger further lives, and as ammunition was nearly exhausted the force had to withdraw.

By his magnificent leadership and complete disregard for his personal safety, Major Lassen had, in the face of overwhelming superiority, achieved his objects. Three positions were wiped out, accounting for six machine guns, killing eight and wounding others of the enemy and two prisoners were taken.

The high sense of devotion to duty and the esteem in which he was held by the men he led, added to his own magnificent courage, enabled Major Lassen to carry out all the tasks he had been given with complete success.

WAR OFFICE
7th September, 1945

Index

393